Low Fertility and Reproductive Health in East Asia

International Studies in Population

VOLUME 11

The International Union for the Scientific Study of Population (IUSSP)

The IUSSP is an international association of researchers, teachers, policy makers and others from diverse disciplines set up to advance the field of demography and promote scientific exchange. It also seeks to foster relations between persons engaged in the study of demography and population trends in all countries of the world and to disseminate knowledge about their determinants and consequences. The members of the IUSSP scientific group responsible for this book were chosen for their scientific expertise. This book was reviewed by a group other than the authors. While the IUSSP endeavours to assure the accuracy and objectivity of its scientific work, the conclusions and interpretations in IUSSP publications are those of the authors.

International Studies in Population (ISIP) is the outcome of an agreement concluded by the IUSSP and Springer in 2004. The joint series covers the broad range of work carried out by IUSSP and includes material presented at seminars organized by the IUSSP. The scientific directions of the IUSSP are set by the IUSSP Council elected by the membership and composed for 2014–2017 of:

Anastasia Gage (Sierra Leone/United States), President
Tom LeGrand (Canada), Vice President
France Meslé (France), Secretary General and Treasurer

Sajeda Amin (Bangladesh)
Ann Biddlecom (United States)
Parfait Eloundou-Enyegue (Cameroon)
Emily Grundy (United Kingdom)
Fátima Juárez (Mexico)

Øystein Kravdal (Norway)
David Lam (United States)
Tom Moultrie (South Africa)
Edith Pantelides (Argentina)
Sureeporn Punpuing (Thailand)

More information about this series at http://www.springer.com/series/6944

Naohiro Ogawa • Iqbal H. Shah
Editors

Low Fertility and Reproductive Health in East Asia

Springer

Editors
Naohiro Ogawa
Population Research Institute
 and College of Economics
Nihon University
Tokyo, Japan

Iqbal H. Shah
Department of Global Health and Population
Harvard School of Public Health
Boston, USA

ISBN 978-94-024-1579-7   ISBN 978-94-017-9226-4 (eBook)
DOI 10.1007/978-94-017-9226-4
Springer Dordrecht Heidelberg New York London

Library of Congress Control Number: 2014948454

© Springer Science+Business Media Dordrecht 2015
Softcover reprint of the hardcover 1st edition 2015 978-94-017-9225-7

This work is subject to copyright. All rights are reserved by the Publisher, whether the whole or part of the material is concerned, specifically the rights of translation, reprinting, reuse of illustrations, recitation, broadcasting, reproduction on microfilms or in any other physical way, and transmission or information storage and retrieval, electronic adaptation, computer software, or by similar or dissimilar methodology now known or hereafter developed. Exempted from this legal reservation are brief excerpts in connection with reviews or scholarly analysis or material supplied specifically for the purpose of being entered and executed on a computer system, for exclusive use by the purchaser of the work. Duplication of this publication or parts thereof is permitted only under the provisions of the Copyright Law of the Publisher's location, in its current version, and permission for use must always be obtained from Springer. Permissions for use may be obtained through RightsLink at the Copyright Clearance Center. Violations are liable to prosecution under the respective Copyright Law.
The use of general descriptive names, registered names, trademarks, service marks, etc. in this publication does not imply, even in the absence of a specific statement, that such names are exempt from the relevant protective laws and regulations and therefore free for general use.
While the advice and information in this book are believed to be true and accurate at the date of publication, neither the authors nor the editors nor the publisher can accept any legal responsibility for any errors or omissions that may be made. The publisher makes no warranty, express or implied, with respect to the material contained herein.

Printed on acid-free paper

Springer is part of Springer Science+Business Media (www.springer.com)

Preface

The chapters in this volume originated from papers presented at the International Conference on Low Fertility and Reproductive Health in East and Southeast Asia, organized by the Nihon University Population Research Institute (NUPRI) in cooperation with the World Health Organization (WHO), the United Nations Population Fund (UNFPA), the International Union for the Scientific Study of Population (IUSSP), and the Mainichi Daily Newspaper. The conference took place in Tokyo, Japan, from 12 to 14 November 2008 and brought together more than 50 experts from such fields as demography, economics, sociology, anthropology, and medicine.

We are grateful for the financial support received under the "Academic Frontier Project" for Private Universities: matching fund subsidy from MEXT (Ministry of Education, Culture, Sports, Science and Technology), 2006–2010, granted to the Nihon University Population Research Institute (NUPRI). We also wish to express our gratitude for the sustained support of Nihon University and the World Health Organization at all stages of the project and in organizing the 2008 conference on which this publication is based. In addition, in preparing this book we have received outstanding logistical support from NUPRI's staff, including Ilja Musulin, Maki Ogawa and Naomi Makabe. We gratefully acknowledge the support received from the International Union for the Scientific Study of Population (IUSSP) and the helpful comments and suggestions of the IUSSP reviewer of the manuscript. We also thank the reviewers of each chapter included in this volume and Dr. Robert Retherford, who assisted the editors in reviewing multiple versions of many of the chapters. Last but not least, Sandra Ward has effectively helped us edit the manuscript.

Tokyo, Japan	Naohiro Ogawa
Boston, USA	Iqbal H. Shah

Contents

1. **Introduction** 1
   Naohiro Ogawa, Iqbal H. Shah, and Gayl D. Ness

2. **Social Norms, Institutions, and Policies in Low-Fertility Countries** 11
   Anne H. Gauthier

3. **Very Low Fertility and the High Costs of Children and the Elderly in East Asia** 31
   Naohiro Ogawa, Andrew Mason, Sang-Hyop Lee,
   An-Chi Tung, and Rikiya Matsukura

4. **The Effects of Daycare Center Use on Marital Fertility in Japan** 59
   Sang-Hyop Lee, Naohiro Ogawa, and Rikiya Matsukura

5. **What Are the Prospects for Continued Low Fertility in Japan?** 75
   Vegard Skirbekk, Rikiya Matsukura, and Naohiro Ogawa

6. **Low Fertility: Choice or Chance?** 101
   Paul F.A. Van Look

7. **Trends in Male Reproductive Health and Decreasing Fertility: Possible Influence of Endocrine Disrupters** 117
   Tina Harmer Lassen, Teruaki Iwamoto, Tina Kold Jensen,
   and Niels E. Skakkebæk

8. **The Sexual Behavior of Adolescents and Young Adults in Japan** 137
   Ryuzaburo Sato and Miho Iwasawa

9. **Sexless Marriages in Japan: Prevalence and Reasons** 161
   Yoshie Moriki, Kenji Hayashi, and Rikiya Matsukura

10 **Community-Level Effects on the Use of Reproductive Health Services in Rural China** 187
Zheng Wu, Shuzhuo Li, Christoph M. Schimmele, Yan Wei, Quanbao Jiang, and Zhen Guo

Index 211

Contributors

Anne H. Gauthier is Senior Researcher, Netherlands Interdisciplinary Demographic Institute (NIDI), The Hague, The Netherlands.

Zhen Guo is Associate Professor, Department of Sociology, Huazhong University of Science and Technology, Wuhan, China.

Kenji Hayashi is President Emeritus, National Institute of Public Health, Saitama, Japan.

Teruaki Iwamoto is Professor, Division of Male Infertility, Center for Infertility and IVF, International University of Health and Welfare Hospital, Nasushiobara, Tochigi, Japan.

Miho Iwasawa is Senior Researcher, Department of Population Dynamics Research, National Institute of Population and Social Security Research, Tokyo, Japan.

Tina Kold Jensen is Professor, Department of Environmental Medicine, University of Southern Denmark, Odense, Denmark, and University Department of Growth and Reproduction, Rigshospitalet, Copenhagen, Denmark.

Quanbao Jiang is Professor, Institute for Population and Development Studies, Xi'an Jiaotong University, Xi'an, China.

Tina Harmer Lassen is Junior Researcher, University Department of Growth and Reproduction, Rigshospitalet, Copenhagen, Denmark.

Sang-Hyop Lee is Professor, Department of Economics, University of Hawaii at Manoa, and Adjunct Senior Fellow, Population and Health Studies, East-West Center, Honolulu, Hawaii, USA.

Shuzhuo Li is Professor and Director, Population Research Institute, Xi'an Jiaotong University, Xi'an, China.

Andrew Mason is Professor, Department of Economics, University of Hawaii at Manoa, and Senior Fellow, Population and Health Studies, East-West Center, Honolulu, Hawaii, USA.

Rikiya Matsukura is Researcher, Population Research Institute, Nihon University, Tokyo, Japan.

Yoshie Moriki is Associate Professor, College of Liberal Arts, International Christian University, Osawa, Mitakashi, Tokyo, Japan.

Gayl D. Ness is Professor Emeritus, Department of Sociology, University of Michigan, Ann Arbor, Michigan, USA.

Naohiro Ogawa is Director, Population Research Institute, and Professor, College of Economics, Nihon University, Tokyo, Japan.

Ryuzaburo Sato is Honorary Researcher, National Institute of Population and Social Security Research, Tokyo, Japan.

Christoph M. Schimmele is a post-doctoral fellow, Department of Sociology, University of Victoria, Victoria, British Columbia, Canada.

Iqbal H. Shah Department of Global Health and Population, Harvard School of Public Health, Boston, Massachusetts, USA.

Niels E. Skakkebæk is Professor, University Department of Growth and Reproduction, Rigshospitalet, Copenhagen, Denmark.

Vegard Skirbekk is Research Group Leader, International Institute for Applied Systems Analysis (IIASA), Laxenburg, Austria.

An-Chi Tung is Associate Research Fellow, Institute of Economics, Academia Sinica, Taipei, Taiwan.

Paul F.A. Van Look is Consultant in Sexual and Reproductive Health, Val-d'Illiez, Switzerland.

Yan Wei is Professor and Director, Institute for Population and Development Studies, Xi'an University of Finance and Economics, Xi'an, China.

Zheng Wu is Professor, Department of Sociology, University of Victoria, Victoria, British Columbia, Canada.

Chapter 1
Introduction

Naohiro Ogawa, Iqbal H. Shah, and Gayl D. Ness

In the last couple of decades, a number of countries in Asia have been posting remarkable economic growth performance. No less phenomenal have been their rapid demographic transformations.

In 2010, Asia's total population was estimated at 4.2 billion (United Nations 2011), which is more than double the size observed in the latter half of the 1960s. The annual population growth rate, however, has been declining continuously since peaking at 2.4 % in the period of 1965–1970. At present the annual growth rate is estimated at 1.1 % (United Nations 2011). As a result of slower population growth beginning in the latter half of the twentieth century, Asia's demographic outlook of today is substantially different from that of only a few decades ago.

Slower population growth in Asia has been due primarily to a significant decline in fertility over the past few decades. In 1965–1970, only one country in Asia (Japan) had below-replacement fertility—that is, a total fertility rate (TFR) of less than 2.1 children per woman. By 2005–2010, the number of East and Southeast Asian countries and areas with below-replacement fertility had increased to 10: China, Hong Kong, Japan, Macao, Myanmar, North Korea, Singapore, South Korea, Thailand, and Vietnam. Moreover, only 5 % of Asians lived in countries or territories with below-replacement fertility in 1965–1970, as compared with 42 % in 1990–1995, when China's fertility rate fell below the replacement level. At present, almost

---

N. Ogawa (✉)
Population Research Institute and College of Economics, Nihon University, Misaki-cho 1-3-2, Chiyoda-ku, 101-8360 Tokyo, Japan
e-mail: ogawa.naohiro@nihon-u.ac.jp

I.H. Shah
Department of Global Health and Population, Harvard School of Public Health, Building 1, Huntington Avenue 665, Boston, MA 02115, USA

G.D. Ness
Department of Sociology, University of Michigan, Ann Arbor, MI 48109, USA

half of Asia's population resides in societies with below-replacement fertility; and, according to a projection by the Population Division of the United Nations, more than 80 % of Asians will live in such societies in the late 2020s, when India is expected to attain below-replacement fertility (United Nations 2011).

Currently, in all countries and territories of East Asia except Mongolia, the TFR is below 1.5 children per woman, which makes East Asia one of the regions with the lowest fertility in the world. Moreover, Hong Kong, Macao, Taiwan, Singapore, and South Korea are classified in the category of lowest-low fertility (i.e., with a TFR below 1.3). In 2010, for example, Taiwan recorded a TFR of only 0.895, the lowest in the world.

Low fertility, which increasingly typifies Asia, particularly its East and Southeast regions, stems not only from reductions in marital fertility but also from later and fewer marriages. The new concern in many societies in East and Southeast Asia is that their fertility is now too low. The governments of Japan, Singapore, South Korea, and Taiwan are trying to raise fertility by encouraging marriage and adopting various measures aimed at increasing the fertility of married couples (Jones et al. 2010).

Although declining fertility has contributed to improvements in infant, child, and maternal survival in Asia, it has also brought new challenges relating to sexual and reproductive health. Premarital sex, premarital pregnancy, and cohabitation before marriage are becoming more common as a result of delayed marriage. As premarital sex becomes socially acceptable, earlier onset of sexual activity without contraception leads to unsafe sex, resulting in a rise in abortion rates and in the incidence of sexually transmitted infections (STIs) among single young adults. At the same time, infertility and childlessness are increasing. The rise in infertility appears to be partly due to falling sperm counts, the causes of which are not yet well understood but are thought to reflect increased exposure to endocrine disrupters in the food supply and elsewhere in the environment. Low fertility is also having profound effects on families, especially on traditional within-family support systems for children and elderly parents. Individuals, families, and governments in various regions of Asia are not well prepared to deal with many of these new challenges, which are often neglected in public discourse and research.

As the realization that very low fertility poses serious problems has started to sink in, keen interest is emerging in the causes – socioeconomic, behavioral and biological – of low fertility and the effects of recent policy efforts to raise it. Of equal importance for policies and programs is the evidence concerning whether high morbidity and mortality that typify high fertility contexts is replaced by new sexual and reproductive health problems in low fertility contexts. The two objectives of the volume are, therefore, to better understand the determinants of low fertility in East Asia, including an assessment of the effectiveness of policies aimed at raising fertility, and to identify and analyze the sexual and reproductive health issues that characterize low-fertility populations in the region.

This volume reflects that rapidly growing interest, not only of the governments in the region but also of national and international organizations and donor agencies concerned with population and reproductive health issues. The chapters are based on a selection of papers presented at the International Conference on Low Fertility and Reproductive Health in East and Southeast Asia, held in Tokyo in November 2008 and organized by the Nihon University Population Research Institute (NUPRI) in cooperation with the World Health Organization (WHO), the United Nations Population Fund (UNFPA), the International Union for the Scientific Study of Population (IUSSP), and the Mainichi Daily Newspaper of Japan.

These chapters make a valuable scientific contribution by addressing a number of under-researched issues and by covering an important region. In addition, the volume provides a unique blend of evidence on fertility determinants and reproductive health from authors with multidisciplinary academic backgrounds and expertise. The application of novel analytical approaches in dealing with complex issues and the description of their implications also make this volume unique. The relevance of findings presented in various chapters reaches beyond East Asian countries. Indeed, there is no other book that comes close to the distinctive coverage, design and content of this volume.

Besides this introduction, the volume consists of nine chapters, which fall into two groups: economic and social aspects of low fertility, and sexual and reproductive health aspects of low fertility. Chapters in the first group examine the effects of state policies aimed at raising fertility, and the nexus between various institutional and socioeconomic factors and declining fertility in East Asia. Chapters in the second group focus on a variety of low-fertility issues from the viewpoint of reproductive health and biomedicine.

The first four chapters deal with the economic and social aspects of low fertility. Chapter 2, by Anne Gauthier, uses a cross-national perspective to examine whether the societies of East and Southeast Asia are indeed unique, or whether a combination of factors found in other regions too can explain their observed very low levels of fertility. To address this challenging question, the author identifies five key themes: financial obstacles to having children, work-related obstacles, gender inequality in paid and unpaid work, normative obstacles, and other obstacles. Gauthier's extensive discussion of these five themes provides insights useful for understanding the rest of the chapters in the first group. She concludes that Asia is unique in that it has a distinctive combination of factors that jointly contribute to very low fertility. Those factors include: (1) a very high direct cost of children (due partly to a competitive education system), combined with very low government financial support for families; (2) a very high opportunity cost of having children owing to considerable normative obstacles that prevent women from staying in the labor market; (3) the persistence of unequal gender norms regarding the division of paid and unpaid work, including the care of children and elderly parents, which makes marriage an unattractive option for single women; (4) increasing uncertainties with respect to financial security; and (5) other norms including consumerism, individualism, and the acceptability of remaining childless. Gauthier emphasizes that although these factors can be observed in other societies outside Asia, what is unique in East and Southeast Asia is the coexistence of all of them, which reinforces their negative impact on fertility.

Chapter 3, by Ogawa et al., draws heavily upon a new methodology called National Transfer Accounts (NTA) to estimate the magnitude of the trade-off between quantity and quality of children. The NTA system takes into consideration not only the private but also the public costs of children. Both are estimated on an age-specific per capita basis. A synthetic life cycle measure based upon the two types of cost is the measure of the quality of children. The data used for statistical analysis are time series, pooled from 24 economies both inside and outside Asia. The computed result shows that a significant trade-off exists between the quantity and the quality of children in the 24 economies included in the pooled data set. The magnitude of the trade-off is particularly large in the case of three East Asian economies (Japan, South Korea, and Taiwan). Moreover, the human capital (health and education) component of public and private costs is found to play an extremely important role in the quantity–quality substitution in East Asia. Finally, using the same data set, the authors examine whether the cost of children is adversely affected by the rising cost of the increasing number of elderly persons in East Asia. They can detect no "crowding out" effect; that is, the two age groups are not competing for limited public and private resources.

Chapter 4, by Lee et al., investigates the effect of daycare center use on marital fertility in Japan. Their study, which uses data from the 2007 National Survey on Work and Family, indicates a substantial positive effect of daycare center use on marital fertility among women living in areas with no waiting lists for admission to daycare centers. For these women, the results indicate that using a daycare center increases the probability of having another child by 10 percentage points for the progression to a second birth and 9 percentage points for the progression to a third birth. By contrast, this effect is not significant for women living in areas where there are waiting lists. Moreover, the two-stage estimation results suggest that there is little effect on fertility when waiting lists are shortened in these areas. This finding suggests that the areal differences in the results (areas with waiting lists versus areas without them) are not due to the waiting lists per se, but rather to other factors such as regional characteristics (urban industrial versus rural agricultural) and women's employment status (i.e., whether women are full-time employees, part-time employees, or nonparticipants in the labor force).

In Chap. 5, Skirbekk et al. consider the prospects for continued low fertility in Japan, using a framework based on the so-called low fertility trap hypothesis (LFTH). The LFTH was developed originally to explain low fertility trends in European countries. The authors justify their decision to test the LFTH's usefulness for explaining Japanese childbearing trajectories by stating that in recent decades Japan has enjoyed economic levels similar to or higher than those observed in Europe, and that Japan's past population trends have shown strong similarities with those in Europe. The authors define the low fertility trap as consisting of three mechanisms and find that in the case of Japan there is clear evidence for the first mechanism (rapidly shrinking reproductive age cohorts), as well as certain evidence for the second (changes in values resulting in further fertility decline) and for the third (declining relative income among young adults, implying postponed and depressed fertility).

Four key findings with significant implications emerge from these four chapters. First, several factors prevail and reinforce each other to depress fertility to low levels in East and Southeast Asia (Chap. 2). Second, the "low fertility trap" caused by rapidly shrinking reproductive age cohorts of 15–49 years is clearly noticeable in Japan which also shows some evidence of changing values and declining income among young adults, all contributing to the low fertility levels in that country (Chap. 5). Third, the access to daycare centers can have positive impact in raising fertility if there are no waiting lists (Chap. 4). However, women's employment status and geographical differences between urban industrial and rural agricultural sectors have more important bearing on fertility than the existence of waiting lists for childcare-centers. Fourth, the application of the new analytical methodology of NTA shows that expenditures to enhance the "quality" of children (through education, health, and other interventions) inevitably leads to a decline in the quantity (the number) of children (Chap. 3). However, it is important to note that the use of limited public and private resources for children is independent of the resources needed to care for the elderly. Thus, it seems that the increasing expenditure on the growing elderly population in the region may not have an impact on the expenditure on children. Taken together, this set of chapters offers little promise for an increase in fertility in East Asia. These chapters also imply that more innovative and efficient approaches than those used thus far in the region are needed to tackle intricate contextual issues such as gender norms in order to raise fertility.

The next five chapters address the much neglected sexual and reproductive health aspect of low fertility. The impact of fertility decline in dramatically reducing infant, child and maternal mortality is well established, as all countries with low fertility show very low levels of infant, child and maternal morbidity and mortality. However, it remains unclear whether different kinds of sexual and reproductive health problems set in and become more pronounced in low-fertility populations. Chapters 7 and 9 provide evidence on two plausible explanations of low fertility. A general decline in male fertility is established in Chap. 7 while Chap. 9 demonstrates exceptionally low frequency of sex among married couples in Japan. Chapter 8 provides new insights on sexual and reproductive health of unmarried adolescents and young adults in Japan. It shows that fewer and delayed marriages are associated with increased sexual activity, number of premarital unintended pregnancies and induced abortions. Chapter 10 explores the issue of quality of care in reproductive health in China.

To set the context for chapters in this section, Chap. 6, by Van Look, examines low fertility as a result of individual and couple choice as opposed to "chance," defined as factors outside a couple's control, in particular involuntary infertility. The number of countries with below-replacement levels of fertility has continued to grow, primarily because of the voluntary use of contraception. In 2010, 63 % of all women in the world who were married or in cohabitating unions were using some method of contraception. Increased use of contraception accounts for 90 % of the decline in fertility. Infertility, that is, the inability to conceive a child, is a less significant factor in the overall low fertility levels in East and Southeast Asia. Where information is available, levels of infertility appeared to have declined over time. The use of assisted reproductive technologies (ART) has increased, but its contribution to raising fertility is shown to be modest. Van Look therefore concludes that the "choice" rather than "chance" is the driving force behind the worldwide demographic shift toward smaller family size. The chapter also highlights the challenges posed by rapidly aging populations with shrinking proportions of young people due to low fertility. Countries facing those challenges need to have sound, equitable, and sustainable social policies to avoid social upheaval. In addition, they need to strengthen their health care systems to deal with increasing caseloads of chronic, noncommunicable diseases such as diabetes and dementia.

Chapter 7, by Harmer Lassen et al., focuses on recent adverse trends in male reproductive health and on the possible effects of endocrine disrupters and lifestyle on fertility. Although the observed fertility decline is due mainly to changes in social and economic conditions, it may also be due to a decrease in the ability to conceive. Harmer Lassen et al. document various factors that potentially account for a decline in male fertility. These include declining semen quality, an increase in the incidence of testicular cancer, an increase in congenital malformations of the male reproductive tract, testicular dysgenesis syndrome, endocrine-disrupting chemicals, genetic factors, and lifestyle factors. The authors conclude that the rise in male reproductive problems and the geographical variations of these problems indicate that exposure to environmental hazards, lifestyle factors, or both, rather than genetic factors, are important contributors. In particular, environmental chemicals with endocrine-disrupting properties are of major concern as they are suspected of having the ability to disturb the development of reproductive organs during fetal life. The implications of the study are of huge significance and widely applicable. The authors recommend that additional studies be done to investigate the effects of endocrine-disrupting chemicals on human reproductive functions, and they encourage collaboration among social scientists and medical scientists when investigating the causes of infertility and of low fertility.

Chapter 8, by Sato and Iwasawa, focuses on sexual and reproductive health of adolescents and young adults in Japan. Using data from nationally representative surveys and documenting the rising levels of premarital sexual activity and unsafe sex among Japanese adolescents and unmarried young people, the authors provide evidence of a sexual revolution in that country. Age at first sexual intercourse has dropped for both men and women, and the gender difference has narrowed mainly because of a steep increase in women's sexual activity. The level of unsafe sex is also on the rise: 20 % of sexually active young people reported not using any contraceptive method during their most recent intercourse. As a result, the numbers of unintended pregnancies and of abortions have increased, and the incidence of sexually transmitted infections has also gone up. Although no comparison of these indicators is made with those in high-fertility populations, it is obvious that delayed marriage and the decline in the percentage of the married in low-fertility populations lead to an onset of sexual activity before marriage. Access to reproductive health services is especially difficult for young people with lower levels of education and for those in tertiary education. The authors make a strong case for extending sex education and reproductive health services to unmarried young people in Japan.

In Chap. 9, Moriki et al. investigate sexual behavior within marriage and among cohabitating partners in Japan. Using data from the 2007 National Survey on Work and Family, the authors report very low frequency of sexual intercourse among married and cohabitating partners. About 45 % of the couples reported not having had sexual intercourse for at least 1 month, and 25 % reported having had no intercourse for more than a year. Even in the young and sexually most active age group of 20–29 years, 21 % of women had sexual intercourse less than once a month. Husbands' long working hours, the presence in the household of children under age 3, and poor marital relations were major determinants of these so-called sexless marriages, which are becoming increasingly common among couples with at least one child. The chapter also provides insights from focus-group discussions conducted in 2009 in the Tokyo Metropolitan Area. For example, Japanese couples, at least in Tokyo, regard "having sex" as a less important activity in their busy schedules than childrearing tasks or work responsibilities. Many respondents indicated that the sole purpose of sex within marriage was to have children; therefore once the desired number of children was reached, their interest in having sex declined. Thus, the chapter provides convincing evidence that one major determinant of low fertility in Japan is sexless marriages.

Moriki et al. also report that sexual activities that used to be confined largely to marriage now occur before marriage. As a result, the number of "shotgun" marriages in Japan has been increasing. Conception preceded marriage among 30 % of those who married in 2005.

In Chap. 10, Wu et al. assess the extent to which community (village) economic and infrastructure and county-level socio-demographic factors affected, independent of the personal background characteristics of married women in rural China, their relative likelihood of having a reproductive-health (RH) checkup. RH checkups are important for diagnosing reproductive health problems, which are found in rural China. The decentralization of funding for health care from the central government to local authorities has produced disparities in access to reproductive health. To explore whether low use of RH services for checkups might be associated with shortcomings in available services, the authors applied a multilevel statistical model to data on village development levels (population size, the presence of a licensed doctor, the existence of a family planning service station, per capita income) and county-level characteristics, such as population size, the total fertility rate, the sex ratio at birth, and the level of female education, which they obtained from the National Population and Reproductive Health Survey and the 2000 census. The RH checkup was defined to include a visit to a health service during the past 18 months for a gynecological exam, breast exam, ultrasound exam, or screening for diseases. The holistic model of predictors included characteristics of the woman and her husband (for example, her age, ethnic minority status, childbearing history, use of contraception, her education, the age difference between spouses, husband's education, husband's training and education in RH and family planning), as well as characteristics of the village and of the county.

The authors report that only 49 % of rural married women of reproductive age had had a RH checkup, and the frequencies for PAP smear (4 %) and for mammogram (5 %) were exceptionally low. The results indicate that the husband's involvement in family planning and RH had a significantly positive effect on a woman's use of services for an RH checkup. Surprisingly, a woman's education was not significantly related to her use of services for an RH checkup, but county-specific contextual variables such as the total fertility rate and women's aggregated level of education (though not village-level characteristics) were significant. The use of a multilevel model provides a more complete and comparative assessment of the determinants of RH checkups in rural China than do models based only on the characteristics of women. As women's status was found to be a crucial dimension of RH checkup use, the authors note the need to better define women's status, as well as other contextual variables. The analysis revealed that differences in the village-level economic and infrastructure factors had little direct impact as compared with county-level variables on the use of RH services by married women in rural China. The chapter by Wu et al. makes an important methodological contribution in studying the determinants of individual health-seeking behavior in the context of community and regional factors as well as providing substantive insights about the relative effects of individual-, community- and county-level factors.

The scientific contribution of the five chapters to a better understanding of the low-fertility context are enormous. Chapter 6 considers both voluntary (choice) and involuntary (chance) factors by taking into account behavioral and biological aspects and concludes that low and declining fertility is mainly due to behaviors such as use of contraceptive methods. The increase in premarital sex, pre-marital conceptions and unintended pregnancies shown in Chaps. 8 and 9 can, in theory, lead to an increase in fertility. However, social taboos against having children outside marriage exert powerful checks. Given that abortion is legally available on request and generally accessible in the region, most premarital pregnancies end in induced abortions rather than in raising fertility. Thus, the fertility-increasing effect of premarital sex is cancelled out by the stigma and taboo against having children outside marriage. On the other hand, declining male fertility as shown in Chap. 7, coupled with low frequency of sex and a high number of sexless marriages (Chap. 9), generates an overall low fertility. The study from China (Chap. 10) dispels the perception that access to reproductive health services and care will improve with a decline in fertility.

Besides the topics covered by this volume and by the seven papers that appeared in a special issue of *Asian Population Studies* (Retherford and Ogawa 2009), a number of academically stimulating papers dealing with socioeconomic issues and sexual and reproductive health in the context of Asia's declining and low fertility were presented at the Tokyo International Conference. Some of them shed light on premarital sex, premarital pregnancy, and cohabitation before marriage, all of which have recently become more common as a result of delayed marriage in East and Southeast Asia. The absence of siblings was noted to have contributed to unsafe sex and other risky behaviors among adolescent boys and girls in Thailand. Other papers examined such problems as an increase in unsafe sex, rising induced-abortion rates, and a growing incidence of sexually transmitted infections, which have been induced by earlier onset of sexual activity as premarital sex has become more socially acceptable in Asia. Case studies focusing on one or another aspect of low fertility were presented for a number of countries and areas, including China, Hong Kong, Japan, Mongolia, South Korea, Thailand, and Vietnam. Several papers covered such neglected topics as premarital pregnancies and their consequences among migrant workers in Hong Kong, fertility among foreign wives in South Korea, and the HIV/AIDS situation and responses to it in East and Southeast Asia. There were also substantial discussions of the rise in infertility, which could be due in part to falling sperm counts. Finally, the conference was unique in providing opportunities for medical researchers and social scientists to exchange their ideas about the causes and implications of declining and low fertility in economically developed societies.

References

Jones, G., Straughan, P. T., & Chan, A. (Eds.). (2010). *Ultra-low fertility in Pacific Asia: Trends, causes and policy issues*. London/New York: Routledge.

Retherford, R. D., & Ogawa, N. (Eds.). (2009). Special issue: Low fertility in East and Southeast Asia: Economic, social and policy influences. *Asian Population Studies, 5*(3), 211–369.

United Nations. (2011). *World population prospects: The 2010 revision*. New York: United Nations, Department of Economic and Social Affairs, Population Division.

Chapter 2
Social Norms, Institutions, and Policies in Low-Fertility Countries

Anne H. Gauthier

2.1 Introduction

The reach and persistence of very low levels of fertility in the industrialized world are unprecedented and have led numerous governments to question how best to support individuals in their fertility decisions, and especially how to allow them to reach their desired family size (Gauthier and Philipov 2008). Such concerns about low fertility have been especially acute in some East and Southeast Asian countries where very low levels of fertility are perceived negatively by governments and have even led in some cases to the adoption of pronatalist policies (Chamie 2004). Despite these concerns and policy interventions, the low levels of fertility remain, leading some scholars to characterize as unique such countries and areas as Japan, South Korea, Singapore, Hong Kong, and Taiwan (Family Planning Perspectives 1987; McDonald 2008). This chapter reflects on the determinants of low fertility and its related policies. Its more specific aim is to situate East and Southeast Asia in a cross-national perspective and to consider whether Asia is indeed unique or whether a combination of factors, common to other countries, can explain the observed very low levels of fertility observed there.

The chapter is organized around five themes: financial obstacles to fertility, work-related obstacles, gender inequality in paid and unpaid work, normative obstacles, and other obstacles. Before examining these themes, I present some recent data on fertility in order to distinguish the regions to which I will be referring throughout the chapter.

A.H. Gauthier (✉)
Netherlands Interdisciplinary Demographic Institute (NIDI), P.O. Box 11650,
NL-2502 AR The Hague, The Netherlands
e-mail: gauthier@nidi.nl

2.2 Regional Fertility Patterns

Table 2.1 presents data on total period fertility rates for East and Southeast Asian countries, along with comparative data for five other geographical regions: Nordic countries, English-speaking countries, Western Europe, Southern Europe, and Eastern Europe.

Obviously the East and Southeast Asian regions are very heterogeneous in their levels of development. If the analysis is restricted to higher-income countries, the average number of births per woman drops to 2.0 for Southeast Asia and to 1.2 for East Asia. These levels clearly place these two Asian regions in the category of very low fertility from a cross-national perspective. These figures, however, likely underestimate, in most countries, their true cohort fertility levels. For example, in 2003 the tempo-adjusted rates were estimated to be 1.52 for South Korea and 1.46 for Japan (Suzuki 2005, p. 25), clearly higher than the nonadjusted rates, but still in the low fertility range.[1]

In the rest of the chapter I turn to an examination of the obstacles to fertility. In doing so, I maintain the cross-national perspective but for some indicators restrict

Table 2.1 Total period fertility rates, arranged by decreasing order within each region: around 2006

Southeast Asia	East Asia	Other developed regions[a,b]
(Average = 2.8)[a]	(Average = 1.5)[a]	
Timor-Leste = 6.7	Mongolia = 2.3	Nordic countries = 1.90
Laos = 4.5	North Korea = 2.0	English-speaking = 1.88
Cambodia = 3.5	China = 1.6	Western Europe =1.59
Philippines = 3.3	*Japan = 1.3	Southern Europe =1.37
Indonesia = 2.6	*South Korea = 1.3	Eastern Europe = 1.37
*Malaysia = 2.6	Taiwan = 1.1	
Myanmar = 2.2	*Hong Kong = 1.0	
Vietnam = 2.1		
*Brunei = 2.0		
Thailand = 1.6		
*Singapore = 1.4		

Sources: For Southeast and East Asia: Population Reference Bureau (2008). For all other developed countries, see Table 2.2 in the Appendix
*Indicates countries that were classified by the United Nations as having a high level of human development on the basis of the UN's Human Development Index. This information was not available for Taiwan
[a]The regional averages are unweighted for the size of each country
[b]Detailed data for all other developed countries are provided in Table 2.2 in the appendix

---

[1] See Table 2.2 for more information on the tempo-adjusted total fertility rates.

my analysis only to selected Asian countries (because of data availability). I also focus mainly on low-fertility countries and neglect the Asian countries that have still not completed their fertility transition.

2.3 Financial Obstacles to Fertility

In the economic model of fertility developed by Gary Becker in the 1960s, it is assumed that individuals weigh the cost of children, their own income, and their preference for children (as opposed to other "consumer goods") when deciding whether or not to have a child (Becker 1991). Financial constraints, along with a major increase in the cost of children, are thus, according to this model, the main reason for the decline in fertility to very low levels. The questions therefore are: How much do countries differ in these financial obstacles to fertility? And to what extent can these differences account for the observed cross-national differences in fertility?

Let us start with the income constraint. In contrast to the 1950s and 1960s, when economies were growing rapidly and job opportunities were numerous, the trends over recent decades have been characterized by numerous ups and downs. Not only is there less economic certainty in today's world, as illustrated by the recent financial crisis, but also earnings for some segments of the population have not kept pace with inflation. For example, the earnings of unskilled workers have stagnated since the 1970s and have even declined (in real terms) in numerous countries (OECD 1997). This differential trend in earnings translates into very large differences between individuals in their financial obstacles to fertility. Similarly, high levels of unemployment observed in some countries, especially among young adults, have reduced the purchasing power of individuals and have likely forced them to postpone or to reduce their childbearing plans.[2] The rising cost of living, high unemployment, and uncertainties regarding governmental support for families are likely part of the explanation for the very low fertility levels currently observed in Central and Eastern Europe (Rostgaard 2004; Stewart and Huerta 2006; Saxonberg and Szelewa 2007). In contrast, the relatively low unemployment, stable economies, and stable financial support for families that characterize the Nordic countries appear to be associated with much higher levels of fertility (Gauthier and Philipov 2008). What about Asia? Could financial constraints be one of the reasons for the observed levels of fertility there?

There is no unanimity in the literature regarding the direct cost of children, and there are hardly any cross-national estimates.[3] What we have, however, are data on governmental financial support for families in the form of cash transfers and tax relief. Figure 2.1 graphs the data for a two-child, two-earner family with

---

[2] One counter-example is the case of low-income individuals in the United States, who have above-average fertility despite their financial circumstances.

[3] For Asia, readers are referred to Ogawa et al. (2009) and their more recent work presented in Chap. 3 of this volume. For Europe, see Diprete et al. (2003).

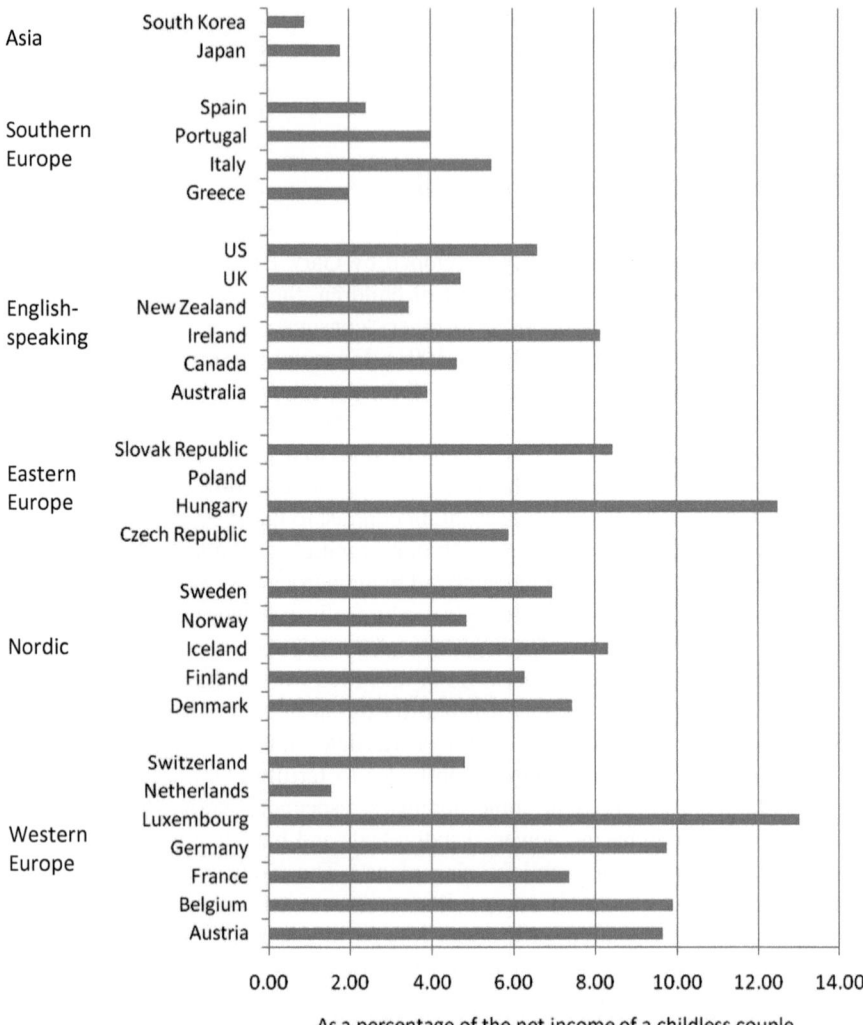

Fig. 2.1 Cash benefits to families: selected OECD countries, 2006 (Source: OECD (n.d. a). Notes: The data refer to the additional disposable income of a dual-earner, two-child family as compared with the disposable income of a dual-earner childless family; in both cases one of the spouse earns 100 % of the average earnings and the other 67 %. The benefits include both direct cash transfers to families with children and tax relief)

an average income as compared with an equivalent childless couple. Across all countries for which data are available, the average value is 5.9 %, which should be interpreted as the additional disposable income of two-child families as compared with childless couples. In other words, it is the amount of governmental financial support for families with children. The cross-national differences are wide, with higher values (on average) observed in Western Europe and lower values in Southern Europe, Japan, and South Korea.[4] On the basis of these data, it is tempting to draw a causal relationship between cash support for families and fertility, since countries that provide higher levels of cash support for families tend also to be those where higher-than-average fertility levels are observed. The correlation is less than perfect, however, and does not explain, for example, the presence of higher levels of fertility in the English-speaking region despite average to low levels of cash support for families.[5]

The above figures capture governmental support for families and not the cost of children itself. As mentioned above, there are no cross-nationally comparable estimates of the total cost of children in all countries. What we do know, however, is that when it comes to the cost of education, there are very large differences across countries. For instance, data from the Organisation for Economic Co-operation and Development (OECD) reveal that the share of private expenditures on education in South Korea and Japan by far exceeds that of all European countries. While across all OECD countries the share of private expenditures is about 15 %, it reaches about 30 % in Japan and 40 % in South Korea (OECD 2008). Moreover, when the data are restricted to tertiary education, the share of private expenditures reaches 65 % in Japan and 75 % in South Korea, as compared with less than 30 % in most European countries.[6] In other words, when planning to have a child, parents and parents-to-be in Japan and South Korea anticipate having to spend a considerable amount of money for their children's education. In fact, the above figures likely underestimate the total private expenditures on education as they exclude expenditures outside educational institutions, such as private tutorials. This is a non-negligible component in countries like Japan and South Korea, where the competitive nature of the schooling system compels parents to enroll their children in after-school study programs and to hire private tutors. In large metropolitan areas in Japan, the estimates are that 70 % of middle-school age children are enrolled in after-school programs (Tsuya and Bumpass 2004).

---

[4] In Fig. 2.1 the US appears to have a higher level of cash support for families than do countries such as Japan, despite the absence of a universal family allowance program in the US. The explanation lies in the fact that the index captures both direct cash transfers to families and tax relief. The data in the figure are also very specific to the type of family chosen—that is, a dual-earner family with two children and average wages.

[5] Other studies (e.g., Bradshaw and Finch 2006) have also pointed to the bivariate correlation between fertility and cash support for families.

[6] Even in absolute figures, tuition rates for higher education in Japan and South Korea are among the highest in OECD countries (OECD 2008).

2.4 Work-Related Obstacles

The indirect cost of children, also known as the opportunity cost, is perhaps an even bigger barrier to fertility in view of its larger magnitude than the direct cost of children. The estimates for a first child vary, but figures from Australia put it at USD $250,000, or 31 % of lifetime potential earnings (Breusch and Gray 2004). Of course, theoretically the opportunity cost of children could be zero if a woman is eligible for maternity leave, if the benefits paid during this leave totally compensate her for the loss of earnings, if she can resume the same job after her maternity leave ends, if she does return to work after the end of her leave, if she does not experience any loss of promotion during her maternity leave or shortly after, and if she experiences continuous employment thereafter. The reality, however, is far from this "no cost" scenario for a large proportion of women. As shown by Sigle-Rushton and Waldfogel (2007a, b) the penalty associated with motherhood is non-negligible and varies widely among countries, being smallest in the Nordic countries and largest in Continental and Southern Europe.[7] It is true that not all women want to resume work after their maternity leave, some of them preferring instead to stay at home to take care of their young children. It remains that in today's economy a second earner is a must in many families. It is also encouraged by several governments.

Not surprisingly then, governments in most industrialized countries have put in place measures to make it easier for parents to combine work and family responsibilities and to reduce the opportunity cost of children. Those measures include maternity and parental-leave schemes, the provision of childcare facilities, and subsidies for childcare. Figure 2.2 presents data on the combined maternity and parental-leave schemes in various countries. The data are expressed as full-time week equivalents in that they take into account both the duration of the leave and the cash benefits received during the leave. The cross-national differences are very large, with high support provided in the Nordic countries and some Eastern European countries and low support in the English-speaking countries and Southern Europe. In this graph, Japan and South Korea appear in the middle of the distribution. This is a new situation and reflects the recent adoption or extension of parental and childcare leave in those two countries.

The data tell us only one part of the story, however. Issues of eligibility for maternity and parental leave, job security after the period of leave, and possible job discrimination against young women need also to be taken into account in order to get the full picture. We do not have cross-nationally comparable data on all these dimensions. What we do know, however, is that a very high percentage of women

---

[7]The analyses by Sigle-Rushton and Waldfogel (2007a, b) do not include estimates for Japan or other Asian countries. Considering the strong tendency for women in countries such as Japan to withdraw from the labor market after childbirth, however, we can expect the wage penalty for motherhood to be high in those countries.

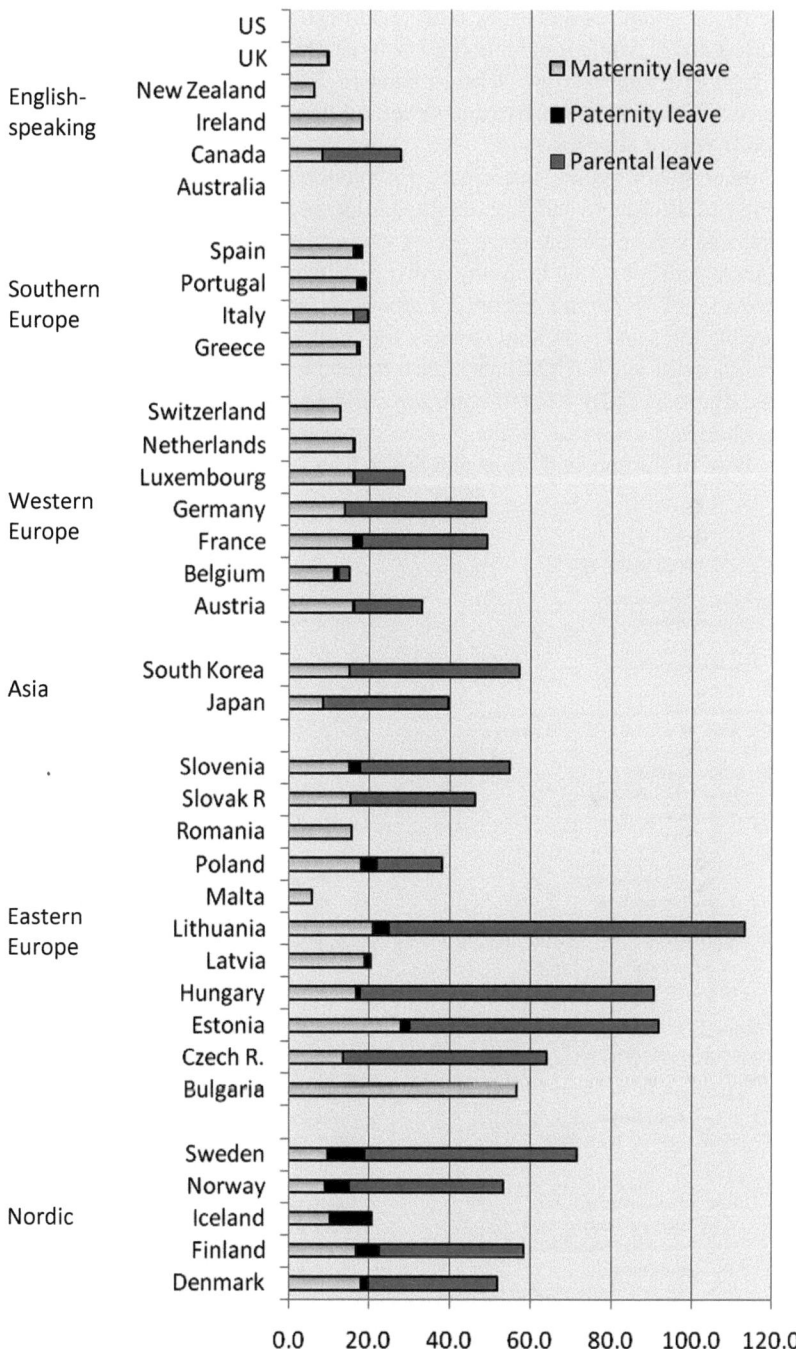

Fig. 2.2 Maternity and parental leave benefits: selected OECD countries, 2006–2007 (Note: All forms of leave are expressed as equivalent full-paid weeks (number of weeks of leave multiplied by the percentage of wage or earnings received during the leave). Source: OECD (n.d. b, table PF7.1))

in some Asian countries quit work after childbirth. In Japan the estimate is about 70 % (Atoh 2008), while it is around 20 % in Europe (Del Boca 2003). And while such a high exit rate from the labor market in Japan may reflect a combination of obstacles, including normative and structural ones, it considerably increases the opportunity cost of children.

The other major policy instrument for reducing the cost of children is the availability of affordable and high-quality childcare arrangements. During the past 20 years, many governments have put in place measures to support the creation of childcare facilities and to partly subsidize them through direct subsidies or through tax relief for parents. Figure 2.3 reports the enrollment of children in formal childcare facilities and preschool services for children under the age of 3 (left-hand side) and those of age 4 (right-hand side). Regional and cross-national differences are very large, especially when it comes to children under age 3, with higher-than-average childcare provision in the Nordic countries and lower ones in Southern Europe, Eastern Europe, and Japan and South Korea.

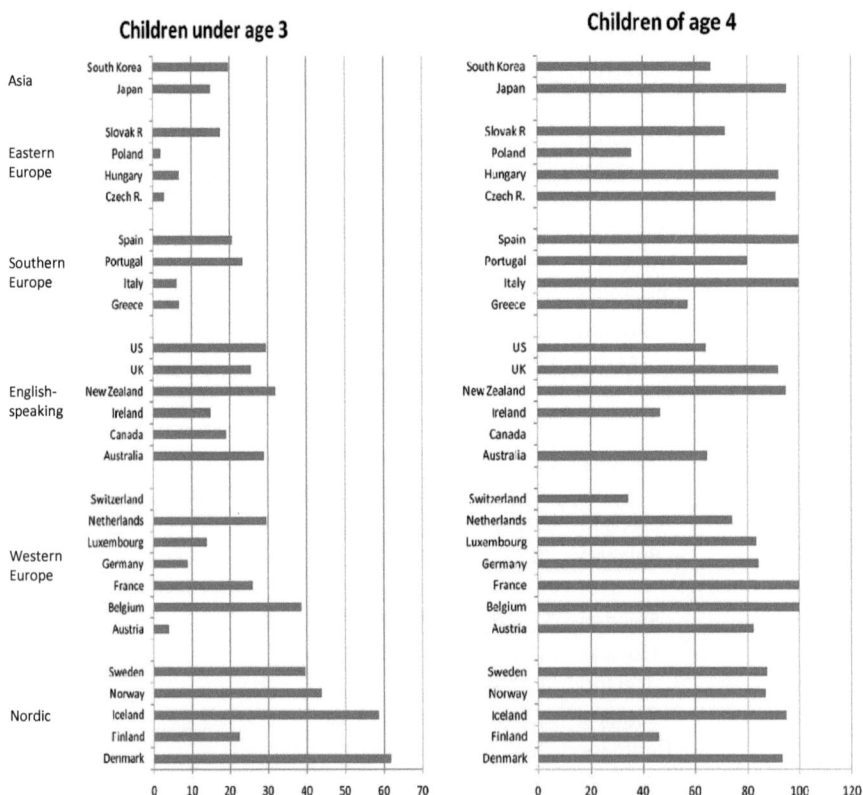

Fig. 2.3 Enrolment of children in formal childcare and preschool: selected OECD countries, 2000–2005 (Source: OECD (n.d. b, table PF11.1). Notes: Enrolment in daycare and preschool. The actual year of the data varies across countries, but all fall in the period 2000–2005)

Affordable childcare on its own is not sufficient, as parents may experience difficulties when their child is ill or when the care-giver himself or herself is ill.[8] While some employers will accommodate parents in such situations by allowing them to take time off, others will not. The struggle of working parents to look after a sick child is one of the key themes that emerged from interviews conducted by Jody Heymann (2006) and her team with mothers in several countries, including Russia, Vietnam, and the US. Their situation contrasts sharply with that of parents in countries like Sweden, where parents are eligible for numerous days off each year to take care of a sick child.

2.5 Gender Inequality in Paid and Unpaid Work

The provision of measures to help parents combine work and family responsibilities is important. But even when these are provided, parents may still face one additional barrier resulting from the combination of their paid job with their unpaid work at home. The term "second shift" was coined by Hochschild and Machung (1989) in their influential book, thus drawing attention to the very unequal gender division of household work.[9] It is not unusual for women to combine their 7 or 8 h of daily paid work with 4 or 5 h of unpaid work at home. The situation has been changing in recent years in some countries where men have increased their contribution to housework and childcare (Gershuny and Robinson 1988; Fisher et al. 2007). However, the division remains very unequal in most countries.

Figure 2.4 reports data on the ratio of father's to mother's time spent in childcare activities as calculated from time-use surveys. More equal gender contributions to childcare are observed in this graph in the Nordic countries, whereas less equal contributions are observed in Eastern Europe and especially in Japan. An unequal division of household labor between men and women can result from several factors, including time availability (itself linked to the number of hours of paid employment) and cultural norms regarding the roles of men and women. What is important to note again is the geographical ranking of countries and its plausible correlation with fertility.

Gender inequality, as a determinant of low fertility, has been discussed widely in the literature, the theoretical argument being that inconsistencies between norms and practices of gender equity in different institutional settings have a negative effect

---

[8]Many childcare centers will not keep a sick child and will instead require the parents to pick up the child.

[9]I treat gender inequality here in a separate subsection, but it is also a normative obstacle.

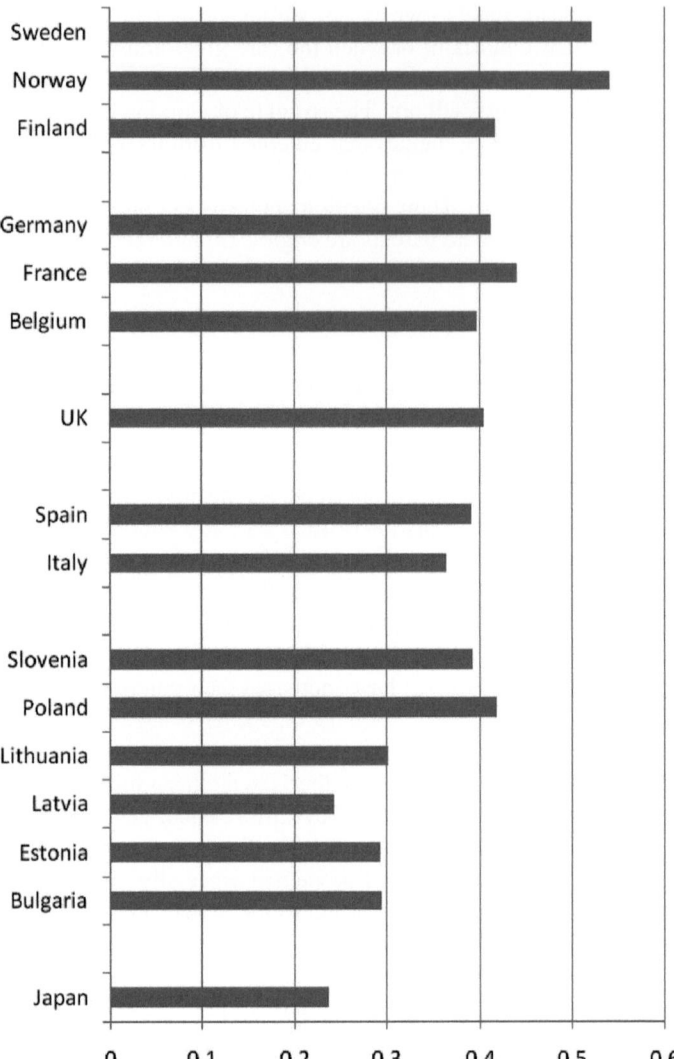

Fig. 2.4 Ratio of fathers' to mothers' time spent daily in childcare activities: selected OECD countries, around 2000 (Sources: Europe: Data computed by the author using the HETUS (n.d.). https://www.h2.scb.se/tus/tus/. Accessed 22 Mar 2010). Dataset, Japan: calculated from Japan, Statistics Bureau (2006). Notes: The data for European countries refer to married or cohabiting parents whose youngest child was under the age of 7. Childcare activities, as defined here, refer to time directly engaged with the child—for example, playing with or reading to the child as well as transporting the child. The data for Japan refer to married couples (regardless of the child's birth order))

on fertility (McDonald 2000). The persistence of very unequal gender norms in the private and public spheres in countries like Japan and South Korea is therefore undoubtedly part of the explanation for the observed very low levels of fertility in those countries. Again, a graphical illustration may be useful. Figure 2.5 shows the correlation between the gender equality index (as computed by the World Economic Forum) and fertility. The correlation is less than perfect, but what is very noticeable is the position of Japan, South Korea, and Singapore at the low end of the continuum, with low levels of both gender equality and fertility.

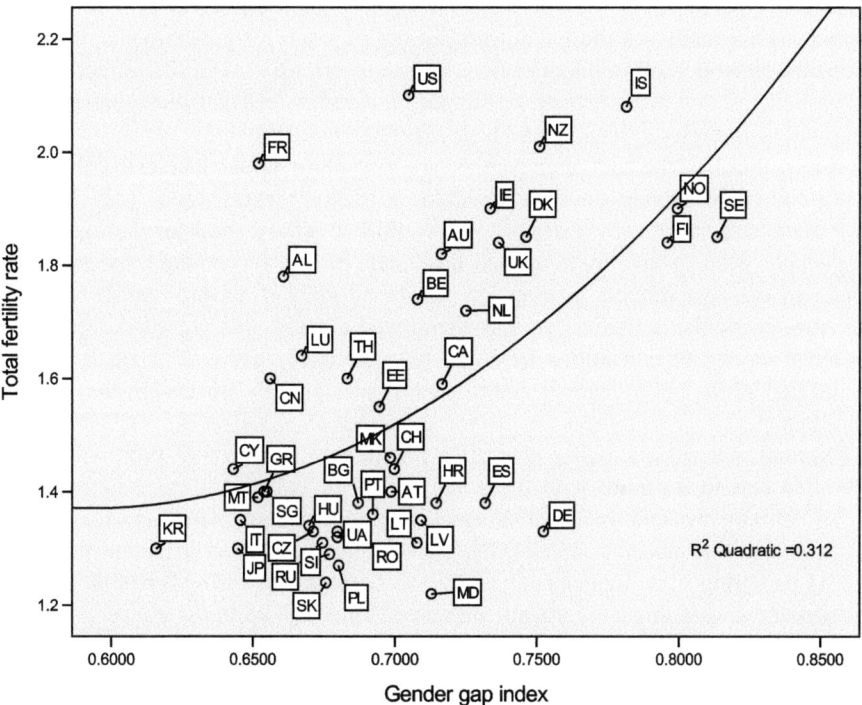

Fig. 2.5 Correlation between fertility and gender inequality: selected countries, 2006 (Sources: Total fertility rates: (Table 2.2 in the Appendix); Gender-gap index: World Economic Forum (2006). Note: Only countries with a total fertility rate equal to or less than 2.1 are included here. Country codes: Albania (AL); Andorra (AD), Armenia (AM), Australia (AU), Austria (AT), Belarus (BY), Belgium (BE), Bosnia-Herzegovina (BA), Bulgaria (BG), Canada (CA), China (CN), Croatia (HR), Cyprus (CY), Czech Republic (CZ), Denmark (DK), Estonia (EE), Finland (FI), France (FR), Germany (DE), Greece (GR), Hong Kong, Hungary (HU), Iceland (IS), Ireland (IE), Italy (IT), Japan (JP), Latvia (LV), Liechtenstein (LI), Lithuania (LT), Luxembourg (LU), Macedonia (MK), Malta (MT), Moldova (MD), Montenegro (ME), Netherlands (NL), New Zealand (NZ), Norway (NO), Poland (PL), Portugal (PT), Romania (RO), Russian Federation (RU), South Korea (KR), Serbia (RS), Singapore (SG), Slovakia (SK), Slovenia (SI), Spain (ES), Sweden (SE), Switzerland (CH), Taiwan (TW), Thailand (TH), United Kingdom (UK), Ukraine (UA), United States (US), Vietnam (VN), Brunei (BN))

2.6 Normative Obstacles

In the economic model of fertility, the preference for children is a key element. This element is rarely the subject of investigation by economists, however, their attention being focused instead on more tangible obstacles to fertility, such as financial and work-related ones. Nevertheless, elements of the normative systems of societies influence not only the desired or expected number of children, but also their "quality"—that is, the amount of money, time, and energy that parents are expected to devote to their children. These norms, it may be argued, have changed and have contributed to the current below-replacement fertility levels. And while some—if not most—of these elements are out of reach for governments, they are nonetheless important to understand as they can seriously curtail the effectiveness of policies aimed at increasing or supporting fertility.[10] I call these barriers the normative obstacles to fertility and have identified five of them.

First, there is the fact that parents are nowadays under increasing pressure to spend more money on their children, a pressure spurred not only by our consumerism, but also by a desire to give children what is best for them. Parents especially want to give them a good head start in life, for example by enrolling them in the best schools, paying for private tutorials if needed, enrolling them in extra-curricular activities, etc. As mentioned already, this pressure, especially when it comes to education, seems to be particularly acute in some East and Southeast Asian countries and contributes to substantially increasing the cost of children.[11]

Second, parents are under normative pressure to spend more time with their children and to do more with them and for them. For centuries, societies have been defining what is good parenting (see, e.g., Johansson 1987). Especially in economically advanced countries, the expectations have risen in recent decades. Good parenting is no longer defined only as feeding and caring for children, but is also about spending a significant amount of time with children: conversing with them, involving them in family decisions, exposing them to culture and politics at a young age, etc.[12] Not all parents have the luxury of conforming to these pressures, and it is unclear whether the pressures are felt equally in different countries. But

---

[10]To consider the possibility that governments can change norms would require a much lengthier discussion. It is certainly true that numerous examples exist in the developing world of governments that have fully endorsed family planning programs, and their endorsement may have indirectly contributed to changing norms toward smaller family size. Examples from the developed world of governments that may have succeeded in changing norms toward larger ideal family size would be much more difficult to find.

[11]Some authors (e.g., Ogawa et al. 2009) have used the term "success-oriented" societies in referring to this phenomenon.

[12]Evidence of such parenting pressures comes mainly from popular studies (e.g., Rosenfeld and Wise 2000).

where they are felt they may be raising the cost of children to parents and causing couples to revise downward their fertility intentions.[13]

Third, there are social pressures and expectations regarding the importance of achieving certain milestones prior to starting a family. For example, many young people, mainly from middle-class families, expect to have not only a good job prior to having children, but also to have traveled, to have found out "who they are" and what they are passionate about, and to have accumulated enough savings to buy a house or at least to rent a house or apartment in a comfortable and family-friendly neighborhood. And once they have children, they aspire (and are expected) to pursue their own development through such activities as fitness exercise, lifelong learning, and social activities. Obviously, these social pressures are difficult to reconcile with an early entry into parenthood and with having a large family. Of course, not all individuals are sensitive to these normative pressures, and different norms and expectations exist in different countries and even among different subgroups within the same society. Granting these differences, we should nevertheless not be surprised by a median age at first birth close to 30 years in some countries, nor by a low level of fertility.

Fourth, in some countries the social norm or expectation is still for couples to have children within marriage, following a traditional pattern of entry into parenthood. As young people increasingly favor cohabitation as a precursor, or even as an alternative, to marriage, such a social norm may act as an obstacle to fertility. Suzuki (2008, p. 37) even argues that it is the "weak familism in north-west Europe and English-speaking advanced countries that [has] prevented lowest-low fertility." In contrast, in Japan and South Korea the marriage norm, along with normative expectations about caring for elderly parents (Atoh 2008), may act as a deterrent to fertility.

Finally, there are social norms regarding ideal family size. Until recently social scientists considered such norms to be mechanisms for keeping fertility around the replacement level. But recent studies indicate that the "ideal" family size appears to have dropped below replacement, for example in such countries as Austria and Germany (Goldstein et al. 2003). The explanation given is part of the so-called fertility-trap hypothesis, which states that the persistence of low levels of fertility has affected societal perceptions of what is acceptable and desirable, thus lowering "ideal" fertility, and in turn contributing to keeping fertility at low levels (Lutz et al. 2006). Similarly, it has been argued that when entire societies adjust to very low levels of fertility—for example, in terms of their standard of living, the stock of small houses, etc.—falling fertility may in itself be self-enforcing (see, e.g., Retherford and Ogawa 2006).

---

[13]This argument is consistent with the quantity–quality trade-off hypothesized by Becker and Lewis (1973).

2.7 Other Obstacles

Other obstacles to fertility exist beyond those reviewed above. Among them are health-related problems, including the physiological difficulty of conceiving a child. It is difficult to quantify this obstacle. In the 2006 Eurobarometer survey, 13 % of men and 20 % of women in Europe identified health problems as one of the reasons why they were unable to fulfill their fertility desires (Testa 2006). Results of a similar magnitude were reported from the 2003 German Population Acceptance Survey among childless women and men (Hara 2008). Empirical evidence suggests an increase in the use of assisted reproductive technologies (ART) in recent years. The use of such technologies varies widely across countries, partly as a result of national differences in the rules regarding their use and their coverage by public health insurance (Billari et al. 2007). Other obstacles are the lack of a stable partnership or marriage that some individuals may face when considering whether to have children, and disagreement between spouses about family size. It is difficult to quantify these obstacles or to even say whether they have increased over time. In Germany, around 60 % of childless men and women identified not having a steady partner as one of the reasons for not having children (Hara 2008). In Japan, around 40 % of never-married men and women identified not having a suitable partner as one reason for not being married (Hara 2008). And since marriage and childbearing continue to be closely linked in countries like Japan, obstacles to marriage are in turn also obstacles to fertility. Some scholars have interpreted these statistics as a reflection of an imperfect marriage market. Countries like Singapore have even taken steps to correct the situation by providing governmental matchmaking services (Singapore Government 2008). Others have interpreted these statistics as a reflection of other obstacles, including the gap between men's and women's norms and expectations regarding gender roles (Jones 2007).

Finally, the labor market should be singled out as a potential obstacle to fertility in some countries. The limited availability of part-time work (and the benefits associated with them) and the rigidity of labor markets in not accommodating exit and re-entry—especially after an absence of some years to look after a young child—are examples of factors that may adversely affect the career trajectories of women and their fertility decisions.[14] Labor market rigidities such as those observed in Japan, South Korea, and some European countries may therefore contribute to low fertility. In contrast, the more flexible labor markets of the US and other English-speaking countries may help explain their higher levels of fertility.[15]

---

[14] In addition, Japan is a salient example of how very long working hours and peer pressure in the workplace negatively affect the work-fertility nexus. See Chap. 9 of this volume.

[15] To this factor one could also add the opening hours of stores, which may act as an obstacle to working parents. The differences between the US (with very liberal opening hours) and parts of Europe (with very traditional opening hours) are wide and may help explain differences in fertility.

2.8 Conclusion

Why do people still want and still have children today despite all the obstacles identified here? A similar question was posed by Schoen and colleagues (1997). Although this is an important question, it is one for which we have only a partial answer. It has been argued that some people still have children for the emotional satisfaction they provide, including the pleasure of nurturing, loving, and caring for a fragile human being. Others have children for more utilitarian reasons: to help consolidate a union or marriage, to build and create social capital, or to ensure companionship and support in old age. Pronatal and antinatal factors play out differently in various cultural settings and among various groups within those settings. The obstacles to childbearing appear to be particularly strong in some East and Southeast Asian countries and have resulted in unprecedentedly low levels of fertility.

One of the questions I posed at the beginning of this chapter was whether East and Southeast Asia is unique or whether a combination of factors (common to other countries) can explain its observed very low levels of fertility. On the basis of the evidence reviewed here, I would argue that the answer is both: The region is unique in that it has a unique combination of five factors that together contribute to very low levels of fertility.[16] First, there is the very high direct cost of children (which is in part the result of a competitive education system), combined with very low governmental financial support for families. Second, there is the very high opportunity cost of children that results from normative obstacles that prevent women from staying in the labor market after childbearing, together with a labor market that requires long hours of work, and low governmental support in the form of maternity and parental-leave schemes. Third, there is the persistence of very unequal gender norms regarding the division of paid and unpaid work, including the care of children and elderly parents, which makes marriage an unattractive option for many young women. This factor is not negligible, as an estimated 24 % of Japanese women from the 1990 birth cohort are expected to remain single (Atoh 2008). Fourth, there have been increasing uncertainties about the future, especially about financial security. The economic slump of the 1990s and early 2000s in Asia has substantially changed the labor market, increasing the number of nonregular employees and jeopardizing job insecurity (Atoh 2008; Suzuki 2008). Although we do not yet have data on the 2008–2009 economic crisis, we can expect it to add to the prevailing uncertainty, especially among young adults. Finally, other norms discourage family formation and fertility, including consumerism, individualism, and the acceptability of childlessness. And while these factors have been observed in other regions, what is unique in East and Southeast Asia is the coexistence of all of them.

---

[16]Throughout this chapter, I have referred to East and Southeast Asia as a single region. The social, economic, political, and demographic differences within the region are large, however.

Is fertility consequently bound to remain at very low levels in countries such as Japan, South Korea, and Singapore? The total period fertility rate may increase slightly in the years ahead as people catch up on postponed births. Nevertheless, reducing the obstacles to fertility would require formidable changes to the labor market, the schooling system, governmental support for families, etc. Furthermore, while some of these obstacles are within the control of governments, others, including normative obstacles, are not.

Implementing pronatalist policies may not be a solution and may even provoke a backlash, as it implies governmental interference in what is perceived to be a fundamentally private decision.[17] A better solution may be the implementation of family-friendly and family-supportive policies, ones that make it easier for parents to combine work and family responsibilities, that reduce the cost of children to parents, and that are sensitive to gender equity.[18] We do not know the exact combination of policies that would most efficiently reduce the obstacles to fertility (Gauthier 2007). What we do know is that governmental interventions, even modest ones, can increase the well-being of parents and children. Such policies, I would argue, may even have a positive effect on fertility, but only if they are designed to truly address the needs and preferences of parents and parents-to-be.

In recent years, Japan, South Korea, and Singapore have bolstered their support for families by providing longer parental and childcare leave, increasing financial support for families, and planning to increase the provision of childcare facilities. It is too early to assess the impact of these policies on the ability of parents to combine work and family responsibilities, and perhaps even their effect on fertility. Some authors have already expressed doubt about their possible benefits in view of the relatively small amounts budgeted and the continued economic uncertainties (e.g., Suzuki 2008). Governments are not the only actor, however. Without normative and policy changes in the labor market, the schooling system, and gender roles, obstacles to fertility will remain, further dampening the desire of young people to form a family.

Acknowledgments An earlier draft of this chapter was presented at a seminar organized by NUPRI in Tokyo in November 2008. I am grateful to the participants of that seminar for their comments. I am also grateful for the comments of the anonymous reviewer and to Professor Ogawa for his careful reading of the current version.

---

[17] Some people may point out that although deciding to have a child is a private decision, children are also a public good in view of their consequences for a country's demographic future. That issue is beyond the scope of this chapter.

[18] Pronatalist policies and family-friendly policies may overlap. For example, a parental-leave scheme may have a pronatalist objective or may be part of a family-friendly policy. What is the chief difference is the stated intention. But there can be other differences, especially if the policies are applied according to the birth order or other criteria.

Appendix

Table 2.2 Total fertility rates arranged by decreasing order within each region: 23 countries, around 2006

Region[a]	Country	TFR,[b] 2006	Adj. TFR[c]	Region[a]	Country	TFR,[b] 2006	Adj. TFR[c]
English-speaking	US	2.10	2.24	Eastern Europe	Albania	1.78	u
	New Zealand	2.01	u		Montenegro	1.62	1.97
	Ireland	1.90	2.14		Estonia	1.55	1.85
	UK	1.84	1.98		Macedonia	1.46	1.88
	Australia	1.82	u		Cyprus	1.44	1.79
	Canada[d]	1.59	u		Serbia	1.42	1.68
					Malta	1.39	1.58
Nordic	Iceland	2.08	2.22		Bulgaria	1.38	1.70
	Norway	1.90	2.01		Croatia	1.38	1.61
	Sweden	1.85	1.96		Latvia	1.35	1.59
	Denmark	1.85	2.00		Hungary	1.34	1.75
	Finland	1.84	1.91		Armenia	1.34	1.62
					Czech Republic	1.33	1.76
Western Europe	France	1.98	2.07		Ukraine	1.33	1.43
	Belgium	1.74	1.86		Romania	1.32	1.75
	Netherlands	1.72	1.82		Lithuania	1.31	1.68
	Luxembourg	1.64	1.82		Slovenia	1.31	1.55
	Switzerland	1.44	1.65		Belarus	1.29	1.47
	Liechtenstein	1.43	u		Russian Federation	1.29	1.52
	Austria	1.40	1.64		Poland	1.27	1.58
	Germany	1.33	1.59		Slovakia	1.24	1.66
					Andorra	1.24	u
Southern Europe	Greece	1.40	1.52		Moldova	1.22	1.36
	Spain	1.38	1.39		Bosnia-Herzegovina	1.19	u
	Portugal	1.36	1.65				
	Italy	1.35	1.48				

Sources: Australian Bureau of Statistics (2007); Statistics Canada (2008); Statistics New Zealand (n.d.); Vienna Institute of Demography (2008)

u—data unavailable

[a] The geographic classification used here partly reflects the conventional typology of countries by welfare regime. The "Eastern European" region, however, is a very broad one and encompasses not only countries traditionally classified (e.g., by the United Nations) as Eastern European but also countries usually classified as Central European or Asian. Excluded from the analysis are Azerbaijan, Georgia, and Turkey

[b] Total period fertility rate (average number of births per woman)

[c] Tempo-adjusted total fertility rate. The data come from the Vienna Institute of Demography (2008). The method used to adjust the total fertility rates is the one suggested by Bongaarts and Feeney (1998)

[d] Canada is here classified among the English-speaking countries despite a nonnegligible French-speaking minority concentrated mainly in the province of Quebec, which displays a significantly different pattern of family formation. Within-country differences are beyond the scope of this analysis

References

Atoh, M. (2008). Family changes in the context of lowest-low fertility: The case of Japan. *International Journal of Japanese Sociology, 17*(1), 14–29.

Australian Bureau of Statistics. (2007). *Births 2007*. http://www.abs.gov.au/AUSSTATS/abs@.nsf/DetailsPage/3301.02007. Accessed 22 Mar 2010.

Becker, G. S. (1991). *A treatise on the family: Enlarged edition*. Cambridge, MA: Harvard University Press.

Becker, G. S., & Lewis, H. G. (1973). On the interaction between the quantity and quality of children. *Journal of Political Economy, 81*(S2), S279–S288.

Billari, F. C., Kohler, H.-P., Andersson, G., & Lundstrom, H. (2007). Approaching the limit: Long-term trends in late and very late fertility. *Population and Development Review, 33*(1), 149–170.

Bongaarts, J., & Feeney, G. (1998). On the quantum and tempo of fertility. *Population and Development Review, 24*(2), 271–291.

Bradshaw, J., & Finch, N. (2006). Can policy influence fertility? In H. Emanuel (Ed.), *Ageing and the labour market: Issues and solutions* (pp. 151–167). Antwerp: Intersentia.

Breusch, T., & Gray, E. (2004). New estimates of mothers' foregone earnings using HILDA data. *Australian Journal of Labour Economics, 7*(2), 125–150 (Special issue).

Chamie, J. (2004, April 2). *Low fertility: Can governments make a difference?* Paper presented at the annual meeting of the Population Association of America, Boston, MA, USA.

Del Boca, D. (2003). *Why are fertility and participation rates so low in Italy (and Southern Europe)?* The Italian Academy for Advanced Studies in America, Columbia University. http://www.italianacademy.columbia.edu/publications/working_papers/2003_2004/paper_fa03_DelBoca.pdf. Accessed 16 Apr 2009.

Diprete, T. A., Morgan, S. P., Engelhardt, H., & Pacalova, H. (2003). Do cross-national differences in the costs of children generate cross-national differences in fertility rates? *Population Research and Policy Review, 22*(5–6), 439–477.

Family Planning Perspectives. (1987). Japan's fertility trends linked to late marriage, unique social factors, heavy reliance on abortion. *Family Planning Perspectives, 19*(4), 166–167.

Fisher, K., Egerton, M., Gershuny, J. I., & Robinson, J. P. (2007). Gender convergence in the American heritage time use study (AHTUS). *Social Indicators Research, 82*(1), 1–33.

Gauthier, A. H. (2007). The impact of family policies on fertility in industrialized countries: A review of the literature. *Population Research and Policy Review, 26*(3), 323–346.

Gauthier, A. H., & Philipov, D. (2008). Can policies enhance fertility in Europe? *Vienna Yearbook of Population Research, 2008*, 1–16.

Gershuny, J., & Robinson, J. P. (1988). Historical changes in the household division of labor. *Demography, 25*, 537–551.

Goldstein, J., Lutz, W., & Testa, M. R. (2003). The emergence of sub-replacement family size ideals in Europe. *Population Research and Policy Review, 22*(5–6), 479–496.

Hara, T. (2008). Increasing childlessness in Germany and Japan: Toward a childless society? *International Journal of Japanese Sociology, 17*(1), 42–62.

HETUS [Harmonized European Time-Use Surveys]. (n.d.). https://www.h2.scb.se/tus/tus/. Accessed 22 Mar 2010.

Heymann, J. (2006). *Forgotten families: Ending the growing crisis confronting children and working parents in the global economy*. New York: Oxford University Press.

Hochschild, A., & Machung, A. (1989). *The second shift*. New York: Viking Penguin.

Japan, Statistics Bureau. (2006). *2006 Survey on time use and leisure activities—Statistical tables*. http://www.stat.go.jp/english/data/shakai/2006/h18kekka.htm#1. Accessed 22 Mar 2010.

Johansson, S. R. (1987). Centuries of childhood/centuries of parenting: Philippe Ariès and the modernization of privileged infancy. *Journal of Family History, 12*(1), 343–365.

Jones, G. W. (2007). Delayed marriage and very low fertility in Pacific Asia. *Population and Development Review, 33*(3), 453–478.

Lutz, W., Skirbekk, V., & Testa, M. R. (2006). The low fertility trap hypothesis: Forces that may lead to further postponement and fewer births in Europe. *Vienna Yearbook of Population Research, 2006*, 167–192.

McDonald, P. (2000). Gender equity, social institutions and the future of fertility. *Journal of Population Research, 17*(1), 1–16.

McDonald, P. (2008). Very low fertility: Consequences, causes and policy approaches. *The Japanese Journal of Population, 6*(1), 19–23.

OECD [Organisation for Economic Co-operation and Development]. (1997). *Employment outlook 1997*. Paris: Organisation for Economic Co-operation and Development.

OECD [Organisation for Economic Co-operation and Development]. (2008). *Education at a glance 2008: OECD indicators*. Paris: Organisation for Economic Co-operation and Development.

OECD [Organisation for Economic Co-operation and Development]. (n.d. a). *Online tax-benefit calculator*. http://www.oecd.org/document/30/0,3343,en_2649_34637_39717906_1_1_1_1,00.html. Accessed 14 Jan 2010.

OECD [Organisation for Economic Co-operation and Development]. (n.d. b). *Family policy database*. http://www.oecd.org/els/social/family/database. Accessed 22 Mar 2010.

Ogawa, N., Mason, A., Chawla, A., Matsukura, R., & Tung, A.-C. (2009). Declining fertility and the rising cost of children: What can NTA say about low fertility in Japan and other Asian countries? *Asian Population Studies, 5*(3), 289–307.

Population Reference Bureau. (2008). *The 2008 world population data sheet*. http://www.prb.org/publications/datasheets/2008/2008wpds.aspx. Accessed 14 Jan 2010.

Retherford, R. D., & Ogawa, N. (2006). Japan's baby bust: Causes, implications and policy responses. In F. Harris (Ed.), *The baby bust: Who will do the work? Who will pay the taxes?* Portland: Rowman & Littlefield.

Rosenfeld, A., & Wise, N. (2000). *The over-scheduled child: Avoiding the hyper-parenting trap*. New York: St. Martin's Press.

Rostgaard, T. (2004). *Family support policy in Central and Eastern Europe: A decade and a half of transition* (Early childhood and family policy series, No 8 – 2004), UNESCO education sector. http://unesdoc.unesco.org/images/0013/001337/133733e.pdf. Accessed 16 Apr 2009.

Saxonberg, S., & Szelewa, D. (2007). The continuing legacy of the Communist legacy? The development of family policies in Poland and the Czech Republic. *Social Politics: International Studies in Gender, State & Society, 14*(3), 351–379.

Schoen, R., Kim, Y. J., Nathanson, C. A., Fields, J., & Astone, N. M. (1997). Why do Americans want children? *Population and Development Review, 23*(2), 333–358.

Sigle-Rushton, W., & Waldfogel, J. (2007a). The incomes of families with children: A cross-national comparison. *Journal of European Social Policy, 17*(4), 299–318.

Sigle-Rushton, W., & Waldfogel, J. (2007b). Motherhood and women's earnings in Anglo-American, Continental European, and Nordic countries. *Feminist Economics, 13*(2), 55–91.

Singapore Government. (2008). *2008 marriage & parenthood package*. http://fcd.ecitizen.gov.sg/MarriageNParenthoodPackage. Accessed 16 Apr 2009.

Statistics Canada. (2008, September 26). *The Daily*. http://www.statcan.gc.ca/daily-quotidien/080926/dq080926a-eng.htm. Accessed 22 Mar 2010.

Statistics New Zealand. (n.d.). *Birth tables*. http://www.stats.govt.nz/methods_and_services/access-data/tables/births.aspx. Accessed 22 Mar 2010.

Stewart, K., & Huerta, C. (2006). *Reinvesting in children? Policies for the very young in South Eastern Europe and the CIS* (Innocenti Working Paper, 2006–01), UNICEF, Innocenti Research Centre. http://www.unicef-irc.org/cgi-bin/unicef/Lunga.sql?ProductID = 422. Accessed 16 Apr 2009.

Suzuki, T. (2005). Why is fertility in Korea lower than in Japan? *Journal of Population Problems, 61*(2), 23–39.

Suzuki, T. (2008). Korea's strong familism and lowest-low fertility. *International Journal of Japanese Sociology, 17*(1), 30–41.

Testa, M. R. (2006). *Childbearing preferences and family issues in Europe* (Special Eurobarometer 253/Wave 65.1). European Commission. http://ec.europa.eu/public_opinion/archives/ebs/ebs_253_en.pdf. Accessed 16 Apr 2009.

Tsuya, N. O., & Bumpass, L. L. (Eds.). (2004). *Marriage, work, and family life in comparative perspective: Japan, South Korea, and the United States*. Honolulu: University of Hawaii Press.

Vienna Institute of Demography. (2008). *European demographic data sheet 2008*. http://www.oeaw.ac.at/vid/datasheet/. Accessed 22 Mar 2010.

World Economic Forum. (2006). *The global gender gap report 2006*. http://www.weforum.org/pdf/gendergap/report2006.pdf. Accessed 22 Mar 2010.

Chapter 3
Very Low Fertility and the High Costs of Children and the Elderly in East Asia

Naohiro Ogawa, Andrew Mason, Sang-Hyop Lee, An-Chi Tung, and Rikiya Matsukura

3.1 Introduction

In the recent past, Ogawa et al. (2009a) attempted to elucidate the effect of direct public and private costs of raising children on fertility in Japan and other selected countries in Asia. One of the criticisms leveled against their study was that it had not analyzed the interrelationships between the cost of children and that of the elderly. In response to this criticism, we attempt here to shed light on the relationship between children and the elderly in the pattern of allocated resources through the following two steps: (1) using a pool of time-series data primarily from three low-fertility East Asian economies (Japan, South Korea, and Taiwan), we examine the nexus between the direct public and private costs of children and the number of children that parents would raise during their reproductive span; and (2) we analyze whether or not there exists a competing relationship between the young and the aged in the allocation of private and public financial resources to these two age groups in the three economies.

The chapter is structured as follows. In the next section, we briefly highlight fertility, mortality, and age compositional transformations over the last few decades in East Asia. In the subsequent section we present some of the basic features of the system of National Transfer Accounts (NTA), which serves as the basic analytical framework for this study. On the basis of the NTA approach, we then analyze, for illustrative purposes, Japan's changing pattern of intergenerational transfers, both public and familial, over the past two decades, especially from the angle of the cost of children as well as from the standpoint of the cost of the elderly. By combining computational results for Japan with those for South Korea and Taiwan, we estimate the relationship between the cost of children and the fertility rate in the three economies. In addition, by employing a pooled data set on the cost of children and the cost of the elderly, we test the applicability of the "crowding out" effect to the East Asian economies. The final section summarizes our major findings.

3.2 Declining Fertility and Population Aging in East Asia

At present, 21 Asian economies have below-replacement fertility. Many of these low-fertility economies are located in East Asia, which has been undergoing continual rapid fertility reduction since the latter half of the 1960s. With the emergence of such rapid fertility declines, today's demographic prospect of East Asia is markedly different from that of only a few decades ago.

In 2010, East Asia's lowest total fertility rate (TFR) was recorded by Taiwan at 0.895, followed by South Korea (1.23) and Japan (1.39), as plotted in Fig. 3.1. These recent fertility rates substantiate the validity of the claim that East Asia currently has the lowest fertility in the world (McDonald 2009). In hopes of raising fertility, the three East Asian governments have been implementing a wide range of pronatalist policies and programs, but have had only limited success so far (Retherford and Ogawa 2009).

Although Japan currently has the highest TFR among these three East Asian economies, it was the first in the region to experience a steep fertility decline. Furthermore, the magnitude of Japan's TFR decline, which occurred after World War II, was one of the greatest among all the industrialized nations. In fact, after a short baby-boom period (1947–1949), Japan's TFR sank by more than 50 %, from 4.54 to 2.04 births, during 1947–1957. This substantial reduction of fertility over a single decade was the first such experience in human history. Subsequently, there were only minor fluctuations around the replacement level until the first oil crisis struck in 1973. Thereafter, the TFR started to fall again, hitting the 1.26 mark in 2005, which was an all-time low in Japan's modern history. After 2005, however, Japan's TFR slowly recovered, reaching 1.39 in 2010. Nonetheless, if fertility were to remain constant at that level, the size of each new generation would decline by 33 %.

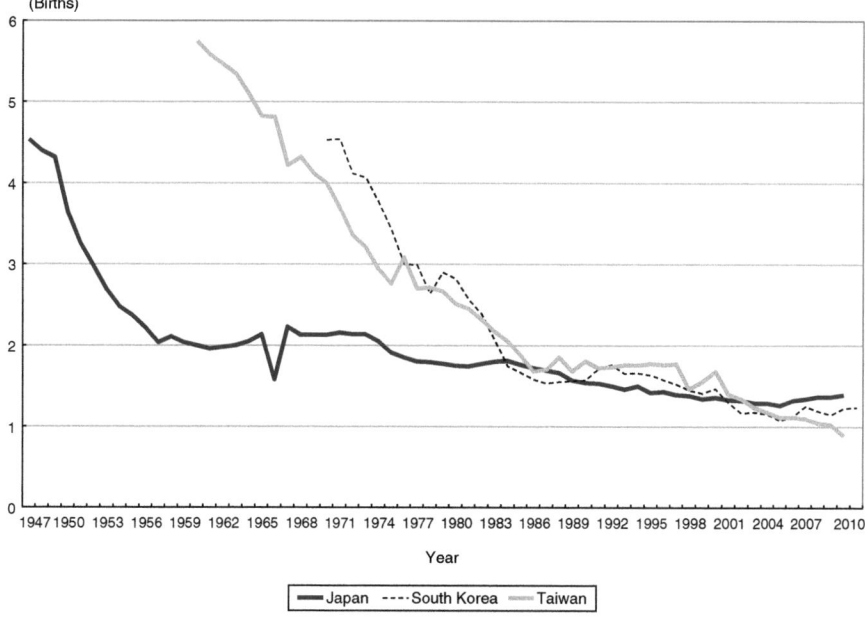

Fig. 3.1 Total fertility rate of Japan, South Korea, and Taiwan, 1947–2011 (Sources: Japan, Ministry of Health, Labour and Welfare (various years); Statistics Korea (n.d. b); Taiwan, Council for Economic Planning and Development (2010a); Taiwan, Department of Statistics (n.d.))

East Asia's very low fertility has been attracting a great deal of attention both inside and outside the region. In contrast, a relatively limited amount of attention has been paid to the rapidity of the mortality transition that has been under way in the region over the past several decades. Japan's unprecedented mortality transition is a good illustration. Japan's life expectancy at birth in 1960 was 65.3 years for men and 70.2 years for women, and these two values were the lowest life expectancies among the OECD member countries at that time (Mason and Ogawa 2001). By the mid-1970s, however, Japanese life expectancy for both sexes combined was one of the highest among the OECD members. In 2010, Japan's male life expectancy at birth reached 79.6 years, to become the fourth highest in the world, while its female life expectancy rose to 86.4 years, the highest in the world (The Nikkei 2011). As regards South Korea and Taiwan, the corresponding figures for females in 2010 were 84.1 and 82.5 years, respectively, and for males, 77.2 and 76.1 years (Statistics Korea n.d.; Taiwan, Department of Statistics n.d.).

Because of such long-term transformations in both fertility and mortality, the age structures of the three East Asian economies have been shifting to a marked extent, as displayed in Fig. 3.2. In the case of Japan, the proportion of those aged 65 and over increased from 4.9 % in 1950 (not shown in Fig. 3.2) to 23.0 % in 2010, indicating that Japan's population is currently the oldest national population in the world. In sharp contrast, the number of those aged below 15 has been declining for 31 consecutive years, from 1982 to 2012, and Japan now has fewer children than at any time in the past 100 years.

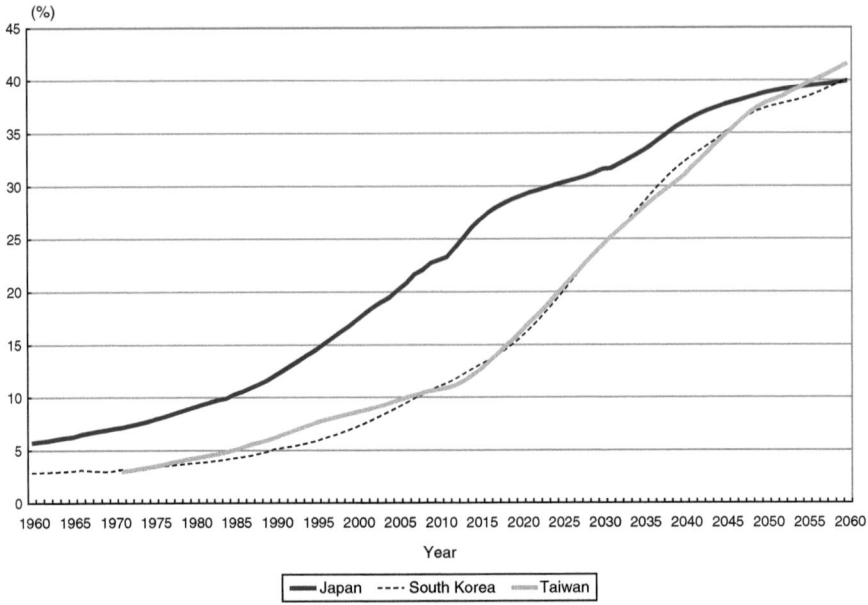

Fig. 3.2 Proportion of the elderly (ages 65+) recorded and projected in the total population: Japan, South Korea, and Taiwan, 1960–2060 (Sources: Japan, Statistics Bureau (various years a, b); NIPSSR (2012); Statistics Korea (n.d. a); Taiwan, Council for Economic Planning and Development (2010a, b))

More importantly, although Japan's aged population reached the 10 % level in 1984 and was the last to do so among the industrialized nations, Japan became the first industrialized country in which the aged comprised more than 20 % of the total population. The length of time required for the increase from 10 to 20 % was only 21 years. Compared with European countries such as Sweden and Norway, Japan is aging at a tempo approximately three times as fast. In addition, as can be seen from Fig. 3.2, in the first half of the twenty-first century, despite a delayed onset of the population aging phenomenon, both South Korea and Taiwan are projected to age faster than Japan, with Taiwan catching up with Japan by 2054, and South Korea by 2059.

3.3 Basic Features of the National Transfer Accounts (NTA) System

To analyze a host of socioeconomic and demographic problems caused by age structural transformation, an international collaborative research project was launched around the turn of this century. At the time of our writing this chapter, a total of 37 countries have participated in this global project. One of its principal objectives is to develop the National Transfer Accounts (NTA), a system for measuring economic flows across age groups. These flows arise because in any viable society, dependent members of the population—those who consume more than they produce—are supported by members of the population who produce more than they consume.

Although societies take different approaches to reallocating resources from surplus to deficit ages, there are two possible methods. One of them relies on capital markets. Namely, individuals accumulate capital during their working ages, and when they are no longer productive they support their consumption in old age by relying on capital income (interest, dividends, rental income, profits, etc.) and by liquidating their assets. The other method relies on transfers from those at surplus ages to those at deficit ages. Some of these transfers are mediated by the public sector. Important examples are public education, publicly financed health care, and public pension programs. In addition, many of the transfers are private transfers, of which familial transfers are most important. The material needs of children are provided mostly by their parents. In Asian societies, familial transfers between adult children and the elderly are also very important. Some of these transfers are between households, but intrahousehold transfers are much more important, since family members in Asia tend to form multigenerational households that engage in large intergenerational transfers.

National Transfer Accounts provide a comprehensive framework for estimating consumption, production, and resource reallocations by age.[1] The accounts are constructed so as to be consistent with and complementary to National Income and Product Accounts. The NTA are being constructed with sufficient historical depth to allow for analysis of key features of the transfer system, and they can also be projected to analyze the economic and policy implications of future demographic changes. Furthermore, sectoral disaggregation allows the analysis of public and private education and health care spending. It should be noted, however, that gender differentiation is not incorporated into the NTA system except in an experimental way.

A fuller explanation of the NTA's basic concepts, the crucial computational assumptions used, and definitions of other key variables are available on the NTA website (http://www.ntaccounts.org). Moreover, a volume containing many NTA country reports together with several chapters on the foundations of NTA and intercountry comparative analysis on selected topics has been published in the recent past (Lee and Mason 2011).

---

[1] It should be noted, however, that the NTA do not include voluntary care work and other services produced inside the household.

3.4 Measuring the Private and Public Costs of Children and the Elderly Within the NTA Framework

3.4.1 The Nexus Between the Direct Costs of Children and the Elderly

In recent years, the gloomy demographic scenarios set for most of the East Asian countries for the next few decades have given rise to a great deal of concern at all levels of their societies.[2] Japan is a salient example. In the hope of raising marital fertility to mitigate a host of adverse effects of population decline and aging, the Japanese government has been implementing, as listed in Table 3.1, a wide range of programs and policy measures since 1972 (Retherford and Ogawa 2006; Ogawa

Table 3.1 Major Japanese government measures aimed at raising fertility, by year

TFR	Year	Action
2.14	1972	Establishment of child allowances (no pronatalist intent at first)
1.54	1990	Establishment of interministry Committee for Creating a Sound Environment for Bearing and Rearing Children
1.53	1991	Enactment of Child Care Leave Act
1.50	1994	Announcement of the Angel Plan for FY 1995–1999
1.42	1995	Enactment of Child Care and Family Care Leave Act
1.34	1999	Announcement of the New Angel Plan for FY 2000–2004
1.33	2001	Amendment to the Employment Insurance Law, specifying that 40 % of salary should be paid to regular full-time employees during child care leave
1.32	2002	Announcement of the Plus One Plan
1.29	2003	Enactment of the Next-generation Law
		Enactment of Law on Basic Measures to Cope with Declining Fertility Society
1.29	2004	Cabinet approval of An Outline of Measures to Cope with Declining Fertility Society
		Announcement of the New Angel Plan for FY 2005–2009
		Revision of Child Care and Family Care Leave Act
1.26	2005	Extension of child care leave to part-time workers, with some limitations
1.32	2006	Announcement of New Policy to Cope with Low Fertility
1.34	2007	Announcement of Work–life Balance Charter and Guidelines
1.37	2008	Announcement of New Strategy for Eliminating Kindergarten Waiting Lists
1.39	2010	Cabinet office formulation of the Vision for Children and Child Rearing for FY 2010–2014
		Establishment of new child allowances
		Formulation of the Project for Early Elimination of Kindergarten Waiting Lists

Source: Compiled by authors from Japan, Cabinet Office (2011)

---

[2]For example, the Chinese government is already concerned about the adverse effects of the cessation of the first demographic dividend in that country, which is projected to end in 2014, and the possibility that China will be facing the "aging before affluence" situation in the 2010s (See Ogawa and Chen 2013).

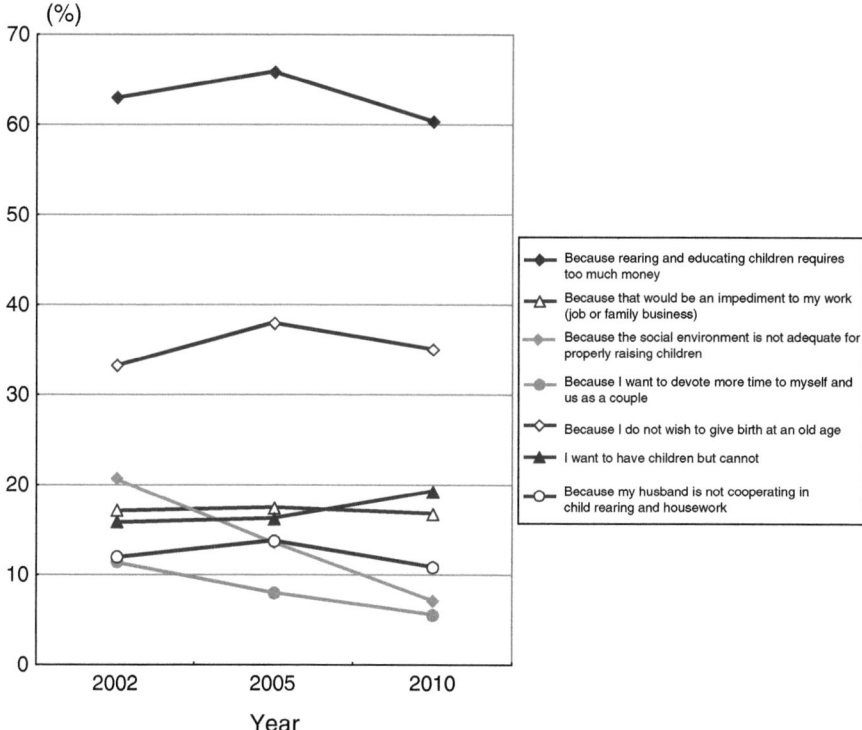

Fig. 3.3 Reasons why the intended number of children is smaller than the ideal number: Japan, currently married women under age 50 (Sources: NIPSSR (2003, 2007, 2011). Note: The authors selected 7 out of 13 precoded responses for this figure)

et al. 2009b).[3] A cursory look at this table reveals that most of these programs and policy measures have been intended to lower both the financial and nonfinancial costs of bearing and rearing children.

According to the data gleaned in the most recent three rounds (2002, 2005, and 2010) of the Japanese National Fertility Survey conducted by the National Institute of Population and Social Security Research (NIPSSR), the high cost of children remains the most important reason for having fewer children among married women of reproductive age below 50. The respondents of the National Fertility Survey were asked to select as many as they wished out of 13 precoded responses to explain why they did not intend to achieve their ideal number of children. The response category that attracted the largest number of responses was "rearing and educating children requires too much money," as illustrated in Fig. 3.3.

---

[3]Most of the government policies measures in Japan mainly focus on women, but some efforts have been directed at men, too. For example, in recent years the government has been encouraging married men to utilize childcare leave. However, the impact has been virtually nonexistent, since the proportion of men taking advantage of the scheme has been around 1 %.

This survey-based result is in line with what Becker's economic theory of fertility (1960, 1981) states. According to an essential idea of the Becker model, the psychological satisfaction that parents obtain from children is directly related to the number of children they have and the amount of resources they spend on them. If parents spend a greater amount of resources on a child, they derive greater satisfaction if the child is of "higher quality." In Becker's fertility model, to increase the amount of satisfaction in the conditions where there is a higher private cost of having children, the parents opt for the substitution of quality for quantity of children, thus operating to decrease fertility. Consequently, Becker's model suggests that there exists a trade-off between the number of children in the family and the quality of those children. Besides private costs of children, public spending on children may play an important role in determining the quality and quantity of children that parents have. For example, subsidizing the quality of children reduces the private costs of rearing high-quality children, thus leading to higher fertility.

The trade-off between spending and the number of children has other implications too. One of them is related to generational equity. Preston (1984) raised the possibility that population aging will lead to a decline in the welfare of children relative to the welfare of the elderly. In Japan, the cost of the elderly has been rising alongside the cost of children, partly owing to the maturity of the pension programs (Ogawa and Retherford 1997; Ogawa et al. 2010a). In addition, the argument has been advanced with respect to the allocation of public resources that, as a consequence of both the increased political power of the elderly induced by rapid population aging and the severe constraints on the Japanese government's budgetary resources, it is conceivable that a "crowding out" effect may be occurring between the resources directed to the young and to the elderly. Another important macroeconomic consideration pertaining to the costs of children is related to the trade-off between the number of children and human-capital spending per child (Becker et al. 1990; Lee et al. 2008).

3.4.2 Per Capita Private and Public Consumption Profiles for Children and the Elderly

Because the direct cost of raising children to adulthood and of supporting elderly persons in retirement is one of the key variables in this chapter, it is worth discussing how the direct public and private costs of rearing children and supporting the elderly are computed. In the NTA system, consumption, both private and public, comprises education, health care, and other consumption (food, clothing, housing, durables, etc.). Moreover, because the young population, particularly at school-going ages, has little or no labor income, its consumption is virtually equal to the direct costs

3 Very Low Fertility and the High Costs of Children and the Elderly in East Asia

of raising children. In contrast, the direct living costs of the elderly need to be calculated as a difference between their consumption and their labor income.[4]

We first discuss the computation of per capita private costs of children and the elderly. We estimate the age-specific profile of the per capita private education costs by applying the following equation to the microlevel data gathered in national representative household income and expenditure surveys. In the case of Japan, we have applied the equation to the five rounds (1984, 1989, 1994, 1999, and 2004) of the National Survey of Family Income and Expenditure (NSFIE), carried out by the Statistics Bureau of Japan:

$$\tau_{jx}^{e+} = \sum_f \beta_f N_{fj}, \qquad (3.1)$$

where N_{fj} = the number of enrolled members in age group f in the household j, τ_{jx}^{e+} = sector x (education) expenditure of household j, and β_f = the average expenditure of age group f.

Similarly, we have estimated the age-specific profile of the per capita cost of private health care on the basis of the same survey data, using the following equation:

$$\tau_{jx}^{e+} = \sum_f \beta_f N_{fj}^e, \qquad (3.2)$$

where N_{fj}^e = the number of household members in age group f, τ_{jx}^{e+} = sector x (health) expenditures of household j, and β_f = the average expenditure for age group f.

The age-specific profile of the per capita cost of private consumption, excluding private education and health care, is estimated by a relatively simple *a priori* method, as shown in Eq. 3.3:

$$\alpha(a) = 1 - 0.6 \times D\,(4 < a < 20) \times \left[\frac{20-a}{16}\right] - 0.6 \times D\,(a \leq 4), \qquad (3.3)$$

where $\alpha(a)$ = the equivalence scale of age group a and $D(z)$ is a dummy variable that takes the value of one when condition z is met but is otherwise zero. The computed equivalence scales at varying ages are as follows: 0.4 for the age group 0–4, and 1.0 for the age group 20 and over, whereas the scale values for the age group 5–19 increase linearly with age.

The values used in the NTA system are substantially different from the various results for the age-specific profile of per capita direct private consumption

---

[4] Although foregone income is an important part of costs to be incurred in raising children and taking care of elderly persons, it falls outside the scope of this chapter.

previously computed for Japan.[5] It should be stressed, however, that both education and health care are excluded from the equivalence scales used in the NTA system, which is why we cannot rigidly compare the results derived from these different modeling approaches.

We now discuss the procedure for computing per capita public costs of children and the elderly. The age-specific profile of the per capita public education cost has been computed from the published data on the government's expenditure for each level of education and the number of pupils and students at each level of education in 1984, 1989, 1994, 1999, and 2004. We have estimated the age-specific profile of the per capita health care cost on the basis of the government's published data concerning age-specific outpatient and inpatient costs per case and the age-specific incidence of receiving such medical treatments. In the case of the per capita cost of public consumption in general (e.g., government employees' salaries, road maintenance costs, national defense, etc.), we have assumed that every person consumes equally, and have simply divided the total annual expenditure for each component of public consumption, except for education and health care, by the total population.

Using these computed results of age-specific profiles of various components of consumption, we have estimated the age-specific profile of per capita consumption for 1984, 1989, 1994, 1999, and 2004, private and public sectors combined. In Fig. 3.4, we have plotted for illustrative purposes the estimated results of per capita total consumption for three of those years (1984, 1994, and 2004). For comparative purposes, we have also plotted the corresponding age-specific profiles of per capita production (labor income) for the three selected years. (For a more detailed methodological explanation of the per capita production profiles, see Ogawa et al. 2010b). These estimated results are expressed in the year 2000 constant prices.

As shown in Fig. 3.4, the magnitude of the upward shift in the estimated age-specific profiles of per capita production from 1994 to 2004 is relatively small. This seems to reflect the influence of "Japan's lost decade" (Yoshikawa 2002). In addition, the upward shift in the profiles from 1984 to 1994 captures the effect on labor income of substantial economic growth during the "bubble economy" phase.

A few more points of interest can be derived from this graphical exposition. First, by drawing upon information contained in Fig. 3.4, we can calculate the size of income and consumption deficits by age in 1984, 1994, and 2004. Throughout the period under review, there are sizable income and consumption deficits at both young and older life cycle stages, as shown in Fig. 3.5. Obviously, these life cycle deficits (LCDs) must be covered, with reallocations coming largely from the surplus of income generated at the life cycle surplus stage during the current period or from assets accumulated during previous periods.

Second, Fig. 3.5 shows that the age at which an average individual shifts from a net consumer to a net producer gradually increased from 23 years in 1984 to

---

[5]Suruga (1993) used the Prais–Houthakker model, Nagase (2001) employed the Engel model, and Oyama (2004) drew upon the Rothbarth equivalence scale model.

3 Very Low Fertility and the High Costs of Children and the Elderly in East Asia 41

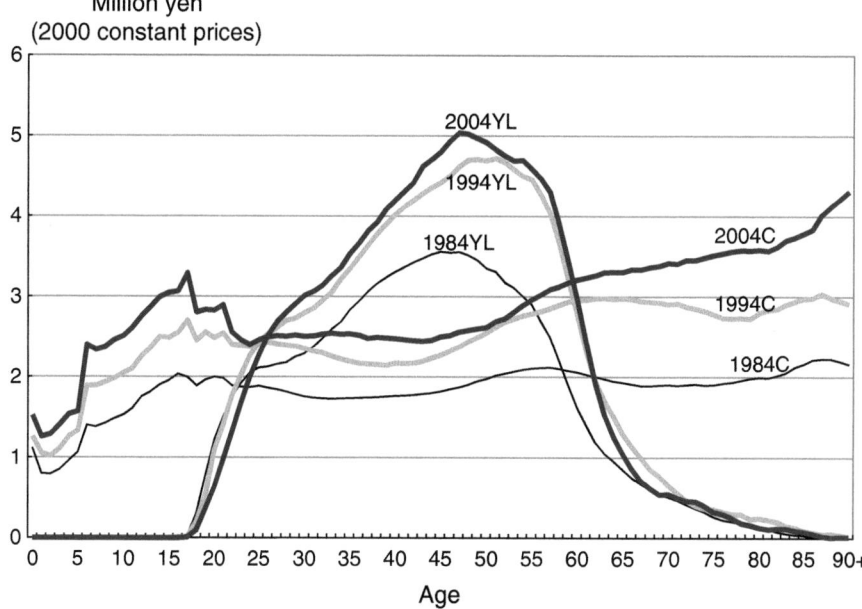

Fig. 3.4 Age-specific profiles of per capita consumption and production: Japan, 1984, 1994, and 2004 (Note: YL denotes labor income, whereas C denotes consumption)

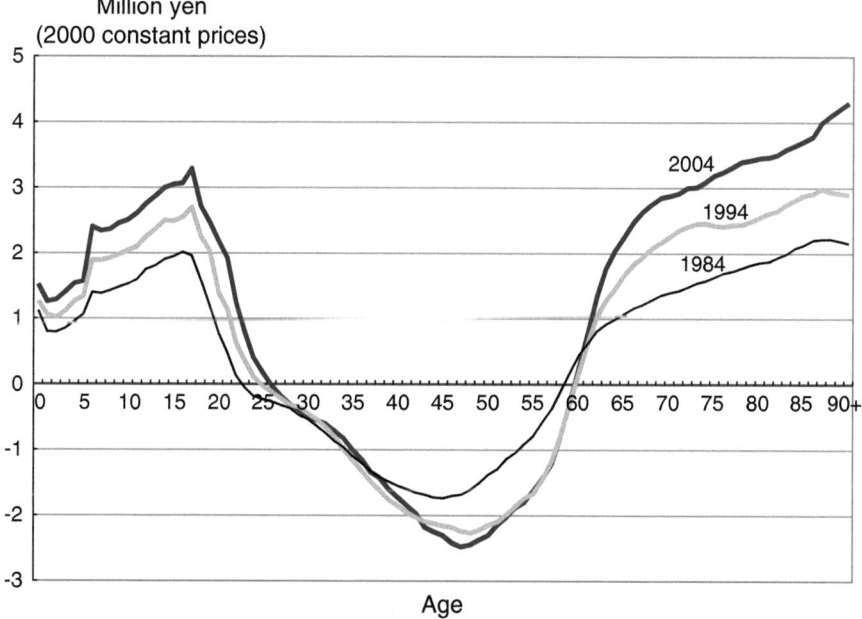

Fig. 3.5 Life cycle deficits: Japan, 1984, 1994, and 2004

25 years in 1994, and to 26 years in 2004. At the other end of the life cycle, the age transition from a net producer to a net consumer was postponed only marginally, from 58 years in 1984 to 60 years in 2004. The fact that the shift in the crossing age at the later stage of life cycle was small is attributable to the existence of Japan's mandatory retirement age.[6] These results indicate that the length of time during which an average individual is financially self-supporting ranges only from 34 to 35 years, which is a relatively short period, corresponding only to approximately two fifths of the average life span.

Third, unlike per capita production, the age profiles of per capita consumption were rising almost continuously over time. The 1984 and 1994 age profiles show a mildly shaped double hump, being high at both young and older ages. The first peak corresponds to the high costs of the young, whereas the second peak is related to the high costs placed upon household heads under multigenerational living arrangements. Moreover, per capita consumption rose distinctly among those aged 65 and over in 2004. This seems to be due to the implementation of Long-term Care Insurance (LTCI) starting in 2000. In that year, in-home care for the frail elderly, which had until then been informally provided by their family members, became formalized as a part of the market economy. As a result, Japan's per capita consumption profiles have started to look increasingly similar to those of the US, Sweden, and Costa Rica, among the NTA member countries (Tung 2011).

Fourth, as widely discussed elsewhere (Mason 2001, 2007; Mason and Lee 2006), one of the important linkages between demographic structural transformations and economic growth is the role of demographic dividends in the process of economic development. When a country's fertility begins to fall, the first demographic dividend arises if changes in the population age structure lead to an increase in the working ages relative to nonworking ages. That is, the first demographic dividend is the rate of growth of the economic support ratio, which rises or falls, subject to the transformation of the age composition in the process of the demographic transition. During a demographic transition, when the economic support ratio rises, income per effective consumer increases, provided that there is no change in productivity. As the economic support ratio declines, however, income per effective consumer falls and the first demographic dividend disappears, which means that the increase in income per effective consumer is transitory.

With a view to identifying the timing and duration of the first demographic dividend for Japan, we have calculated the change in the economic support ratio over the period 1975–2025, and have done so by applying the age-specific profiles of per capita consumption and production observed in the year 2004 as statistical weights to adjust the entire population. This implies that the computational results reflect solely the effect of age structural change on the economic support ratio. In addition, we have used the 2010 United Nations population projection as the source of demographic data for the computation. The results are shown in Fig. 3.6. As can

---

[6]As a result of recent legislation, however, from 2006 the age of retirement was gradually raised from 60 years and became 65 years in 2013.

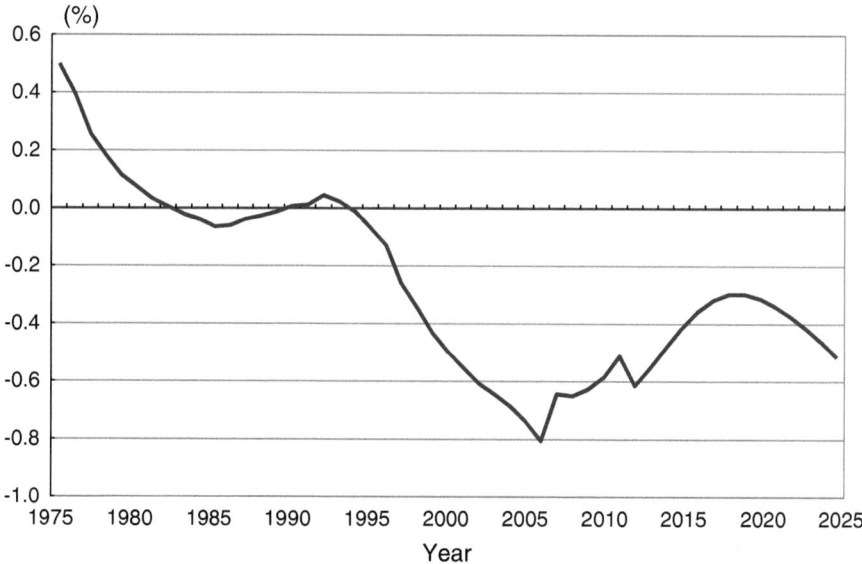

Fig. 3.6 First demographic dividend: Japan, 1975–2025

be observed in this graph, Japan's first demographic dividend came to an end over the period 1982–1995, after which Japan entered into the phase of population aging, where it is expected to continue during the rest of the projected period.[7]

3.4.3 Life Cycle Deficits and Life Cycle Allocations

As has been widely reported in numerous publications about the NTA system, the accounts measure intergenerational flows for a certain period of time (usually a calendar or fiscal year) and are governed by the following relationship:

$$y^l + y^A + \tau_g^+ + \tau_f^+ = C + S + \tau_g^- + \tau_f^-, \tag{3.4}$$

where y^l = labor income, y^A = asset income, τ_g^+ = public transfer inflows, τ_f^+ = private transfer inflows, C = consumption, S = saving, τ_g^- = public transfer outflows to the government, and τ_f^- = private transfer outflows. By rearranging the terms in Eq. 3.4, we see that the LCD, which is the difference between consumption

---

[7]By applying the same computational procedure to each economy's data, we have computed the timing and duration of the first demographic dividend for Taiwan and South Korea. As shown in Appendix Fig. 3.12, in the case of South Korea, the first demographic dividend phase ended in 2007, whereas Taiwan reached the end of its first dividend stage in 2013.

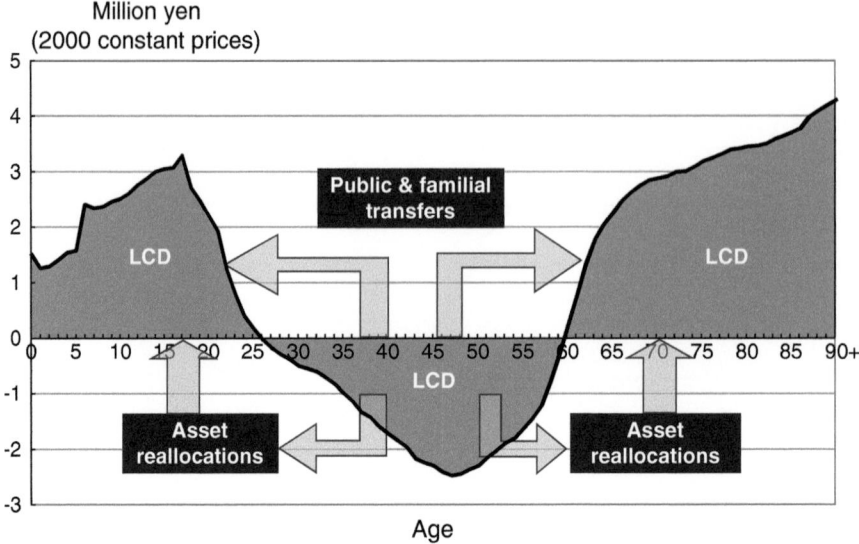

Fig. 3.7 Total reallocations: Life cycle deficits (LCD)

and production, is matched by age reallocations consisting of reallocations through assets and net transfers, as expressed in Eq. 3.5:

$$\underbrace{C - y^l}_{\text{Lifecycle deficit}} = \underbrace{y^A - S}_{\text{Asset reallocations}} + \underbrace{\tau_g^+ - \tau_g^-}_{\text{Net public transfers}} + \underbrace{\tau_f^+ - \tau_f^-}_{\text{Net private transfers}}$$

$$\underbrace{}_{\text{Net transfers}}$$

$$\underbrace{}_{\text{Age reallocations}}$$

(3.5)

To gain further insight into Eq. 3.5, we can express the mathematical relationship by using the relevant data for 2004 as illustrated in Fig. 3.7.[8] In this graph, the vertical scale represents the age-specific per capita deficit, which corresponds to the difference between per capita consumption and per capita production at each age. Note that a graph depicting the age-specific aggregate-level deficit (containing the total number of persons at each age) would indicate a pattern substantially different from the one displayed in Fig. 3.7.

By applying the time-series data for Japan to Fig. 3.7, we have produced Fig. 3.8, which shows how the pattern of three components of reallocation of the LCD changed in Japan over the two decades beginning in 1984. The three components

---

[8]Two points should be noted. First, the terms "familial transfers" and "private transfers" are used interchangeably in this chapter; both of them refer to private transfers received by households from any source, of which the predominant share is surely familial transfers. Second, although net private transfers consist of bequests and *inter vivo* transfers, the computation of the bequest

3 Very Low Fertility and the High Costs of Children and the Elderly in East Asia 45

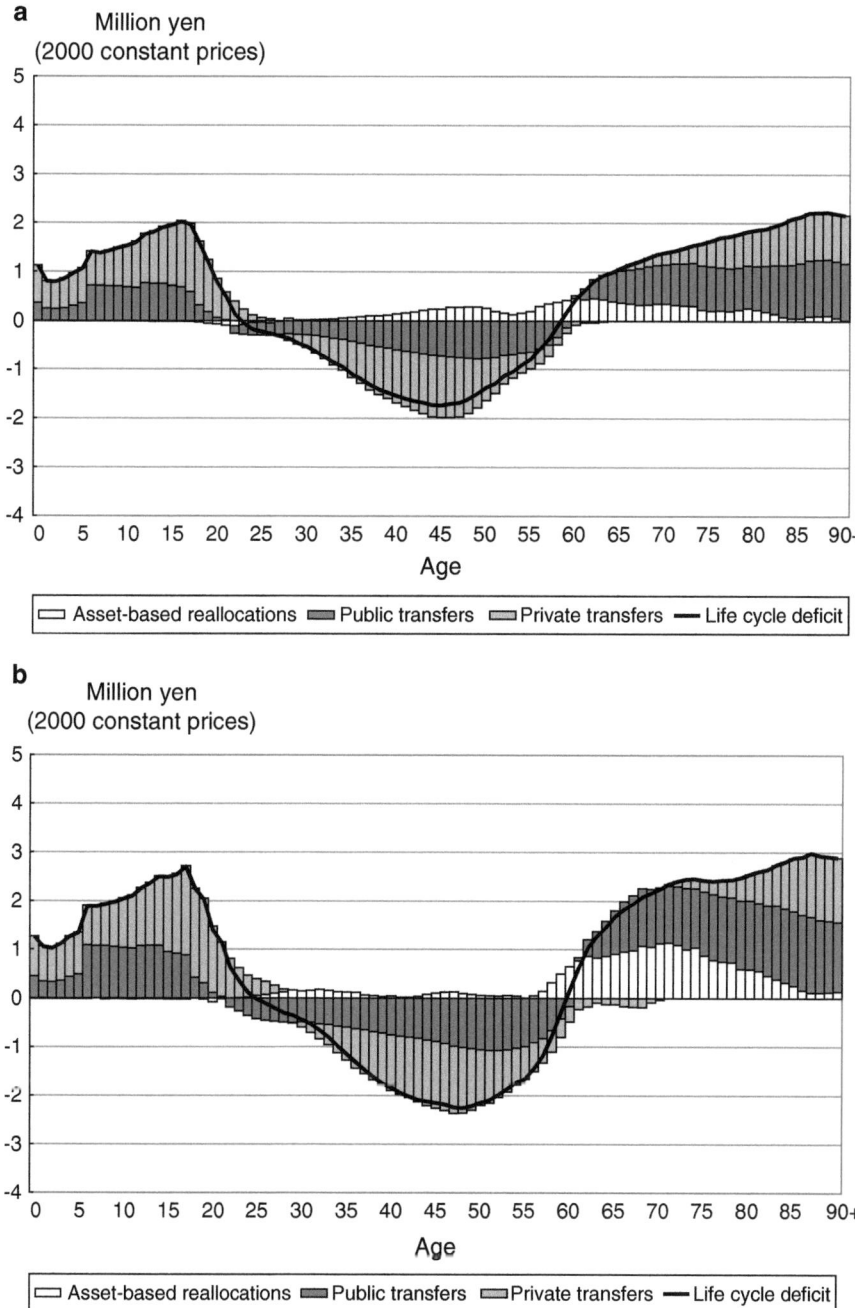

Fig. 3.8 Changing pattern of three components of per capita reallocation of life cycle deficit@: Japan, (**a**) 1984, (**b**) 1994, and (**c**) 2004

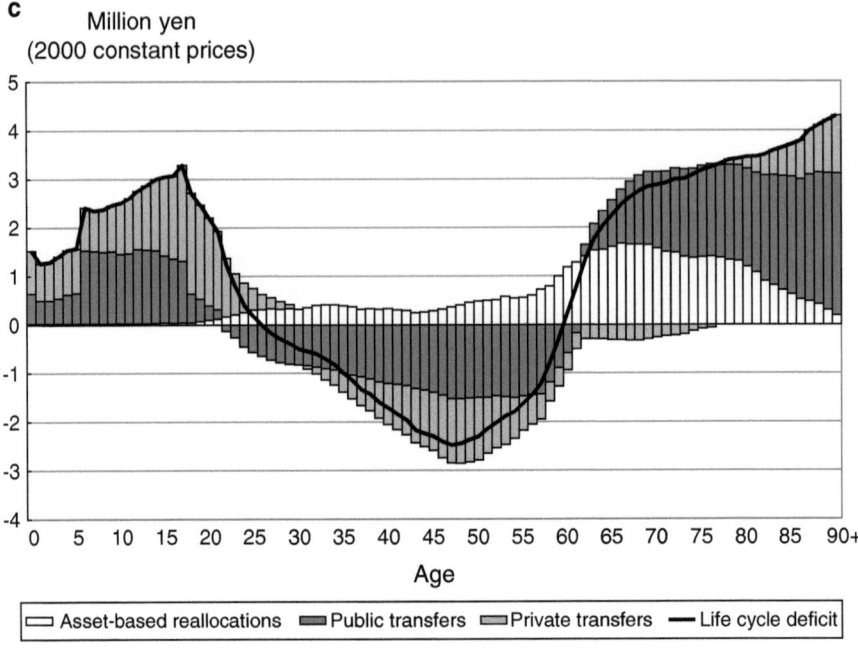

Fig. 3.8 (continued)

are reallocations through assets, public transfers, and private transfers, measured on an annual basis. Panels (a), (b), and (c) illustrate annual reallocations of the LCD observed in 1984, 1994, and 2004.

3.5 Increased Per Capita Costs of Children and the Elderly Over Time in East Asia

To facilitate the analysis that follows in this section, we introduce and define two new variables, the child LCD and the elderly LCD. The child LCD represents the per capita direct cost of raising children up to a self-sufficient age, i.e., the age at which the age-specific LCD shifts from positive to negative, based upon the NTA system. The elderly LCD represents the per capita direct cost of the elderly from the age at which they cease to be self-sufficient up to the age of their death.[9] The

---

component has not been completed at the time of our writing this chapter. For this reason, bequests are excluded from the computational results reported here.

[9]In the quantitative exercise that follows, each of the three economies (Japan, Taiwan, and South Korea) experiences during the period under review a rising trend in the direct cost of raising children up to their self-sufficient ages. In Japan the age increases from 23 years in 1984 to

per capita direct cost of the elderly corresponds to the sum of the age-specific LCD, computed as consumption minus production.

3.5.1 Spending per Child and the Number of Children in the Three East Asian Countries

As briefly discussed earlier in this chapter and fully described elsewhere (Ogawa et al. 2009a), one of the key concepts in the economics of fertility is the trade-off between the spending per child and the number of children; and this idea is fully embedded in Becker's model of fertility decision-making (Becker 1960, 1981). In its simplest form, Becker's theory states that higher income leads to an increase in the demand for higher quality in children and a more modest increase in the demand for the number of children (quantity). But because higher-quality children are costly, couples tend to substitute quality for quantity. In other words, the basic trade-off has to do with private costs of children, i.e., costs borne by the fertility decision-makers (parents). Public spending on children may also play an important role. For instance, the provision of government subsidies for improving the quality of children reduces the private cost of raising high-quality children and consequently boosts fertility.

As briefly described above, the child LCD is the consumption (both public and private) by children, minus the value of children's labor, i.e., the cost that children themselves cover. The child LCD is calculated for single years of age and can be used to construct a synthetic cohort measure of the cost of children. It represents the direct cost of children, assuming that they are raised from birth to adulthood consuming and producing at the same age-specific rates that prevailed in the year in question.

We normalize the child LCD by dividing it by the mean labor income of prime-age adults aged 30–49. Doing this facilitates comparison across countries but also indirectly controls for the effects of income on child spending. To allow for mortality risks in childhood, we have also adjusted the normalized child LCD by using appropriate life table values. Thus, the computed values can be interpreted as the years of prime-age adult labor devoted to rearing a child from birth to economic independence, or to the child's death, should that occur during childhood.

Using the computed results of the child LCD per person below a self-sufficient age and the mean income of adults aged 30–49 for Japan, we have calculated the normalized per capita child LCD, adjusted for survivorship from birth to the

---

26 years in 2004 and Taiwan records a comparable rise from 1981 to 2005, whereas South Korea experiences the same shift more swiftly from 1996 to 2005. In contrast, each of the three economies shows a different pattern of change over time as regards the age at which the elderly cease to be self-sufficient. In both Japan and South Korea, this age remains stable: around 58–59 years for Japan and 55 years for South Korea. In Taiwan, however, the age at which the LCD shifts from negative to positive gradually declines from 63 years in 1981 to 53 years in 2005.

self-supporting age in 1984, 1989, 1994, 1999, and 2004. The calculated values increased monotonically over time, namely, 9.8 years of labor income in 1984, 10.6 years in 1989, 11.5 years in 1994, 12.9 years in 1999, and 14.3 years in 2004. We have carried out the same computation for Taiwan (1981–2005) and South Korea (1996–2005). In the case of Taiwan, the normalized per capita child LCD adjusted for survivorship increased almost continuously, from 7.8 years in 1981 to 16.7 years in 2005. In the case of South Korea, the corresponding value rose linearly from 9.0 years in 1996 to 12.6 years in 2005.

With a view to quantitatively examining the trade-off between the spending on children and the number of children, we have pooled the results for the child LCD derived from the three economies and have linked them to the time-series data on TFR for each economy under investigation. In Japan, the TFR declined continuously, from 1.81 in 1984 to 1.29 in 2004. Taiwan's TFR declined substantially from 2.46 to 1.12 from 1981 to 2005, whereas South Korea's TFR fell from 1.60 to 1.10 during the period 1996–2005.

Figure 3.9 plots a total of 33 data points of the normalized per capita child LCD for the three economies for various years, coupled with the TFR for the corresponding years. As displayed in this graph, we have fitted the data by regressing the natural logarithm of the normalized per capita child LCD onto the natural logarithm of the TFR; hence, the coefficient is the elasticity of the quality–quantity trade-off.

As is well-known, a coefficient of -1 implies that a 1 percentage-point decrease in the number of children is accompanied by a 1 percentage-point increase in the cost of children and, hence, the total change in spending by adults on childrearing

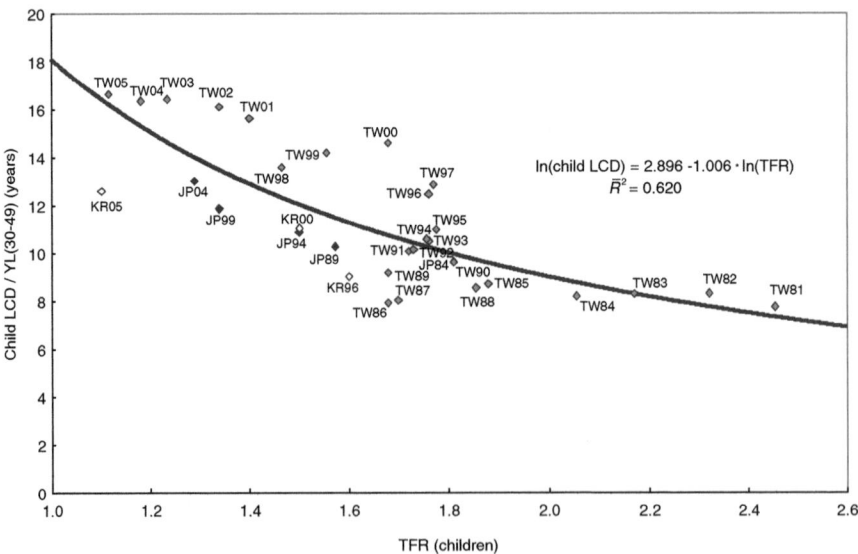

Fig. 3.9 TFR versus normalized per capita LCD for children: Japan, South Korea, and Taiwan

3 Very Low Fertility and the High Costs of Children and the Elderly in East Asia   49

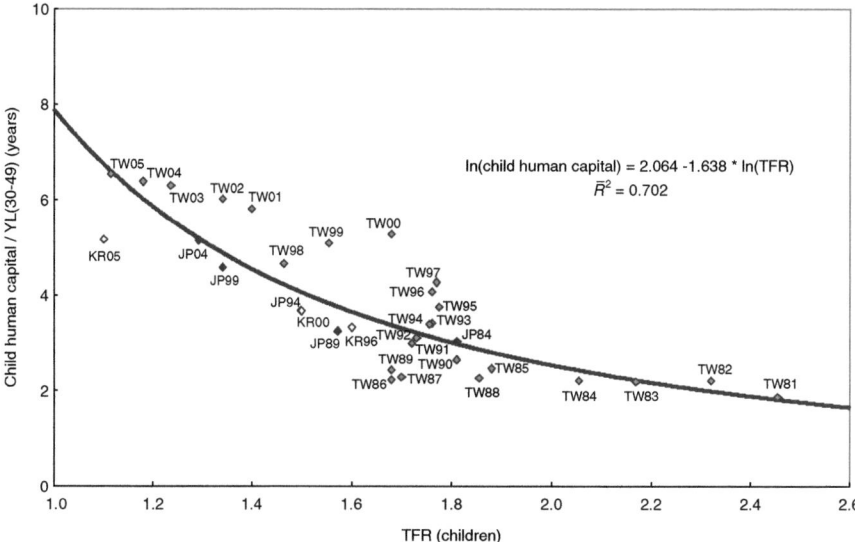

Fig. 3.10 TFR versus normalized per capita human capital spending for children: Japan, South Korea, and Taiwan

remains constant. Figure 3.9 shows that the estimated elasticity for the three East Asian economies combined is −1.01, implying that a decrease in the TFR leads to essentially no change in the total cost of childrearing per adult.

Furthermore, we have undertaken a regression analysis, as displayed in Fig. 3.10, by focusing on the relationship between the human-capital component (education and health costs) of per capita child LCD and the TFR. Except for the fact that we have used the human-capital component of the per capita child LCD in place of the per capita child LCD as a whole, all the data points plotted in Fig. 3.10 have been constructed in the same manner as in Fig. 3.9. The regression result indicates that the computed elasticity (−1.64) is considerably larger than the one shown in Fig. 3.9 for the total cost of children. This elasticity is also much larger than the cross-sectional elasticity reported by Lee and Mason (2010). In addition, the goodness of fit, as measured by adjusted R^2, is better in the case of the computed result shown in Fig. 3.10 than that in Fig. 3.9. Hence, the health and education component of per capita child LCD are more closely linked to fertility change than the other components of child LCD.[10] This finding is consistent with the widely-held view that human-capital factors have been playing an important role in the relationship

---

[10]We have also run the same regressions by adding the 2002 data for China, but the results are basically the same as those for the other three East Asian economies alone. The validity of this observation, however, needs to be carefully assessed as China's time-series data become available.

between economic growth and fertility change in Asian countries, particularly in East Asia (Ogawa et al. 2009a; McDonald 2009).[11]

To shed more light on the nexus between human-capital factors and fertility, we conducted two additional regressions for the three East Asian economies. In one of them, we fitted the data by regressing the natural logarithm of normalized per capita *public* human-capital spending onto the natural logarithm of the TFR. In the other, we regressed the natural logarithm of normalized per capita *private* human-capital spending on the natural logarithm of the TFR. The results of these regressions, not detailed here, indicate that both the public and private components of human-capital spending have similar associations with fertility, i.e., the elasticity of -1.62 for public human-capital spending and the elasticity of -1.49 for private human-capital spending.

These computational results appear to be inconsistent with those obtained in the work recently undertaken by Lee and Mason. In their recent analysis of NTA data from 19 economies (not only in Asia, but also in Europe and Latin America), they have found that the quantity–quality trade-off is very strong for public spending (particularly on education) but not for private human-capital spending (Lee and Mason 2010). As can be seen in Table 3.2, however, private human-capital spending (particularly on education) tends to be very large, and even exceeds public human-capital spending in East Asian economies such as South Korea, Taiwan, and China. Primarily because East Asian societies are "success-oriented," parents in those societies are prone to spend vast amounts of financial resources on their children's education (McDonald 2008). We believe that our two elasticity results, one on public human-capital spending and the other on private human-capital spending, have turned out to be fairly comparable to each other precisely because of the cultural emphasis on success in the three East Asian societies, and that this explains why our results differ from those obtained by Lee and Mason, whose data came from a wide spectrum of societies.

The regression results presented thus far appear to conform to the view that there is a distinctive trade-off between the number of children and the combined (familial and public) spending per child in East Asia. Caution should be exercised in interpreting these fitted results, however. All the regressions for East Asia are based upon a mixture of cross-sectional and time-series data that are heavily dominated by Taiwan. Given such limitations of the data, the fixes that are usually employed to deal with well-known statistical problems that limit the value of aggregate

---

[11] Aside from these two regressions for the three East Asian economies, we have also run additional regressions by employing data from other countries that were available on the NTA website at the time of writing this chapter. The following eight economies have been incorporated into the additional regressions: Chile (1997), Costa Rica (2004), France (2001), Hungary (2005), the Philippines (1999), Slovenia (2004), the US (2003), and Uruguay (2004). The computed values of elasticity for this expanded data set are -0.77 for per capita child LCD and -1.56 for the human capital component of per capita child LCD. These additional results show that the computed elasticity values are smaller when all the economies are combined than when the three selected East Asian economies are examined separately from the others.

Table 3.2 Proportion of private spending in per capita educational costs for children and youths of ages 0–24: selected economies

Country	Year	Percentage
Sweden	2003	3.1
France	2001	5.0
Austria	2000	5.8
Slovenia	2004	8.7
Hungary	2005	11.1
US	2003	17.0
Costa Rica	2004	22.3
Japan	2004	26.0
Chile	1997	39.4
Indonesia	2004	39.6
Uruguay	1994	46.4
Philippines	1999	48.2
South Korea	2005	51.6
Taiwan	2005	69.4
China	2002	71.2

Source: Authors' calculations

regression estimates are not practical in this case. Furthermore, these regression results do not represent causal relationships. That is, the variable on the right hand of the regressions is not necessarily an explanatory variable, nor is the variable on the left hand of the regressions necessarily a dependent variable. Hence, the regressions estimated in this chapter should be treated only as a descriptive device, thus making causal interpretation indefensible.

3.5.2 The Role of the First Demographic Dividend in Determining the Interrelationship Between the Per Capita Child LCD and the Number of Children in East Asia

In the foregoing analysis, we have examined the nexus between the normalized per capita child LCD and the number of children in the three East Asian economies. It should be stressed that a rise in the economic support ratio has accompanied the decline in total fertility. It may be that spending on children is rising because of the favorable support ratio rather than (or in addition to) the decline in the number of children per se. As discussed earlier in this chapter, fertility decline induces a higher economic support ratio, which in turn leads to an increase in the normalized per capita child LCD. Despite this important linkage between the fertility decline and the economic support ratio, no empirical work has been conducted yet on the relationship among the cost of children, the number of children, and the economic support ratio. Taking into account the importance of the economic support ratio

Table 3.3 Estimated results for the four regressions with the economic support ratio (ESR) variable incorporated for Japan, South Korea, and Taiwan

Left-hand side variables	Right-hand side variables			
	ln (TFR)	ln (ESR)	Constant	Adjusted R^2
ln (Per capita child LCD)	−0.47	1.48	2.42	0.97
ln (Per capita child human capital, public and private combined)	−0.97	1.84	1.48	0.93
ln (Per capita child human capital, public)	−1.23	0.90	1.01	0.64
ln (Per capita child human capital, private)	−0.43	2.89	0.38	0.67

in determining the relationship between the cost of children and the number of children, we expand our regression analysis by adding the economic support ratio to the two key variables (the per capita cost of children and the number of children).

Table 3.3 presents the estimated results for pooled data from the three East Asian economies. Four variables are treated as dependent variables: (1) normalized per capita child LCD, (2) the human-capital component (public and private combined) of normalized per capita child LCD, (3) the public human-capital component of normalized per capita child LCD, and (4) the private human-capital component of normalized per capita child LCD. A brief glance at the estimated results of the four regressions reveals that the economic support ratio positively affects all four variables representing the per capita cost of children. In addition, in each regression, the value of the estimated coefficient for the TFR variable is considerably smaller than its corresponding value in each of the earlier regressions without the economic support ratio, as indicated by the regression results reported in Figs. 3.9 and 3.10. This result is consistent with the view that fertility change and the economic support ratio are related to each other to a significant extent.

The results reported in Table 3.3 for the economic support ratio are interesting in their own right. The elasticity of the economic support ratio is 0.90 in the case of the public human-capital component of normalized per capita child LCD, but it is much larger (2.89) in the case of the private human-capital component of normalized per capita child LCD. This is an interesting pattern that warrants further investigation.

3.5.3 The Interrelationship Between the Per Capita Child LCD and the Per Capita Elderly LCD

In recent years, numerous studies (e.g., Takegawa 2005) have shown that the cost of the elderly has also been rising in aging Asia, particularly in East Asia. The question therefore arises: Is there a "crowding out" effect between the resources going to the young and those allotted to the elderly? To shed light on this question, we have calculated, on a time-series basis, (1) how many years of the mean labor income of prime-age adults aged 30–49 are needed to finance the per capita LCD for a child,

3 Very Low Fertility and the High Costs of Children and the Elderly in East Asia

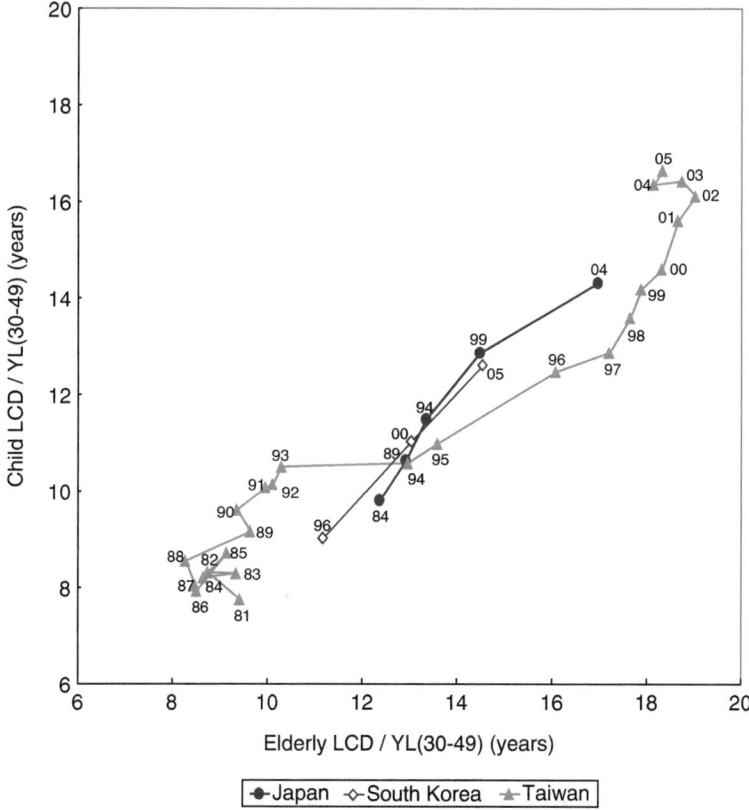

Fig. 3.11 Relationship between the cost of children and the cost of the elderly: Japan, South Korea, and Taiwan

and (2) how many years of prime-age mean labor income are required to finance the per capita LCD for an elderly person. The data for the computation have been prepared for Japan, South Korea, and Taiwan in the same manner as in our foregoing analysis pertaining to the cost of children and fertility.

The computed results are plotted in Fig. 3.11. The pattern emerging from this graph indicates that both the cost of a child and the cost of an elderly person grow in the same direction, thus suggesting that there is no "crowding out" effect in these three East Asian economies.[12] This result suggests that in those three economies, working-age adults are sandwiched between their elderly parents and their children, and rely heavily on assets to meet their own material needs as well as their familial and social obligations to the older and younger generations.

---

[12] The simple correlation coefficient between the two variables shown in Fig. 3.11 amounts to 0.96.

Besides these three East Asian economies, we have calculated the cost of a child and the cost of an elderly person for NTA member countries in other regions. Although omitting relevant graphs, we can safely make the following observations. On the one hand, in both Latin America and Africa we found virtually the same pattern as the one prevailing in the three East Asian economies. On the other hand, European countries show a totally different pattern from that in the developing economies; and the cross-sectional data gleaned from the European countries involved in the NTA project indicate that there is no significant relationship between the costs of the two age groups. It is conceivable that, because many of the European countries have had welfare systems for a long time, the per capita benefits that elderly retirees receive there are more stable and larger than in the developing countries. At any rate, we should reassess this statistical result when the NTA data for the European countries become available on a time-series basis.

3.6 Concluding Remarks

In this chapter we have examined the relationship between the cost of raising children up to self-supporting ages and the number of children parents have, by drawing heavily upon the computed results for Japan, South Korea, and Taiwan. The results suggest that the two variables in question have a negative association in the case of the three East Asian economies, and that the calculated elasticity is -1.01, which implies that a decrease in the TFR leads to essentially no change in the total cost of childrearing per adult. More importantly, as regards the per capita child human-capital costs and the TFR, the calculated elasticity amounts to -1.64, which suggests that, in the three economies under examination, the health and education components of the per capita child LCD are more closely linked to fertility change than are other components. In addition, a difference between the results obtained from this study and those derived from earlier ones (Lee and Mason 2010; Ogawa et al. 2009a) is that our estimate controls for the economic support ratio. No other research undertaken so far has examined the role of the economic support ratio in the analysis of the cost of raising children and the number of children that parents have.

So, what can these three East Asian societies do to restore their fertility levels in the years to come? The fact that higher-quality children are costly leads couples to substitute quality for quantity. This basic trade-off between the quality and quantity of children plays a crucial role in determining the private cost of children borne by parents. Public spending on children also plays a vital role in this respect. By subsidizing the quality of children via public resources, for example, a government reduces the cost to parents of rearing higher-quality children, and thus encourages higher fertility.

Apart from providing subsidies for pronatalist purposes, a government can reduce the child LCD by lowering the self-supporting ages—for example, by creating more stable full-time job opportunities for young workers. In the case of a shrinking population such as that of Japan, hourly labor productivity can be raised through better vocational and on-the-job training. Encouraging women's labor force participation is another option for increasing productivity, but methods for ameliorating the potentially negative impact of female paid employment on fertility need to be carefully considered before this policy option is implemented.

The trade-off between the cost of children and the number of children has implications not only for fertility policies but also for generational equity. As hypothesized by Preston (1984), population aging induced by reduced fertility and extended longevity should lead to a decline in the welfare of children relative to the elderly. However, in the three East Asian economies we have examined in this study, the "crowding out" phenomenon posited between children and the elderly competing for limited public and private resources is not observed.

Acknowledgments Research for this study was partially funded by two grants from Nihon University: the Nihon University Multidisciplinary Research Grant 2011 and the Collaborative Research Grant of the Research Institute of Economic Science, the College of Economics.

Appendix

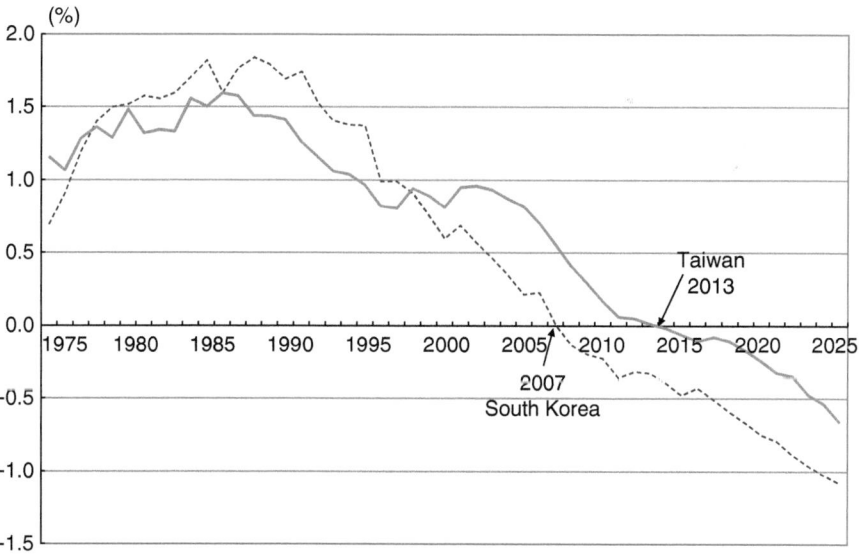

Fig. 3.12 First demographic dividend: South Korea and Taiwan, 1975–2025

References

Becker, G. S. (1960). An economic analysis of fertility. In *Demographic and economic change in developed countries* (National Bureau of Economic Research special conference series, Vol. 11, pp. 209–231). Princeton: Princeton University Press.

Becker, G. S. (1981). *A treatise on the family*. Cambridge, MA/London: Harvard University Press.

Becker, G. S., Murphy, K. M., & Tamura, R. (1990). Human capital, fertility, and economic growth. *Journal of Political Economy, 98*(5), Prt 2, S12–S37.

Japan, Ministry of Health, Labour and Welfare. (Various years). *Vital statistics of Japan*. Tokyo: Health and Welfare Statistics Association.

Japan, Statistics Bureau, Ministry of Internal Affairs and Communications. (Various years a). *Population census of Japan*. Tokyo: Japan Statistical Association.

Japan, Statistics Bureau, Ministry of Internal Affairs and Communications. (Various years b). *Population estimates*. Tokyo: Statistics Bureau, Ministry of Internal Affairs and Communications.

Japan, Cabinet Office. (2011). Kodomo kosodate hakusho (Whitepaper on children and child-rearing). http://www8.cao.go.jp/shoushi/whitepaper/w-2011/23pdfhonpen/23honpen.html. Accessed 25 July 2011.

Lee, R., & Mason, A. (2010). Fertility, human capital, and economic growth over the demographic transition. *European Journal of Population, 26*(2), 159–182.

Lee, R., & Mason, A. (Eds.). (2011). *Population aging and the generational economy: A global perspective*. Cheltenham/Northampton/Ottawa: Edward Elgar and International Development Research Centre.

Lee, R., Lee, S.-H., & Mason, A. (2008). Charting the economic life cycle. In A. Prskawetz, D. E. Bloom, & W. Lutz (Eds.), *Population aging, human capital accumulation, and productivity growth. Supplement to population and development review* (Vol. 34, pp. 208–237). New York: Population Council.

Mason, A. (Ed.). (2001). *Population change and economic development in East Asia: Challenges met, opportunities seized*. Stanford: Stanford University Press.

Mason, A. (2007). Demographic transition and demographic dividends in developed and developing countries. In Population Division, Department of Economic and Social Affairs, United Nations (Ed.), *Proceedings of the United Nations Expert Group meeting on social and economic implications of changing population age structures, Mexico city, 31 August – 2 September 2005* (pp. 81–101). New York: United Nations.

Mason, A., & Lee, R. (2006). Reform and support systems for the elderly in developing countries: Capturing the second demographic dividend. *GENUS, 62*(2), 11–35.

Mason, A., & Ogawa, N. (2001). Population, labor force, saving and Japan's future. In M. Blomström, B. Gangnes, & S. La Croix (Eds.), *Japan' new economy: Continuity and change in the twenty-first century* (pp. 48–74). Oxford: Oxford University Press.

McDonald, P. (2008, Nov 12–14). *Low fertility as a macro-sociological issue: An application to East Asia*. Paper presented at the international conference on low fertility and reproductive health in East and Southeast Asia, organized by Nihon University Population Research Institute in cooperation with WHO, UNFPA, IUSSP, & The Mainichi Daily Newspapers, Tokyo, Japan.

McDonald, P. (2009). Explanations of low fertility in East Asia: A comparative perspective. In G. Jones, P. Tay Straughan, & A. Chan (Eds.), *Ultra-low fertility in Pacific Asia: Trends, causes and policy issues* (pp. 23–39). Abingdon: Routledge.

Nagase, N. (2001). Kodomo-kosuto no Suikei: Kakei oyobi Shisan-men karano Bunseki (Estimation of the cost of children: Using Japanese household expenditure and asset data). *Jinkogaku Kenkyu (The Journal of Population Studies), 28*, 1–14.

National Institute of Population and Social Security Research (NIPSSR). (2003). *Heisei 14 nen dai 12 kai shussho doko kihon chosa (Kekkon to shussan ni kansuru zenkoku chosa), Dai ichi hokokusho: Waga kuni fufu no kekkon katei to shusshoryoku* (Report on the Twelfth Japanese National Fertility Survey, 2002: Marriage process and fertility of Japanese married couples), Vol. 1. Tokyo: National Institute of Population and Social Security Research.

National Institute of Population and Social Security Research (NIPSSR). (2007). *Heisei 17 nen dai 13 kai shussho doko kihon chosa (Kekkon to shussan ni kansuru zenkoku chosa), Dai ichi hokokusho: Waga kuni fufu no kekkon katei to shusshoryoku* (Report on the Thirteenth Japanese National Fertility Survey in 2005: Marriage process and fertility of Japanese married couples), Vol. 1. Tokyo: National Institute of Population and Social Security Research.

National Institute of Population and Social Security Research (NIPSSR). (2011). *Dai 14 kai shussho doko kihon chosa: Kekkon to shussan ni kansuru zenkoku chosa, fufu chosa no kekka gaiyo* (Press release on the results of the Fourteenth Japanese National Fertility Survey) 21 Oct 2011. http://www.ipss.go.jp/ps-doukou/j/doukou14/doukou14.pdf. Accessed 22 Oct 2011.

National Institute of Population and Social Security Research (NIPSSR). (2012). *Nihon no shorai suikei jinko (Heisei 24 nen 1 gatsu suikei) suikei kekka hyo* (Projection of future population for Japan [Jan 2012]: List of estimation results). http://www.ipss.go.jp/syoushika/tohkei/newest04/sh2401shk.html#chapt20-1. Accessed 2 Feb 2012.

Ogawa, N., & Chen, Q. (2013). The end of the first demographic dividend and possible labor market response in China and other Asian countries. *China and World Economy, 21*(2), 78–96.

Ogawa, N., & Retherford, R. D. (1997). Shifting costs of caring for the elderly back to families in Japan. *Population and Development Review, 23*(1), 59–94.

Ogawa, N., Mason, A., Chawla, A., Matsukura, R., & Tung, A.-C. (2009a). Declining fertility and the rising cost of children: What can NTA say about low fertility in Japan and other Asian countries? *Asian Population Studies, 5*(3), 289–307.

Ogawa, N., Retherford, R. D., & Matsukura, R. (2009b). Japan's declining fertility and policy responses. In G. Jones, P. Tay Straughan, & A. Chan (Eds.), *Ultra-low fertility in Pacific Asia: Trends, causes and policy issues* (pp. 40–72). Abingdon: Routledge.

Ogawa, N., Chawla, A., & Matukura, R. (2010a). Changing intergenerational transfers in aging Japan. In K. Eggleston & S. Tuljapurkar (Eds.), *Aging Asia: The economic and social implications of rapid demographic change in China, Japan, and South Korea* (pp. 43–62). Baltimore: The Brookings Institution.

Ogawa, N., Mason, A., Chawla, A., & Matsukura, R. (2010b). Japan's unprecedented aging and changing intergenerational transfers. In T. Ito & A. K. Rose (Eds.), *The economic consequences of demographic change in East Asia* (NBER-EASE, Vol. 19, pp. 131–160). Chicago/London: The University of Chicago Press.

Oyama, M. (2004). Kodomo no yoiku kyoiku hiyo to shusshoritsu teika (Cost of raising children and recent fertility decline in Japan). *Jinkogaku kenkyu (The Journal of Population Studies), 35*, 45–57.

Preston, S. H. (1984). Children and the elderly: Divergent paths for America's dependents. *Demography, 21*(4), 435–458.

Retherford, R. D., & Ogawa, N. (2006). Japan's baby bust: Causes, implications, and policy responses. In F. R. Harris (Ed.), *The baby bust: Who will do the work? Who will pay the taxes?* (pp. 5–47). Lanham: Rowman & Littlefield.

Retherford, R. D., & Ogawa, N. (2009). Guest editors' introduction. *Asian Population Studies, 5*(3), 211–213.

Statistics Korea. (n.d. a). Population projections and summary indicators for Korea (population items). Data downloaded from Korean Statistical Information Service. http://kosis.kr/eng/database/database_001000.jsp?listid=A&subtitle=Population/Household. Accessed 8 May 2012.

Statistics Korea. (n.d. b). Vital statistics (number and rate). Data downloaded from Korean Statistical Information Service. http://kosis.kr/eng/database/database_001000.jsp?listid=A&subtitle=Population/Household. Accessed 16 Mar 2012.

Suruga, T. (1993). Estimation of equivalence scale using Japanese data. *The Economic Studies Quarterly, 44*(2), 169–177.

Taiwan, Council for Economic Planning and Development. (2010a). *Population projections for R.O.C (Taiwan): 2010–2060*, Appendixes. http://www.cepd.gov.tw/encontent/m1.aspx?sNo=0001457. Accessed 5 Aug 2011.

Taiwan, Council for Economic Planning and Development. (2010b). *Population projections for R.O.C (Taiwan): 2010–2060*, Medium Variant. http://www.cepd.gov.tw/encontent/m1.aspx?sNo=0001457. Accessed 27 Jan 2011.

Taiwan, Department of Statistics, Ministry of the Interior, Republic of China (n.d.), *Statistical yearbook of interior*. http://sowf.moi.gov.tw/stat/year/elist.html. Accessed 5 Aug 2011.

Takegawa, S. (2005). Japan's welfare-state regime: Welfare politics, provider and regulator. *Development and Society, 34*(2), 169–190.

The Nikkei. (2011). *Josei, mosho de jumyo chijimu: Sekai ichi iji 86.39sai, dansei wa 79.64sai* (Women's life span shortened by sizzling heat, but despite that remains longest in the world at 86.39 years of age, while men record 79.64). 28 July.

Tung, A.-C. (2011). Consumption over the lifecycle: An international comparison. In R. Lee & A. Mason (Eds.), *Population aging and the generational economy: A global perspective* (pp. 136–160). Cheltenham/Northampton/Ottawa: Edward Elgar and International Development Research Centre.

Yoshikawa, H. (2002). *Japan's lost decade*. Tokyo: International House of Japan.

Chapter 4
The Effects of Daycare Center Use on Marital Fertility in Japan

Sang-Hyop Lee, Naohiro Ogawa, and Rikiya Matsukura

4.1 Introduction

Many families with young children rely on daycare centers and services. This can be a sizable financial burden, particularly for poor families. The financial burden may affect the couple's decision-making about continuous childbearing. This chapter analyzes the effect of daycare center services on the continuous childbearing for the case of Japan, where the government has adopted several programs over the last two decades to support childbearing and childrearing.

Japan substantially expanded daycare centers in the late 1990s. As is well described in Retherford and Ogawa (2006), the major expansion started with the "Angel Plan" for 1995–1999, which the government introduced in 1994. The subsidized daycare centers were funded out of the Ministry of Health, Labour, and Welfare's annual budget. As a result of the Angel Plan, daycare center capacity in Japan for children of ages 0–2 increased from 451,000 in FY 1994 (ending on 31

S.-H. Lee (✉)
Department of Economics, University of Hawaii at Manoa, 2424 Maile Way, Honolulu, HI 96822, USA

Population and Health Studies, East-West Center, Honolulu, HI, USA
e-mail: Leesang@hawaii.edu

N. Ogawa
Population Research Institute and College of Economics, Nihon University, Misaki-cho 1-3-2, Chiyoda-ku, 101-8360 Tokyo, Japan

R. Matsukura
Population Research Institute, Nihon University, Misaki-cho 1-3-2, Chiyoda-ku, 101-8360 Tokyo, Japan

March 1995) to 564,000 in FY 1999 (ending on 31 March 2000).[1] Services available under the Angel Plan were means-tested, which usually meant that higher-income parents had to pay more for services. Eligibility criteria varied by locality and are not well documented. It appears that daycare centers established in localities where there was not much demand for them eased eligibility criteria in order to attract clients. In some urban areas where the demand was not met and there were long waiting lists, higher-income couples were simply rejected. Because many mothers who were eligible for leave under the 1991 Child Care Leave Act were either not eligible for services provided by the Angel Plan or had to pay too much for them because of their high income, daycare services in the private sector also expanded.

In 1999 the original Angel Plan for 1995–1999 was succeeded by a New Angel Plan for 2000–2004. The new plan called for further expansion of daycare centers, and daycare center capacity for children of ages 0–2 subsequently increased from 564,000 in 1999 to 640,000 in 2002 (Retherford and Ogawa 2006: 35). As in the original plan, services under the New Angel Plan for 2000–2004 were made available on a means-tested basis that varied by locality. As a result of this change, the proportion of preschool children who were enrolled in daycare centers (both public and private) increased from 24 to 34 % between 1990 and 2004 (Ogawa 2005: 130).

Daycare centers can increase fertility by lowering the opportunity cost of having children. The opportunity cost of children is conventionally defined as earnings forgone as a result of not working, permanently or temporarily, in order to have and raise children. The waiting list for daycare centers exists because of limited availability. When a public daycare center is built, the opportunity cost of having children is greatly reduced for a mother, since the government bears some of the operating costs, including a subsidy. However, by making work more attractive to women who want children, daycare centers can also draw more housewives into the labor market, which tends to reduce fertility. Nonetheless, expanding public daycare centers appears to be a good way to raise fertility in Japan. Evidence in support of this hypothesis is provided by responses to a direct question intended to shed light on the fertility-enhancing effect of daycare center services, asked in the 2007 National Survey on Work and Family. The survey asked how important good public daycare facilities were for having a child. Sixty-five percent of female respondents said "very important," and another 27 % said "relatively important."

Are daycare centers effective at raising fertility? A growing body of literature in Western countries examines the effect of subsidized daycare centers on fertility (Kravdal 1996; Del Boca 2002; Rosen 2004; Neyer and Andersson 2007; Rindfuss et al. 2007; see also Gauthier 2007 for reviews of related studies) and

---

[1]In addition to daycare centers, the Angel Plan called for more after-school sports and other activities, which were intended to help working women who did not return home until well after the end of normal school hours. The plan also called for the establishment of regional family support centers. For a modest fee that varied by locality, these centers provided services such as picking up children from school and taking them to a daycare center, and arranging for medical care for a sick child until one of the parents could return from work.

on women's labor supply (Ribar 1995; Kreyenfeld and Hank 2000; Powell 2002; Baker et al. 2008; see also Blau 2003 for a review of related studies). In Japan, although evaluating the effectiveness of the aforementioned policy measure has important policy implications, to this day only a few relevant studies exist (e.g., Suruga and Nishmoto 2002; Ogawa 2005).

This chapter provides additional evidence relevant to these issues. It uses the National Survey on Work and Family of 2007, conducted by the Nihon University Population Research Institute in collaboration with the World Health Organization. The survey data include detailed histories concerning childbirth and the use of daycare centers, as well as information on socioeconomic, demographic, and geographic characteristics of respondents. We restrict our sample to women who have experienced childbirth. We created a profile of each woman's childbirth history from the augmented individual data file. Thus, the record for each childbirth includes selected characteristics at the time of childbirth such as the parents' use of daycare facilities, the wife's and the husband's characteristics, and the household and its location.

The remainder of the chapter is organized as follows. Section 4.2 discusses the data and empirical methodology. Section 4.3 presents our results, and Sect. 4.4 offers a conclusion.

4.2 Data and Methods

As already mentioned, our study is based on data from the 2007 National Survey on Work and Family. The survey covered a wide range of topics related to work and family life, including questions about the demographic and socioeconomic characteristics of respondents and their spouses, marriage decisions, childbearing and childrearing, care for the elderly, birth history, working conditions, contraceptive use, experience of infertility, and sexual activity. The target population was both women and men of ages 20–59. A two-stage cluster sample design was used to select 9,000 potential respondents. The questionnaire schedule was left for the prospective respondent to complete and was picked up later by a member of the survey team. Because of a low response rate, the first round of data collection was followed up with a second round using the direct-mail method. Characteristics of respondents in the first and second rounds were found to be similar. The final response rate, however, was only 51.4 % of the original 9,000. To minimize nonresponse bias, we weighted the sample to match the officially published age–sex profile of the Japanese population in 2007.

We considered three models to account for the effect of daycare center use on fertility. They were employment status (Model 1); parity progression (separate models for the progression from one to two children, Model 2A, and for the transition from two to three children, Model 2B); and desire for another child (separate models for women with one child, Model 3A, and for women with two children, Model 3B).

We used Model 1 to estimate how daycare center use was related to women's job status. This model has little to do with estimating the effect of daycare center provision on fertility, but it may show that the provision of daycare centers is a useful policy tool for reducing the burden of childrearing on women. We used Model 2 to measure fertility as parity progression between first and second births (i.e., the fraction of women who had a first birth who went on to have a second) and between second and third births (i.e., the fraction of women who had a second birth and went on to have a third), defining parity in the usual way as the number of children that a woman has ever borne. Higher-order progressions were not considered because very few Japanese women have more than three births. These parity progression percentages are referred to in the demographic literature as parity progression ratios. We did not consider progression from marriage to a first birth because the analysis required a variable indicating whether a couple was using daycare facilities for the starting birth in the progression, and there is no starting birth when a progression is from marriage to a first birth. Because of this restriction, our statistical analysis was confined to married women of ages 20–49 who had had at least one child.

In Model 3, the two dependent variables are whether a woman wanted to have another child, one for married women of ages 20–49 who currently (i.e., at the time of the survey) had one child, and the other for married women of ages 20–49 who currently had two children. Our measurement of the desire for another child was based on the question, "How many more children would you like to have? Please indicate the number of children you *really want*." In this model we do not distinguish between a wife's and a husband's response to this question. Since job status has four indicators, a multinomial logit model is used for estimation. Both Model 2 and 3 are estimated by a logit model.

The predictor variables included in the models are shown in Table 4.1. We based our selection of predictor variables not only on data availability but also on our knowledge of previous theoretical and empirical studies of factors affecting parity progression and the desire for children. Table 4.1 classifies predictor variables in each model into five categories: (A) daycare center use or provision, (B) woman's education, (C) woman's age, (D) woman's time constraint and other household characteristics, and (E) duration of current parity. The predictor variables and subsample sizes varied from model to model, which means that the means and standard deviations shown in Table 4.1 are based on the specific subsamples.

We measured the use of daycare centers from a woman's birth history, which contained information on that variable. However, whether a daycare center was *available* in the region, whether it was *affordable* to most women, or whether a woman actually *used* the daycare center for her child has quite different implications for its effect on fertility. Many studies have used the measure of availability, instead of use as a measure, because the supply of daycare centers is limited in many areas. In particular, the availability of daycare centers in European countries has been found to substantially influence individual behavior (Kreyenfled and Hank 2000). In Japan, too, the supply of daycare centers is inadequate to meet demand in some areas. Especially in large urban areas, waiting lists for public daycare centers can be long, and they are growing longer. According to the Ministry of Health, Labour,

4 The Effects of Daycare Center Use on Marital Fertility in Japan

Table 4.1 Definitions and mean values of variables

Models[a] (X indicates variables are used)							
	Definition (dummy variables take on the value of 1 if the specified condition is met, 0 otherwise)	1	2A	2B	3A	3B	Mean[b]
(A) Daycare center use or provision							
Number of uses	Number of times (children) used a daycare center	X					0.458
Use status	Currently using a daycare center		X	X			0.404
Use experience	Ever used a daycare center				X	X	
Waiting list	District has a waiting list. Used as a predictor for daycare center use in the bivariate probit model		X	X	X	X	0.020
(B) Wife's education[c] (Reference: <high school)							
High school	High school	X	X	X	X	X	0.406
Junior college	Junior college	X	X	X	X	X	0.377
University	University	X	X	X	X	X	0.158
(C) Wife's age							
Wife's age at starting birth	(Reference: 20–24)						
25–27	25–27		X	X			0.327
28–30	28–30		X	X			0.231
31–33	30–33		X	X			0.092
≥34	34+		X	X			0.054
Wife's current age	(Reference: 20–29)						
30–34	30–34	X			X	X	0.266
35–39	35–39	X			X	X	0.261
40–44	40–44	X			X	X	0.175
≥45	45+	X			X	X	0.113
(D) Wife's time constraint and other household characteristics							
Young children	Has at least one child aged 0–6	X			X	X	0.517
Total number of children	Total number of children	X					2.02
Coresidence	Couple co-residing with parents or parents-in-law	X			X	X	0.222
Husband's income (X1,000 yen)	(Reference) Husband not working/no income						
1–3,999	<4 million yen	X	X	X	X	X	0.257
4,000–7,999	4–8 million yen	X	X	X	X	X	0.427
8,000+	8+ million yen	X	X	X	X	X	0.159
Arranged marriage	Marriage was arranged		X	X	X	X	0.137
Childcare leave status	Wife used childcare leave for the starting birth		X	X			0.175

(continued)

Table 4.1 (continued)

Models[a] (X indicates variables are used)		1	2A	2B	3A	3B	Mean[b]
	Definition (dummy variables take on the value of 1 if the specified condition is met, 0 otherwise)						
Childcare leave experience	Wife has ever used childcare leave				X	X	0.190
Current residence (wife)	Urban area	X			X	X	0.898
Childhood residence (wife)	Urban area		X	X			0.746
(E) Duration of current parity							
Duration from starting birth	Duration from starting birth (includes squared)		X	X			3.38
Duration from first birth	Duration from first birth (includes squared)				X	X	5.34

[a]Dependent variables are the following: Model 1: job status (4 indicators), Model 2A: a binary indicator of parity progression from first to second birth, Model 2B: a binary indicator of parity progression from second to third birth, Model 3A: a binary indicator of desire for additional children for parity-1 women, and Model 3B, a binary indicator of desire for additional children for parity-2 women

[b]Means are based on different subsamples. All numbers are based on Model 2A. For variables that do not appear in Model 2A, such as woman's current age, Model 3A is used (except for total number of children). All samples are first restricted to the sample of married women aged 20–49 who had had least one child. Then, these subsamples are further restricted to smaller samples for some models; for example, the first birth for Model 2A, and those who had had only one child for Model 3A

[c]This variable indicates that the wife had completed the specified level of education

and Welfare, the number of children on waiting lists for admission to authorized daycare centers nationwide as of 1 April 2009 was 25,384, an increase of 29.8 % from the same period a year earlier (*Nihon Keizai Shimbun*, 10 September 2009). Japanese daycare centers are heavily subsidized. According to Ministry of Health, in Tokyo in 2000, the average operating cost of public daycare services for infants was about 500,000 yen ($5,000) per infant per month, an amount that exceeded the average male worker's monthly salary in Tokyo of 440,100 yen (Ogawa 2003: 103). Charges to parents using these services come nowhere near covering this cost, and hence it is heavily subsidized by Japanese government.

Does the shortage of daycare centers have a significant effect on couples' decisions regarding their use? Interestingly, previous research has found that the majority of the administrative districts in Japan have relatively short waiting lists for their public daycare centers (Ogawa 2005). The results of the 2007 survey provide supporting evidence. Respondents were asked why many women had never used a daycare center. Those who had never used one were allowed to choose as many as three precoded responses. Fifty-nine percent of the mothers chose the response "because I was a full-time housewife," 31 % chose "I want to raise the child on my own," and 11 % chose the response "relatives or friends are helping". Only

8 % thought that daycare centers were "too costly," just 4 % complained that "there were no vacancies in the center," 2 % stated that there was "no daycare center in the neighborhood," and 1 % expressed dissatisfaction in the sense that a daycare center's service hours did not coincide with their working hours. The seemingly contradictory results are due to the wide regional disparities in supply and demand. More recent figures published by the Ministry of Health, Labour, and Welfare show that five prefectures account for almost two thirds of all children on the waiting lists, and nine prefectures do not have any waiting lists (*Daily Yomiuri Online*, 9 September 2009). That is, a long waiting list is a serious problem for some metropolitan areas, but it is not a pressing matter in many other areas.

Given the existence of waiting lists, the estimated effects of daycare center use on fertility may be biased. In fact, our sample consisted of two groups of women. One group lived in a district with no waiting list, and therefore the estimation results for this group (called the unconstrained group) were not constrained by the limited supply of daycare centers. The other group (called the constrained group) lived in a district with a waiting list, so that the estimation results for this group were constrained by the limited supply of daycare services. Thus, whether a woman had used daycare centers or not may have been affected by the district she was living in. Ignoring this constraint could cause the estimated coefficients to be biased.

There are a couple of ways to handle this problem. A traditional approach is to measure the supply or provision of daycare centers, instead of using the measure of demand for or use of daycare centers. This variable then can be used as an instrument variable in a structural two-stage model to estimate the effect of the provision of daycare centers on fertility. We followed this approach and applied it to the sample of women who lived in areas with waiting lists for admission to daycare services. Because predicted probability is a continuous variable, we calculated predicted probability in the second stage for selected values that play the role of categories. Table 4.1 does not actually show the selected values of predicted probability because they differ between the models. We chose the four selected values to correspond to varying degrees of improvement in the waiting lists: no improvement, 10 % improvement, 25 % improvement, and 50 % improvement in the number of children on the waiting lists.

We used the ratio of the number of children on the waiting lists to the number of children aged 0–4 living in the district as the instrument variable to predict the effect of the waiting lists on the probability of daycare center use. We created this variable by merging the information on waiting lists with the 2007 survey responses by district level. Again, although it appears that some districts had a substantial number of children on their waiting lists, the majority of districts either had no waiting list or a relatively small number of children on their waiting lists. If we divide the number of children on the waiting lists by the total number of children aged 0–4 in each district, 43 % of the districts had no waiting lists, 50 % of the districts had an index of less than 5 %, and only 7 % of the districts showed a measure of over 5 %. The average was 1.1 % for all districts, and 2 % for districts with waiting lists.

Estimating each model required statistical controls for other factors. Wife's education and husband's income were clearly relevant to all the models. We did not control for husband's education because it was strongly correlated with wife's education, creating the problem of multicollinearity. We included wife's age at the starting birth in Model 2 (parity progression) but not in the other models. Instead, wife's current age had to be controlled in the other models. The presence of children aged 0–6 in the household was clearly relevant to Model 1 (employment status) and to Model 3 (desire for another child), but not to Model 2. We did not include this variable in Model 2 because it was effectively controlled by the parity duration from the starting birth. Arranged marriage was relevant to Model 2 (parity progression) and Model 3 (desire for another child), but not to Model 1. Wife's current residence was relevant to Models 1 and 3 but not to Model 2, for which we used wife's childhood residence instead. Models 2 and 3 also include parity duration: Model 2 includes duration from the year of starting birth, whereas Model 3 includes duration from the first birth. This variable, combined with wife's age, also controls for the time trend in fertility.

4.3 Results

4.3.1 The Effect of Daycare Center Use on Women's Job Status

Married women's careers are often interrupted by childbearing and childrearing. The 2007 survey collected information about women's job status 1 year prior to each childbirth and at the time of childbirth. Twenty-three percent of full-time employees and 41 % of part-time employees or self-employed women who were working 1 year before they gave birth were no longer working at the time of any childbirth. Although this result does not indicate whether a woman returned to work soon after giving birth, it does suggest that childbearing has had a negative effect on women's job careers in Japan.

Table 4.2 shows results for the relationship between job status and daycare center use. Panel A shows the result using the sample of women who lived in a district with no waiting list for daycare centers, whereas Panel B shows the results using the sample of women who lived in districts with waiting lists. We report only the results for daycare center use because the other predictor variables function mainly as controls. As the total number of children was controlled in the model, the positive correlation between the number of children and the number of daycare centers used did not affect the results. Alternatively, we used the ratio of the number of daycare centers used to the total number of children as an index of daycare center use, instead of controlling for the total number of children. But the results remain quite similar, and hence the results based on this alternative specification are not reported here.

The results in Table 4.2 indicate the probability of being in each of the possible job statuses (housewife, self-employed, employed part-time, and employed

Table 4.2 Daycare center use and current job status (Model 1)

Daycare center use and predictor variable	Housewife‡	Self-employed	Part-time	Full-time
(A) Used daycare center for which there was no waiting list ($N = 673$)				
None	44.8	5.6***	36.2***	13.4***
One	30.5	7.8***	38.8***	22.9***
Two	18.2	9.7***	37.2***	34.8***
(B) Used daycare center for which there was a waiting list ($N = 926$)				
None	54.9	5.2***	30.7***	9.3***
One	36.4	7.5***	33.9***	22.2***
Two	19.2	8.9***	30.7***	41.1***

Notes: A multinomial logit model was used for the estimations. See Table 4.1 for the other variables included in the models but not shown here
***, **, and * indicate statistical significance at the 1 %, 5 %, and 10 % levels, respectively
‡ indicates the reference category

full-time). Predicted values of the dependent variable thus present the probability of being in a certain job status and indicate the fraction of women who were in that category. These fractions are expressed as percentages. In each column we calculated the probability by varying the indicated predictor variable while holding all the other predictor variables in the model constant at their mean values in the subsample on which the multinomial logit regression was run.

Panel A shows that using a daycare center (for which there was no waiting list) once increased the probability of working full-time by 9.5 % points (22.9–13.4 %). Using daycare center services twice increased the probability by 21.4 % points, as compared with never using a daycare center. Using a daycare center also increased the probability of working as self-employed, but its effect on working part-time was trivial. Using a daycare center substantially decreased the probability of being a housewife—by 14.3 % points for the first use and by 12.3 additional percentage points for the second use.

Panel B shows the results for the constrained sample (i.e., women who lived in a district with a waiting list for admission to daycare centers). The pattern is very similar to Panel A in that having used daycare centers increased the probability of working full-time or working as a self-employed person but decreased the probability of being a housewife. The only difference between the two samples was that the probability of working full-time increased much more rapidly for the constrained sample as those women used more daycare centers. This result should be interpreted with care because it does not necessarily mean a causal relationship existed between daycare center use and job status. The causation could be reversed; that is., it could be that women's employment status determined the amount of daycare center use. If there were more full-time working women in the region, there would be more demand for daycare centers. Nonetheless, the results are informative in that they reveal how women's job status is associated with the use of daycare centers.

4.3.2 Effects of the Provision of Daycare Centers on Fertility

Table 4.3 presents probit regression results for the progression from first birth to second birth (Panel A) and from second birth to third birth (Panel B). Again we report only the results for daycare center use in the table. For the transition, the dependent variable observed for an individual woman is a dummy variable indicating whether she progressed to the next parity (had a next birth) by the time of the survey (1 if yes, 0 if no). Predicted values of the dependent variable are thus parity progression ratios (PPRs), indicating the fraction of women who progressed from the starting parity to the next parity. In each column, PPRs were calculated by varying the indicated predictor variable while holding all the other predictor variables in the model constant at their mean values in the subsample on which the probit regression was run.

We should note several shortcomings of our analysis. PPRs are more appropriately calculated by life table methods. The estimates of PPRs in Table 4.3, therefore,

Table 4.3 Predicted percentages of women progressing to next birth (Models 2A and 2B)

Progression and dependent variable	(1) Women living in districts without waiting	(2) Women living in districts with waiting	(3) Women living in districts with waiting (2SLS)
(A) From 1st to 2nd birth			
Daycare center use			
No‡	74.0	72.4	
Yes	84.4***	75.4	
Reduction in waiting lists			
No improvement			73.5
10 % improvement			73.5
25 % improvement			73.6
50 % improvement			73.7
(B) From 2nd to 3rd birth			
Daycare center use			
No‡	29.0	31.5	
Yes	37.7***	36.2	
Reduction in waiting lists			
No improvement			33.0
10 % improvement			33.0
25 % improvement			33.0
50 % improvement			33.0

Notes: The probit method was used for estimation. For 2SLS, the waiting index was used to predict daycare center use, and predicted probability of using daycare centers in the first stage was used as a new predictor in the second stage. See Table 4.1 for the reference category and other variables included in the models but not shown
***, **, and * indicate statistical significance at the 1 %, 5 %, and 10 % levels, respectively
‡ indicates the reference category

are not very accurate because some women may have progressed to the next parity after the survey date. Nor have we have presented the results by women's job status mainly because of the small sample size. Moreover, the survey did not contain information on women's labor market histories, and hence it was not feasible to estimate the effect by using women's job status at the time of childbirth.

Panels A and B represent parity progression. Column (1) shows the results using the sample of women who lived in a district with no waiting list, whereas column (2) shows the results using the sample of women who lived in a district with waiting lists. Column (3) presents the two-stage estimation results. The results in column (1) of Panel A indicate that using daycare centers had a positive effect on the progression from first to second birth. The predicted percentage of women progressing to a second birth was 84.4 % for women who used daycare centers, but only 74.0 % for those who did not, indicating that using daycare centers was associated with an increased probability of having a second child of about 10.4 % points. When we used the sample of women who lived in a district with a waiting list, however, this effect disappeared by losing its statistical significance. To investigate what caused these different results, we used the index of waiting lists as an instrument variable and estimated how an improvement in waiting lists affected the result.

Column (3) in Panel A shows the result. Quite surprisingly, reducing the number of children on the waiting lists had little effect on the parity progression. The predicted probability of progressing to a second birth was 73.5 % for women with the current waiting list, 73.6 % for women with a 25 % reduction in the waiting lists, and 73.7 % with a 50 % reduction in the waiting lists. The results are insignificant in the first and second stage regressions. They have the same level of statistical significance because there is only one underlying coefficient of predicted probability of daycare center use, and that coefficient is insignificant. This result implies that the current level of waiting for daycare centers may not be an important deterrent for a Japanese woman to have more children. Thus, the difference in results between columns (1) and (2) may not be due to the existence of waiting lists. The disparity in results exists perhaps because women living in areas with waiting lists for admission to daycare centers differ in some way—e.g., job status, attitude toward having children, or regional characteristics—from women living in areas without waiting lists. The disparity also may be related to other factors, besides their limited availability, among Japanese women who do not use them. As the survey revealed, one reason that many respondents gave for not using daycare centers was that raising children in Japan is still considered to be a wife's responsibility. However, as indicated in column (1), this result does not mean that daycare center use has little effect on the probability of progression to a second birth. It just means that an increase in daycare availability from the current level may have only a marginal effect on fertility.

Panel B shows results for the progression from the second to a third birth. Interestingly, the patterns are similar to those for the progression from the first to a second birth for columns (1) and (2) in terms of the changing pattern of significance due to sample selection. When we used the sample of women who were living in a district with no waiting list, the predicted percentage progressing to a third birth was 37.7 % for women who used daycare centers, compared with 29.0 % for those who did not, indicating that using daycare centers increases the probability of having a third child by 8.7 % points. The results for the sample of women living in a district with waiting lists were not significant, as was the case in the progression from the first to a second birth. As with the progression to a second birth, the two-stage estimation results for the progression to a third birth had no significance. The estimated coefficient for the waiting index in the first stage was far from significant.

This result suggests that our instrument variable may not be entirely satisfactory because demand as well as supply may affect the waiting index, although we used it as a measure of supply only. In other words, not only did the availability of a daycare center influence whether a woman used one or not, but also whether she used one or not affected the number of children on the waiting list. If more women were using daycare centers in a district, the district was more likely to have a waiting list, creating a positive correlation between the two variables. Addressing this issue, however, is beyond the scope of this study.

Table 4.4 shows the effects of daycare center use on the desire to have another child. Again, this is reported for two parities, Panel A for parity-1 women, and Panel B for parity-2 women. The desire to have another child obviously differs from actually having another child, but the desire to have another child may be somewhat predictive of whether a woman will have another birth in the future.

The results show that using daycare centers had a substantial positive effect on the desire for another child for women who currently had two children, but no effect at all for those who currently had one child, regardless of the existence of a waiting list. However, when we applied the two-stage method, reducing the number of children on the waiting list had no effect on the desire for another child. On the one hand, again this could be due to our weak instrument variable, or the possibility that women living in areas with waiting lists differ in their desire for having another child or their job status from women living in areas without waiting lists. On the other hand, the results for the desire to have more children may be less reliable than those for the actual transition to the following birth owing to the inherent limitation of the variable.

4.4 Conclusion

Policies that make high-quality daycare centers available and affordable have received considerable attention in Japan. The current debate on policy effectiveness is based on a handful of studies, which provide insufficient evidence for drawing firm conclusions. The lack of policy evaluation makes it difficult to see what steps should be taken next.

This chapter has investigated the effects of daycare center use on marital fertility as measured by parity progression from the first to a second birth and from the second to a third birth, and by the desire for another child. The findings indicate

Table 4.4 Predicted percentage of wives and husbands desiring another child (Models 3A and 3B)

Parity and dependent variable	(1) Women living in districts with waiting	(2) Women living in districts with waiting	(1) Women living in districts with waiting (2SLS)
(A) Currently have one child			
Daycare center utilization experience			
No‡	61.1	63.7	
Yes	62.0	64.5	
Reduction in waiting lists			
No improvement			64.0
10 % improvement			64.0
25 % improvement			64.0
50 % improvement			64.0
(B) Currently have two children			
Daycare center utilization experience			
No‡	12.4	12.9	
Yes	18.9*	19.9*	
Reduction in waiting lists			
No improvement			15.6
10 % improvement			15.5
25 % improvement			15.6
50 % improvement			15.6

The probit method was used for estimation. For 2SLS, the waiting index was used to predict daycare center use and predicted probability of using daycare centers in the first stage was used as a new predictor in the second stage. See Table 4.1 for the reference category and other variables included in the models but not shown
***, **, and * indicate statistical significance at the 1 %, 5 %, and 10 % levels, respectively
‡ indicates the reference category

a strong effect of daycare center use on marital fertility for women living in areas with no waiting list. For those women, the results indicate that using a daycare center increased the probability of having another child by 10 % points for the progression to a second birth and by 9 % points for the progression to a third birth; but this effect was not significant for women living in areas with waiting lists. The two-stage estimation results suggest that there is little effect on fertility of shortening the waiting lists for daycare centers in those areas. This result does not mean that daycare center use has little effect on the probability of progressing to a second birth, however. It just means that a further increase in daycare centers may have little effect on raising fertility from the current level.

The results presented here should be interpreted with caution for several reasons. The survey data do not contain labor market histories. There is no information on women's job history, and hence it is not feasible to estimate what effect the provision of daycare services can have on fertility through a change in women's job status. Moreover, some results do not necessarily mean causation. For example, the estimated results for job status (Model 1) could be biased owing to a potential endogeneity problem. Perhaps the most important limitation is that findings from the two-stage estimates are subject to the validity of the instrument variable. The correlation between the waiting index and daycare center use does not necessarily mean causation between these two variables, because both demand and supply influence the number of children on the waiting list. Despite these limitations, the findings are informative, and they clearly suggest that using daycare centers has a strong positive effect on parity progression for women living in areas with no waiting lists.

Acknowledgments Research for this chapter was funded by a grant from Nihon University Population Research Institute, the "Academic Frontier" Project for Private Universities, and a matching-fund subsidy from the Ministry of Education, Culture, Sports, Science and Technology in Japan.

References

Baker, M., Gruber, J., & Milligan, K. (2008). Universal child care, maternal labor supply, and family well-being. *Journal of Political Economy, 116*(4), 709–745.
Blau, D. M. (2003). Childcare subsidy programs. In R. A. Moffit (Ed.), *Means-tested transfer programs in the U.S* (pp. 443–516). Chicago: Chicago University Press.
Daily Yomiuri Online. (2009, 9 September). *Day care waiting list grows 30 % from '08, tops 25,000*. http://www.yomiuri.co.jp/dy/national/20090909TDY03103.htm. Accessed 9 Sept 2009.
Del Boca, D. (2002). The effect of child care and part time opportunities on participation and fertility decisions in Italy. *Journal of Population Economics, 15*(3), 549–573.
Gauthier, A. H. (2007). The impact of family policies on fertility in industrialized countries: A review of the literature. *Population Research and Policy Review, 26*, 323–346.
Kravdal, Ø. (1996). How the local supply of day-care centers influences fertility in Norway: A parity-specific approach. *Population Research and Policy Review, 15*, 201–218.
Kreyenfeld, M., & Hank, K. (2000). Does the availability of child care influence the employment of mothers? Findings from Western Germany. *Population Research and Policy Review, 19*, 317–337.
Neyer, G., & Andersson, G. (2007). *Consequences of family policies on childbearing behavior: Effects of artifacts?* (MPIDR Working Paper). Rostock: Max Planck Institute for Demographic Research. http://www.demogr.mpg.de/papers/working/wp-2007-021.pdf. Accessed 21 Aug 2009.
Ogawa, N. (2003). Japan's changing fertility mechanisms and its policy responses. *Journal of Population Research, 20*(1), 89–106.
Ogawa, N. (2005). Analysis of policies for the promotion of women's employment and child rearing. In Population Problems Research Council, The Mainichi Newspapers (Ed.), *Perceptions of family in the age of very low fertility* (pp. 107–147). Tokyo: Population Problems Research Council, The Mainichi Newspapers.
Powell, L. M. (2002). Joint labor supply and childcare choice: Decisions of married mothers. *Journal of Human Resources, 37*(4), 106–128.
Retherford, R. D., & Ogawa, N. (2006). Japan's baby bust: Causes, implications, and policy responses. In F. R. Harris (Ed.), *The baby bust: Who will do the work? Who will pay the taxes?* (pp. 5–47). Lanham: Rowman & Littlefield.

Ribar, D. C. (1995). A structural model of child care and the labor supply of married women. *Journal of Labor Economics, 13*, 558–597.

Rindfuss, R. R., Guilkey, D., Morgan, S. P., Kravdal, Ø., & Guzzo, K. B. (2007). Child care availability and first-birth timing in Norway. *Demography, 44*(2), 345–372.

Rosen, M. (2004). Fertility and public policies: Evidence from Norway and Finland. *Demographic Research, 10*, 143–170.

Suruga, T., & Nishimoto, M. (2002). The influence of policies for promoting childcare on child birth-related behavior. *The Quarterly of Social Security Research, 37*(4), 371–379.

Chapter 5
What Are the Prospects for Continued Low Fertility in Japan?

Vegard Skirbekk, Rikiya Matsukura, and Naohiro Ogawa

5.1 Is the Low-Fertility Trap a Threat to Japan?

The low-fertility trap hypothesis may help explain Asian low-fertility childbearing trajectories, among which that of Japan in particular has several similarities to European countries. Japan was the first Asian country to industrialize and in the past several decades has enjoyed economic levels similar to or higher than those observed in Europe. Japan's past population trends have exhibited fundamental similarities to those in Europe. One example is the size of its demographic transition multiplier (DTM)—that is, the ratio of population size after the demographic transition to population size before the demographic transition. In European countries this ratio was found to lie in the range of 3–5, whereas in Japan it is 5. Japan's population, currently around 128 million, is estimated to have been around 26 million in 1800 (United Nations 1973, 2011). This sets Japan apart from other Asian economies, where the DTM is estimated to be considerably higher: 23 in the Philippines, 13 in Thailand, 9 in Indonesia, and 16 in Myanmar (Cleland 2001).

Moreover, the net reproduction rate—the number of daughters per woman who survive and bear children themselves—never exceeded 1.7 during the demographic transition in Japan. This was also the case in France, Germany, Italy, England and

Wales, Sweden, the Netherlands, and Norway, in all of which the net reproduction rate peaked between 1.4 and 1.6. In other Asian countries, however, it tended to reach higher levels: in China it peaked at 2.5, in South Korea at 2.4, in Singapore and Thailand at 2.6, and in the Philippines at 2.7 (Chesnais 1992). Moreover, current fertility patterns suggest that Japan has much in common with Europe in this respect. The total fertility rate (TFR) in Southern and Southeastern Europe ranged from 1.2 to 1.4 in 2004, while the Japanese TFR was 1.3 births (Population Reference Bureau 2007).

Projections by national statistical offices and international bodies such as the UN's Population Division (United Nations 2011) assume that countries with low population growth will see an increase in fertility levels; for example, the UN medium assumption is a gradual shift toward replacement fertility in the longer term. In contrast, population projections made by the Japanese government recently *lowered* their assumptions about future fertility, with the 2006 medium scenario assuming that the TFR would remain at 1.26 births until 2055, while the low scenario assumed a drop to 1.06 births and the high scenario assumed an increase to 1.55 births (Kaneko 2007). Such uniquely low fertility assumptions make Japan an ideal case to investigate whether assumptions about future low fertility are justified and whether Japan will continue to have low fertility levels.

The generally assumed drivers of the fertility decline of the past decades may continue to push fertility in Japan to even lower levels. These range from transformations of traditional family patterns and an increase in female education and opportunity costs to increasing secularization and uncertainty resulting from social and technological change, recent economic downturns, urbanization, and globalization.

The common deviation from the conventional rules of trend analysis must have to do with a belief that somehow a powerful social force will stop and even reverse the downward trend in fertility, and that at the aggregate level human populations will not voluntarily shrink and age to an extent that would be socially disruptive and, in the very long run, cause them to become insignificant as political entities. However, there does not seem to be any "natural law" that would stop fertility from falling further.

The low-fertility trap hypothesis as presented here consists of three independent elements that all work in the same direction and can reinforce each other. Whereas the first one is a demographic accounting truism, the other two are testable subhypotheses. The three mechanisms can be classified as demographic, sociological, and economic. To better distinguish between them, we refer to them as LFT-1, LFT-2, and LFT-3 (Fig. 5.1).

LFT-1 is based on the well-known demographic mechanism by which the age distribution of a population exerts an independent influence on the number of births, or the crude birth rate. A reduction in the number of women of reproductive age implies that the number of births will decline for an extended period of time even if fertility were to instantly jump to the replacement level; that is so simply because there are fewer women who can have children. This process itself causes a downward trend in the number of births.

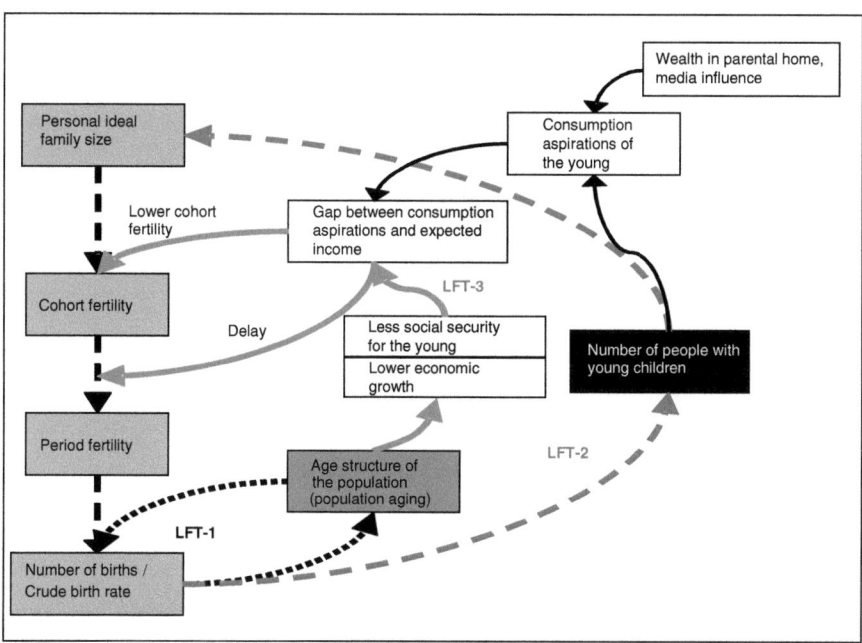

Fig. 5.1 The demographic, sociological, and economic mechanisms of the low-fertility trap hypothesis (Source: Lutz et al. (2006a) with permission)

LFT-2 refers to the concept of personal ideal family size, which is one of the factors that determine actual cohort fertility. The fewer the children belonging to the social environment that young people experience, the smaller the number of children that will be part of their normative view of a desirable adult life. Hence, in Fig. 5.1 the feedback loop goes from the actual number of births in a population to the number of people with young children a few years later. This, in turn, is viewed as a key determinant of personal ideal family size.

LFT-3 refers to the economic gap between personal aspirations for consumption and expected income, which is assumed to correlate with fewer births. A decline in the number of births in a population further results in more rapid aging, which in turn may trigger cuts in social security benefits that seem to affect mostly today's younger cohorts while having less and more gradual effects on the older ones. On the one hand, this can lead to less investment and lower economic growth, resulting in a more pessimistic economic outlook among today's younger generations. On the other, aspirations for material consumption are probably higher today than ever before, following greater exposure to advertising aimed at further raising the aspirations for consumption. There is also a demographic factor at work here: due to the fertility decline since the 1970s, children have shared parental wealth with fewer siblings, a factor that helped to raise the standard of living to which they have now become accustomed.

In Japan, individuals who live for an extended period of their young adulthood with parents are called "parasite singles," a term coined by Yamada (1996) to describe young single persons who work for pay, live with parents, contribute little or nothing to household finances, and therefore have ample money to lead the "good life." They are in no hurry to marry because under current employment conditions in Japan, marriage would likely entail a substantial reduction in their living standard. In 2004 the proportion of single employed women who were living with their parents was 73 % at ages 20–24, 67 % at ages 25–29, and 69 % at ages 30–34 (computed from the National Survey of Population, Families and Generations data).

5.2 LFT-1: Population Aging and Lower Fertility in Japan

Declining fertility has led to smaller female populations of reproductive age, and the first part of the low-fertility trap hypothesis for Japan is clearly supported by data. In 1995 Japan saw large birth cohorts entering peak reproductive ages. Since 1995, however, the larger birth cohorts have been aging, as shown by Fig. 5.2, while fertility has stayed at low levels. Hence, this window of "reproductive opportunity" is about to start closing within the next few years. For example, the 1992 cohort is 60 % smaller than the 1972 cohort, and cohorts born after 1992 are even smaller. Thus, we may safely assume that even if policies are adopted that succeed in raising fertility rates, there will be significantly fewer births in Japan.

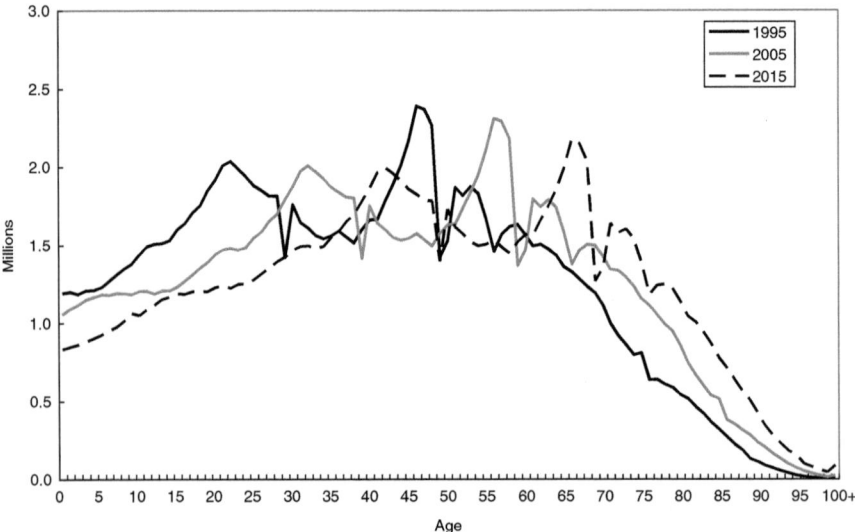

Fig. 5.2 Japanese population structure (in millions) by age and year: 1995, 2005, and 2015 (projected) (Sources: Japan, Statistics Bureau (1996); Japan, National Institute of Population and Social Security (2007))

5.3 LFT-2: Declines in Ideal Family Size

The second element of LFT relates to changes in ideal family size. In demography there has been a long tradition of research based on the assumption that actual fertility is influenced, at least to a certain degree, by fertility preferences (Barber and Axinn 1998; Tan and Tey 1994). Indicators of fertility preferences include the societal ideal, the personal ideal, and expected family size. Couples in modern societies usually have fewer children than they say they would like to have (Demeny 2003). For this reason, stated family-size ideals are also sometimes considered to be an upper bound for actual fertility (Van Peer 2002).

Fertility preferences are dynamic and change over time, mostly in the direction of smaller family size. In many formerly high-fertility countries, rapid declines in desired family size are well documented by the series of World Fertility Surveys and Demographic and Health Surveys (Cleland and Scott 1987; Westoff and Bankole 2002) and are assumed to be an important driver of the observed fertility declines. The question of concern here is whether Japanese fertility norms will continue to decline or be kept from falling below the replacement level by some new development. For decades, population forecasters assumed that fertility would not fall below replacement levels. However, once the number of children that people observe—siblings, friends' children, children in other families, children portrayed in the media—during the process of socialization falls below a certain level, their own ideal family size tends to become smaller; and in due course that in turn may lead to a further decline in actual family size and to even lower ideal family size in the subsequent generation. This scenario follows the same logic as described by Rindfuss et al. (2004: 855) in the context of Japanese marriage behavior: "Changes in attitudes likely create a feedback mechanism influencing behavior; and changes in behavior likely create a feedback mechanism influencing attitudes." For example, Testa and Grilli (2006) have found that, in Europe, in those regions where the mean actual number of children of the older (parents') generations is lower, young individuals have a higher probability of preferring smaller families. In addition, the authors report that the relationship is stronger in areas with below-replacement fertility levels than elsewhere, especially where fertility is below 1.5 births. Only at very low levels of actual fertility does the two-child norm start to fade and the ideal of a one-child family becomes more likely.

Figure 5.3 compares the fertility ideals of both married and unmarried Japanese women in 1981 and 2000. In 1981 their preferences were for 2.5 children or more among all age groups. By 2000, ideal fertility had fallen for all age groups relative to 1981; e.g., for the 15–19-year-olds, ideal fertility was 2.2 children, down by 0.5 since 1981. The decline in family-size preferences is compatible with the low-fertility trap hypothesis, as those who were at the peak of their reproductive ages in 1981 belonged to the cohorts born in the late 1940s and the 1950s, which had fertility above replacement level. By 2000, the average woman of reproductive age had grown up with fewer siblings, and that may have resulted in her idealizing lower fertility.

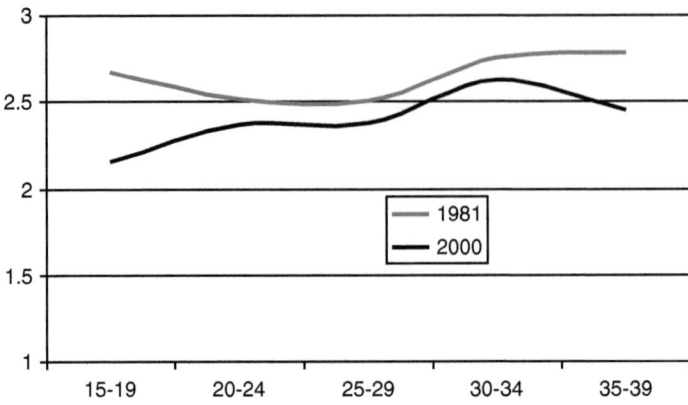

Fig. 5.3 Ideal number of children by age and year: Japanese women aged 15–39, 1981 and 2000 (Source: Computed from Inglehart et al. (2010))

Other multiple-wave surveys show a weaker decline in ideal family size. According to the Japanese National Fertility Survey, for example, the *ideal* number of children for all married couples decreased from 2.61 to 2.48 and the *intended* number of children dropped from 2.17 to 2.11 between 1977 and 2005 (Kaneko et al. 2008). The inclusion of single women could explain some of the discrepancies between the World Value Survey (the source of Fig. 5.3) and the Japanese National Fertility Survey, as singles have much lower fertility ideals. Over the period 1994–2007, when singles' fertility ideals could be observed in the samples, their fertility preferences ranged from 1.9 to 2.2 children, whereas married respondents' preferences were from 2.4 to 2.7 children, an average of 0.5 children more than singles'. Hence, the compositional shift in population following an increase in the proportion of Japanese singles is likely to lead to a decrease in fertility ideals.

Japanese ideals are still higher than in Western Europe, where ideal family size tends to be closer to two children (e.g., Testa and Grilli 2006). The high frequency of the three-child ideal norm, however, may be due to the fact that fertility declined later in Japan than in Europe: in Japan the total fertility rate in 1950–1955 was still above 3.5, a period when it stood at an average of 2.4 births in Western Europe.

Further evidence of a decline in Japanese fertility ideals is given by the 2007 National Survey on Work and Family. The survey covered a wide range of topics related to work and family life, including the demographic and socioeconomic characteristics of respondents and their spouses, marriage decisions, childbearing and rearing, old-age care, birth history, working conditions, contraceptive use, experience of infertility, and sexual activities. The survey targeted males and females of ages 20–59 living in Japan. A total of 9,000 people randomly selected with two-stage cluster sampling methods were contacted about participating in the survey. A questionnaire was left for each prospective respondent to complete and was picked up at a later date. After the first round of data collection, there was a second attempt to reach people by mail who had not been initially contacted (mostly for

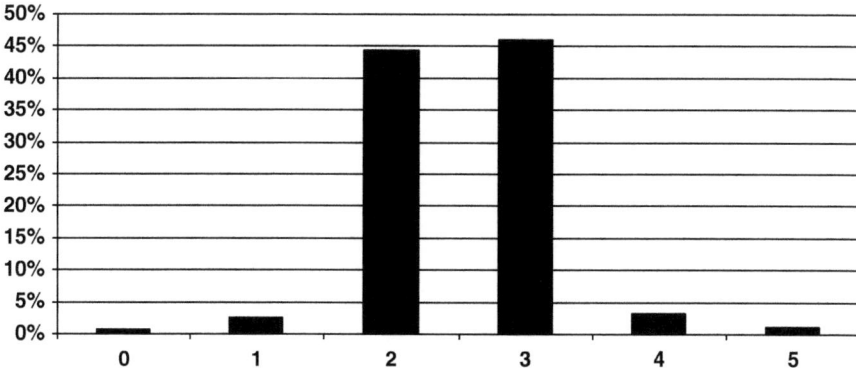

Fig. 5.4 Answers to the question, "Ideally, how many children would you like to have?": Japan, 2007 (Source: Computed from National Survey on Work and Family 2007)

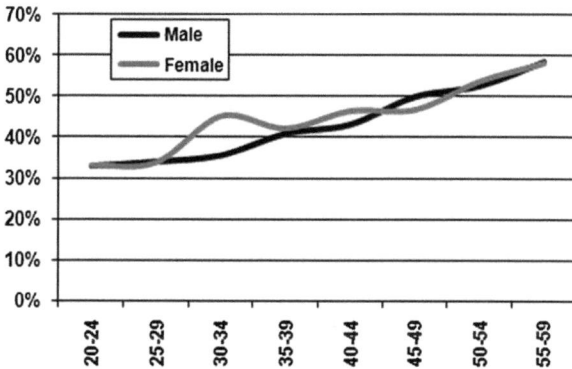

Fig. 5.5 Percentage, by age and sex, of those agreeing that "three children are ideal": Japan, 2007 (Source: Computed from National Survey on Work and Family 2007)

having been absent from home). The final response rate of the survey was 51.4 % (number of returned questionnaires/number of cases contacted). For the following analyses, we have weighted the sample to match the age–sex profile of the Japanese population in 2007. The results indicate that 90.3 % of the respondents preferred two or three children, and 0.8 % regarded childlessness as an ideal (Fig. 5.4).

To identify recent trends in Japanese childbearing ideals, we focused on the age variation among respondents idealizing two and three children (Figs. 5.5 and 5.6). For a majority of men and women aged 50 and over, three children were the ideal, whereas the majority of men and women in their 20s regarded two children as ideal. However, the statements expressing high fertility ideals may reflect what is socially acceptable, rather than what the "true" ideal is (e.g., a statement that one does not want any children may be socially unacceptable). Furthermore, it should be noted that the ideal of two children is not likely to sustain replacement-level fertility because realized fertility tends to be considerably below ideal fertility in low fertility countries. In effect, a substantial proportion of the population of reproductive age needs to have at least three children as a childbearing ideal in order for realized fertility to be around two.

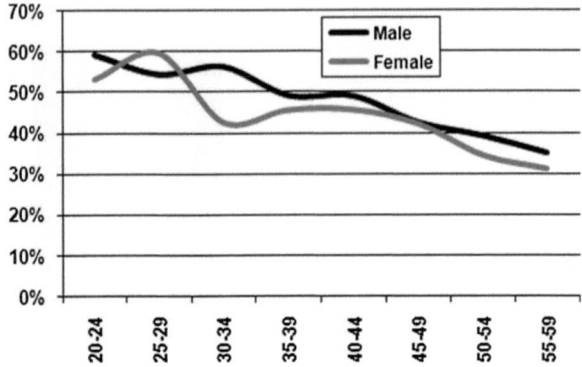

Fig. 5.6 Percentage, by age and sex, of those agreeing that "two children are ideal": Japan, 2007 (Source: Computed from National Survey on Work and Family 2007)

5.4 Changes in Other Values

Other values affecting childbearing trends in Japan could change in several ways. Central to the Japanese case, which is characterized by low levels of premarital childbearing, are the relatively new norms of love marriage rather than arranged marriage, delayed marriage, and delayed childbearing (Atoh 2001; Ogawa 2003). Japan has recently completed the transition from traditional marriages to non-traditional, love marriages. Figure 5.7 shows how traditional arranged marriages have all but disappeared among younger married individuals: Fewer than 5 % of those aged 30–34 had had an arranged marriage, as compared with more than 35 % of those aged 55–59. Younger women and men are now more concerned about compatibility than older individuals when it comes to selecting a partner for marriage or cohabitation (Fig. 5.8).

The greater gap in Japan than in Europe between reported ideal family size and realized fertility may also reflect cultural differences in expressing family-size preferences. In Japan, there may be a stigma against expressing a preference for an "incomplete family"—that is, one with no children or just one child. That there is less acceptance in Japan of such small families suggests that stated ideals conceal some respondents' true feelings. If so, this could partly explain the larger difference between ideal and realized numbers of children in Japan than in Europe. Moreover, some of the mechanisms that pull realized fertility down—high population density, high costs of children, urbanization, very high female education levels, and child-unfriendly cities—are stronger in Japan than in a number of European countries.

Japan is a traditional society that places significant weight on social duties and obligations, a society in which the truth is often concealed by means of polite fiction. It may differ from Europe in the sense that in Japan a person's "real intentions" (*honne*) are traditionally kept separate from "appearances" (*tatemae*) in communication with others (Naito and Gielen 1992; Reggy 2008). These are important points that one needs to be aware of when designing survey questions for Japanese respondents. Several surveys have included questions about the ideal number of children that have taken the following form: "What is your ideal number

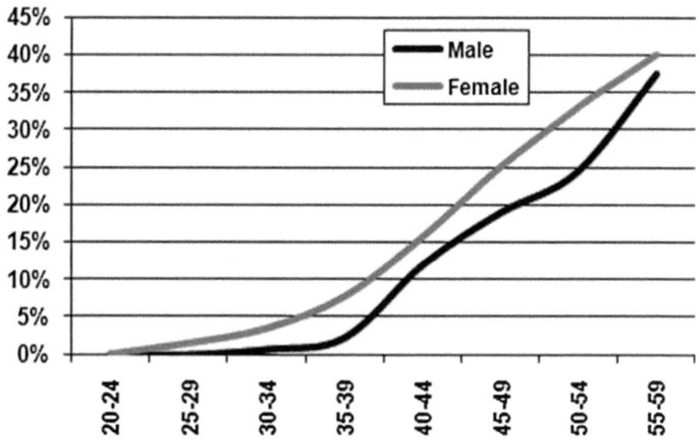

5 What Are the Prospects for Continued Low Fertility in Japan?

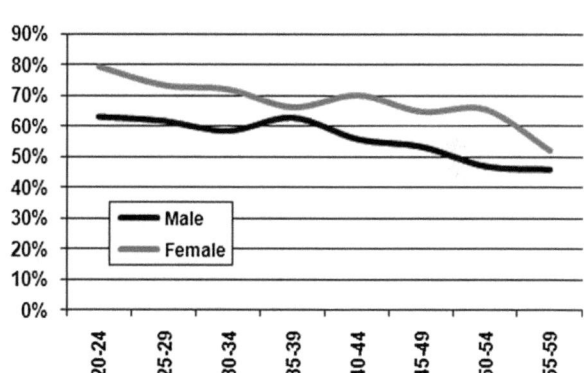

Fig. 5.7 Percentage, by age and sex, of married respondents reporting their marriage had been arranged: Japan, 2007 (Source: Computed from National Survey on Work and Family 2007)

Fig. 5.8 Percentage, by age and sex, of those agreeing that "for marriage (or cohabitation), partner's character is very important": Japan, 2007 (Note: Computed from National Survey on Work and Family 2007)

of children?" In Japan this may be understood to mean either "In general, what do you think is the ideal number of children for a married Japanese couple?" or "Ideally, how many children would *you* like to have?" The interpretation of the question is left to the respondent, which means that the answer may not reflect the real, intended meaning of the question, i.e. the respondent's personal ideal number of children. Therefore, a careful choice of words is needed in designing surveys to distinguish between normative opinions and personal ones.

In the 2007 Survey on Work and Family we endeavored to shed light on this difference and found that among 70 % of the survey subjects the personal ideal number of children was the same as the ideal number of children for Japanese families in general. However, 20 % of the respondents reported that their personal ideal number of children was higher than the ideal for the Japanese in general, and 10 % reported that it was lower. Thus, although it is difficult to assess the extent of the confusion created by the phrasing of survey questions in the past, it is at least clear that a simple comparison between Japanese and European respondents is difficult to make.

In response to a question about whether only the legally married should have children, more than 65 % of Japanese men and women aged 50–54 agreed, while only about 40 % of those 20–24 years old supported this statement (Fig. 5.9).

Fig. 5.9 Percentage, by age and sex, of those agreeing that "only legally married should have children": Japan, 2007 (Note: Computed from National Survey on Work and Family 2007)

Fig. 5.10 Percentage, by age and sex, of those agreeing that "cohabitation is a good thing": Japan, 2007 (Note: Computed from National Survey on Work and Family 2007)

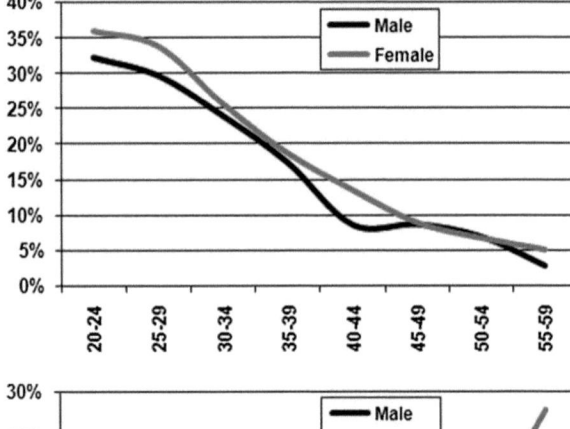

Fig. 5.11 Percentage, by age, of those agreeing that "only those engaged or married should have sex": Japan, 2007 (Source: Japanese Family Planning Association (2008))

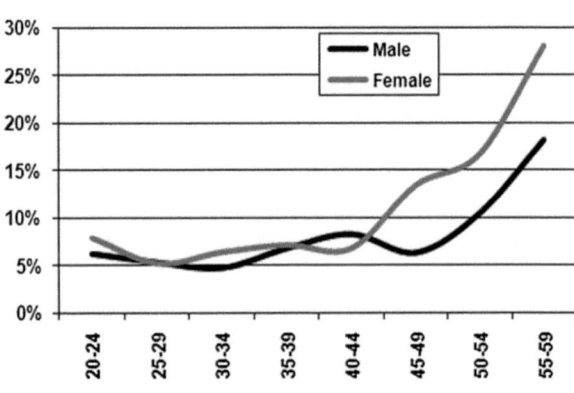

Younger respondents, particularly women, were much more likely to condone cohabitation than were older ones; fully a third of those aged 20–24 approved, but only about 10 % of men over age 45 and of women over age 50 approved (Fig. 5.10). Fewer than 10 % of respondents under age 45 agreed with the statement that only those engaged or married should have sexual relations, whereas nearly 30 % of women and nearly 20 % of men over age 54 agreed (Fig. 5.11).

Atoh (2001) has also reported a decline among younger Japanese in traditional attitudes toward marriage and divorce. In 1992 more than two thirds of those born during 1923–1932 agreed that "women should marry," but less than a third of those born between 1953 and 1972 shared that opinion. Less than half of the 1923–1932 birth cohort agreed with the statement "I may get a divorce if I am not satisfied with my spouse," whereas a majority of the 1953–1972 cohort supported the statement.

Behavioral changes reflect most of the recent changes in attitudes toward premarital sex. The proportion of Japanese high school students who reported having had sexual experience increased from 6 to 30 % (females) and from 10 to 27 % (males) between 1974 and 2005; and the share of university students reporting sexual experience rose from 11 to 62 % (females) and from 23 to 63 % (males) over the same period (Japan Family Planning Association 2008).

Despite the liberalization of sexual attitudes and behavior in Japan, extramarital births are still uncommon (Atoh 2001). As Naito and Gielen (1992) have noted, the coexistence of "modern" values with "traditional" childbearing within marriage is an important characteristic of Japanese society. One reason why the share of children born out of wedlock is small is that they are at a disadvantage when it comes to inheritance. But a low tolerance for extramarital births may be a more salient reason. In any case, greater acceptance of premarital sex has not led to an increase in extramarital births or affected overall fertility in Japan. Rather, the rising share of unmarried Japanese in their 20s and 30s has had a downward effect on fertility levels.

5.5 LFT-3: The Relative Income Argument

The main line of reasoning for this part of the low-fertility trap hypothesis comes directly from Easterlin's (1980) relative income hypothesis. According to Easterlin (1980: 40–41), "The material expectations of young adults are largely the unconscious product of the environment in which they grow up. ... And this environment is very largely shaped by the economic circumstances, or income, of one's parents." Using the income of the father as a proxy for the level of aspirations and the income of the young person as a proxy for expected income, he posited that the ratio of these two income measures of younger workers to older workers should provide a quantitative proxy for relative income. If the ratio increases, then relative income increases and fertility will be higher; if it decreases, then fertility can be expected to decline. Easterlin showed that this could explain the US baby boom after World War II and the subsequent fertility decline.

How relevant is this relative income argument for Japan today? In what follows, we present some empirical evidence indicating that relative income is on the decline in Japan, and that there are no convincing reasons to dismiss Easterlin's hypothesis that declining income contributes to fertility decline. Here, however, we do not refer to the second part of Easterlin's hypothesis, namely, the assumption that smaller cohorts will have higher incomes.

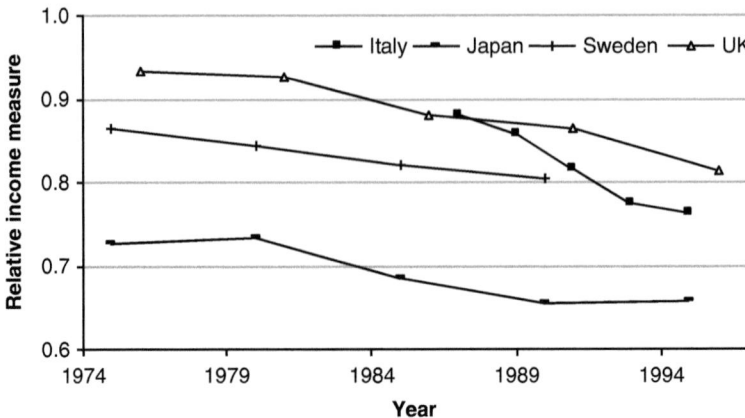

Fig. 5.12 Relative income (income of full-time workers aged 25–34 divided by the income of economically active persons aged 45–54): four countries for which data were available, 1970s–1990s (Source of data: OECD (2001))

Figure 5.12 plots the relative income measure proposed by Easterlin for four European countries for which age-specific income data are available from recent decades. Ideally, the income data for the parents should refer to the period during which the young generation experienced its socialization, and they should be adjusted for changes in purchasing power. Since the necessary data are difficult to find, Easterlin (1980) used only the father's income lagged by 5 years. As a first approximation, we compare the incomes of the two age groups in the same period. The ratio plotted in Fig. 5.12 is the income of economically active men aged 25–34, which refers to those fathering children, divided by the income of economically active men aged 45–54. Among the four nations, the ratio is clearly lowest in Japan. Solely on the basis of these data, which show a decline in relative income from the 1970s to the 1990s, one would expect fertility to decline during the 1970s in Sweden and the UK, and during the 1980s in Italy and Japan. This fits very well with actually observed fertility trends in these countries. But what is also visible from the graph is that relative income does not have a cyclical pattern but rather exhibits a continuous decline. This continuous trend contrasts sharply with Easterlin's expectation, based on the second part of his hypothesis, that relative income would increase for the smaller cohorts entering the labor market. That part of the hypothesis led him to expect a new baby boom in the 1990s. But in all four countries, the young cohorts (those aged 25–34) in 1991–2000 had even lower relative incomes than the same age groups 20 years earlier. In light of these trends in relative income, the continued low fertility in the 1990s comes as no surprise.

The relative income of younger Japanese to prime-age Japanese workers declined from the 1970s to the 1990s. From 1971 to 1986, Japanese male earnings increased monotonically from age 20 up to age 49. In spite of rising education levels among the young, 40–49-year-olds earned increasingly more relative to the

20–24-year-olds, 1.76 times as much in 1971 and 1.92 times as much in 1986 (Clark and Ogawa 1992). Age–earning differences have continued to widen, and Matsukura et al. (2007) found that salary and wage earners in their 40s received on average almost three times as much as 20–24-year-olds by 2002.

Moreover, employment stability is decreasing for young Japanese adults. For 15–24-year-olds, the share of irregular employees rose from 20 % in 1990 to 43 % in 2008 among males and from 21 % in 1990 to more than 51 % in 2008 among females. For the 25–34 age group, it rose from 3 to 13 % for men and from 28 to 40 % for women. For the 25–34 age group (both sexes) the number of *NEETS* (those Not in Education, Employment, or Training) rose from 40,000 in 1993 to 64,000 in 2008, while the number of *freeters* (those in low-paying temporary jobs who often experience periods of unemployment) rose from 1,010,000 in 1992 to 1,700,000 in 2005 (Japan, Statistics Bureau 2009). The irregularity of employment for the young in Japan seems to resemble the case of Spain, where liberalizing the labor market has affected the young in particular and led to very rapid increases in the age at first birth and declining period fertility. It also resembles the case of Germany, where employers resist giving permanent employment to the young since part-timers are cheaper and can be laid off easily (Sanderson 2011).

Other economic factors affecting young people's childbearing decisions in Japan can be found in Oyama's (2006) study exploring why Japanese have fewer children than their ideal number. "Raising and educating children is too expensive" was by far the most common reason given by survey respondents, with more than 75 % of those aged 25–34 agreeing with that statement. In addition, they judged it as far more important than the second most important factor, "Society does not supply [a] safe, sound environment for children" (slightly less than 28 %). Ogawa et al. (2009), using National Transfer Accounts (NTA) research findings for Japan and three other Asian countries and provinces, found that the perceived cost of children and the number of children were negatively and highly correlated at the aggregate level in Japan and East Asia. They noted that the human capital components (health and education) of the cost of children were closely related to the fertility decline in this region, suggesting a trade-off in the quantity and quality of children, with Japanese couples substituting quality for quantity.[1]

What do these findings imply for the future? Can we expect the trend in relative income to be reversed in the near future and young adults to have higher incomes than their parents'? It is possible, of course, that the chosen measure of relative income, comparing two age groups at one point in time, does not give an accurate approximation of the relationship between aspirations and expected income. To explore this possibility, we review some broader evidence and data that relate to the relative income argument, to see whether there are reasons to assume certain trends in the future.

---

[1] A full explanation of the NTA project's basic concepts, the crucial computational assumptions employed, and the definitions of key variables are all available on the NTA website (http://www.ntaccounts.org).

5.6 Economic Aspirations

Although it is very hard to predict how the absolute incomes of younger people will change in Japan and Europe in the future, it seems fair to say that general aspirations for material consumption have been on the rise for quite some time and are unlikely to decline any time soon. This may be due in part to increasing wealth in parental households, and to a penetrating advertising industry that promotes material consumption, especially of expensive brands, as the only avenue to self-worth and happiness. Several surveys have shown that young people are especially susceptible to the influence of advertising (e.g., PEW Research Center 2006). Given the strong increase in consumption aspirations and a more modest increase (or even decline) in the purchasing power of younger workers, personal satisfaction with their level of consumption will possibly never be reached. One might argue that advertisers are likely to set consumption ideals higher (but not unattainably higher) than what individuals currently consume, in order to maximize sales and profits. If this is true, then the gulf between aspirations and expected purchasing power will never be closed for a broad segment of the population. In fact, Stutzer (2004) shows that even as people become richer, their material aspirations increase. Given processes of adaptation and social comparison, their income aspirations also tend to rise as the average income of their communities rises. And Stutzer's analysis shows that higher consumption aspirations decrease wellbeing.

A key economic reason why young Japanese postpone marriage and childbearing seems to be the importance they place on the (potential) husband's income. In particular, younger women regard income level and stability as one of the most important characteristics in a partner (Figs. 5.13 and 5.14). A clear majority of younger respondents to the National Survey on Work and Family (though very few in the more senior age groups) considered the costs of rearing children (particularly the costs of education) as a key barrier to childbearing (Fig. 5.15). Furthermore, it has been demonstrated that in Japan economic booms and busts affect parity progression ratios. For example, Ogawa (2003) has reported a positive relationship between economic downturns and slower and lower transition to

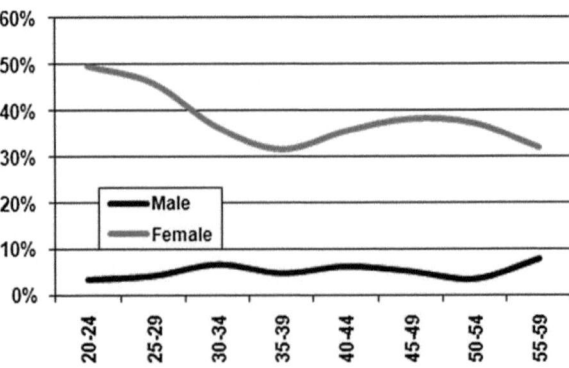

Fig. 5.13 Percentage, by age and sex, of those agreeing that "for marriage (or cohabitation), partner's income level is important": Japan, 2007 (Note: Computed from National Survey on Work and Family 2007)

Fig. 5.14 Percentage, by age and sex, of those agreeing that "for marriage (or cohabitation), partner's income stability is important": Japan, 2007 (Note: Computed from National Survey on Work and Family 2007)

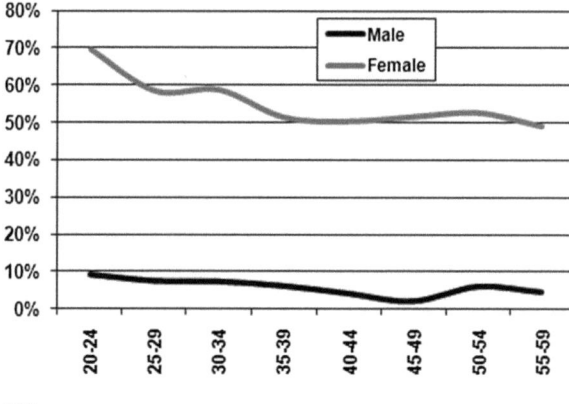

Fig. 5.15 Percentage, by age and sex, of those stating, as a reason for *not* wanting children that "raising children requires a lot of money such as that for their educational expenses": Japan, 2007 (Note: Computed from National Survey on Work and Family 2007)

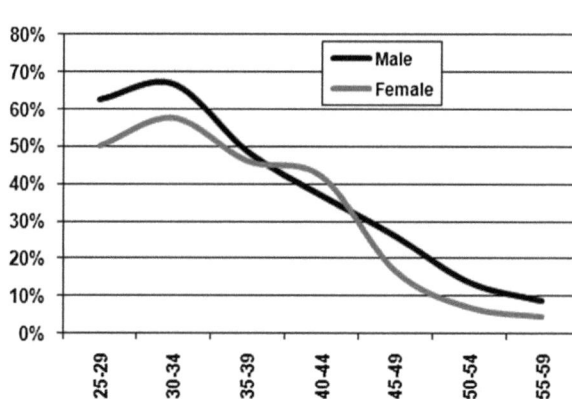

second- and higher-order parities. Similarly, in Sweden the timing of childbearing has been shown to follow economic swings (e.g., Andersson 2002). In sum, very high childbearing costs, growing economic aspirations, and falling relative income among young adults decrease their fertility.

5.7 The Effect of Relative Cohort Size

As already mentioned, Easterlin argues in the second part of his relative income hypothesis that smaller cohort sizes will improve labor market prospects for the young and lead to higher relative incomes. Since most people do not distinguish the second part of Easterlin's hypothesis from the first, which is the one that we have focused on, a brief discussion of the second part is needed to avoid confusion. That part could be seen as an argument for expecting a recovery of relative income, and therefore a recovery of fertility, in Europe over the coming years, when smaller cohorts enter the labor market.

Easterlin (1980) found that in the US during 1950s there were few new labor market entrants and at the same time good labor market prospects, whereas in the

1970s there were many new labor market entrants and poor labor market prospects. He argues that the inverse association between cohort size and labor market opportunities is causal, which is why the assumption of a negative relationship between a cohort's size and aggregate labor market outcomes is often referred to as the "Easterlin hypothesis."

If this hypothesis holds true, there should be a moderating effect on fertility of increasingly smaller cohorts receiving increasingly higher incomes, which would counter the LFT3. Martin and Ogawa (1988) considered the Japanese case and found that the wage ratio of 20–29 to 40–49-year-olds was reduced by 1 % when the share of the former increased by 10 %. Mason et al. (1994) identified a small inverse effect of cohort size on cohort economic success in Japan. Using US data, Shimer (1998) also found a negative cohort-size effect. However, Jimeno and Rodríguez-Palenzuela (2002) analyzed OECD data and found that such an effect—that larger cohort sizes increase unemployment—is evident mostly when labor markets and wages are not flexible enough to adjust to changes in the annual number of new labor market entrants. If such effects of cohort size do exist, they are mostly temporal, disappearing when labor markets have adjusted to changes in the labor supply. Furthermore, in the US the notion that the wages of the young in the 1980s decreased because of their large cohort size was partially abandoned when the wages of the young did not rebound after the baby-bust cohorts entered the labor market (Gottschalk 2001). Moreover, Shimer (2001) found that, regionally, smaller cohorts in the US were associated with lower labor force participation rates and increased unemployment levels, possibly because firms tend to relocate away from where labor supply is expected to decrease and information on cohort sizes of future labor market entrants is readily available. Likewise, regional evidence from Sweden suggests that belonging to a small cohort negatively affects labor market outcomes (Skans 2005).

The possible presence of the effect in which larger cohort size leads to worse conditions for the members of that cohort does not necessarily imply that the reverse will be true and that a smaller cohort size will lead to improved conditions. A survey of 34 countries found that firm start-up activity typically peaks in the young ages of 25–44, which may imply that population aging could cause less job creation (Global Entrepreneurship Monitor 2004). Hence, small cohorts may even negatively affect the overall job market by reducing the number of new enterprises.

5.8 Further Trends that May Lower Japanese Fertility

Several factors of growing importance are likely to imply a further depression of fertility ideals and values, including marriage patterns, education, urbanization, and status seeking. In Japan, the mean age at first birth increased rapidly after the 1970s. Whereas in 1980 it was 26 years, by 2000 it had reached 28 years and has continued to rise since (Fig. 5.16). The development in Japan is similar to that of Western Europe, where some countries, such as the Netherlands, Switzerland, and Sweden,

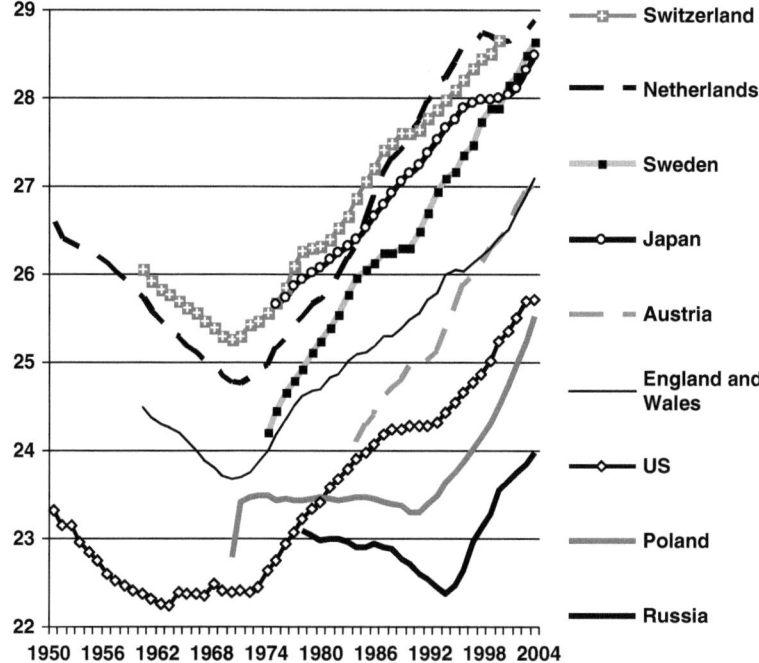

Fig. 5.16 Mean age at first birth: nine countries and areas, 1950–2004 (Source: Computed from Sobotka (2008))

have been seeing ages at first birth rise above 28 years. Furthermore, in Japan the female singulate mean age at marriage rose from below 24 to above 29 years from 1950 to 2005, while for men it rose from around 26 to above 31 years. In Tokyo the mean age at first marriage in 2005 was about 31 years for women and 32 years for men (Retherford et al. 2008).

Rising education levels have been shown to be causally related to postponed marriage and childbearing (see, e.g., Skirbekk et al. 2004). The more educated marry less and later and also postpone and depress their fertility (Retherford et al. 2004; Skirbekk 2008). Hence, a compositional change in the education distribution is likely to have contributed to the postponement of marriage and childbearing. The proportion of Japanese women enrolled in tertiary education (junior college or university) increased from 5 % in 1955 to 20 % in 1970 and to 53 % in 2007; for Japanese men it increased from 15 % in 1955 to 55 % in 2007. The mean age at first marriage was 4.5 years lower for women with junior high school or lower education than for university educated women (Japan, Ministry of Education, Culture, Sports, Science and Technology 2009; own calculations). Ogawa and Retherford (1993) estimated that already in 1990, 22 % of university-educated women were not likely to marry by the age of 40, as compared with only 4 % of women with a junior high school education. They found, however, that, among individuals who married, transitions to first, second, and third parity were not much affected by education.

From 1975 to 2005, Japanese lifetime celibacy rates (defined as never married by age 50) increased from 2 to 16 % for men and from 4 to 7 % for women (Retherford et al. 2008). In urban areas these numbers were even higher; for example, in Tokyo the figure rose from 4 to 21 % for men and from 8 to 13 % for women. The higher male numbers may be explained in part by a greater share of men in the cities. Among 35–39-year-old Japanese, 19 % of women and 31 % of men were never married in 2005, which implies that celibacy rates are likely to increase sharply in the coming years.

The period from marriage to first birth is also increasingly prolonged. Whereas in 1955 the duration was 1.3 years, by the mid-1990s it was 2.1 years (excluding births resulting from "shotgun marriages," i.e., births that took place before the eighth month of marriage (Retherford et al. 1999).

Most Japanese women now work and live alone before entering a formal union. In 1955, 50 % of women worked before marriage, but by the early 1970s more than 90 % did so. Another point of interest is the number of years required to attain median education among women 25–29 years of age. As shown in Fig. 5.17, in order to be in the 50th percentile, one needs increasingly more years of education over

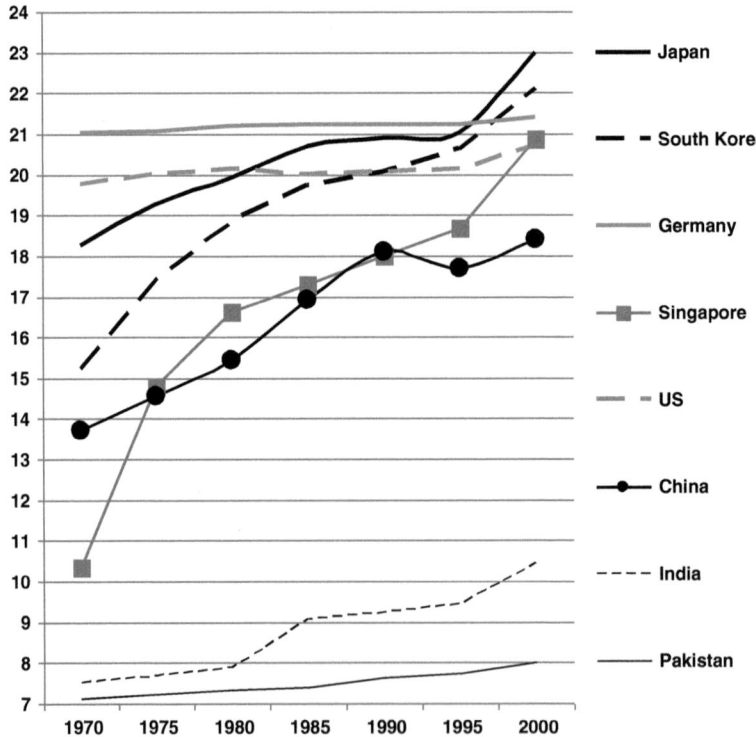

Fig. 5.17 Age at which women, ages 25–29, attained median education: eight countries, 1970–2005 (Source: Skirbekk and KC (2008))

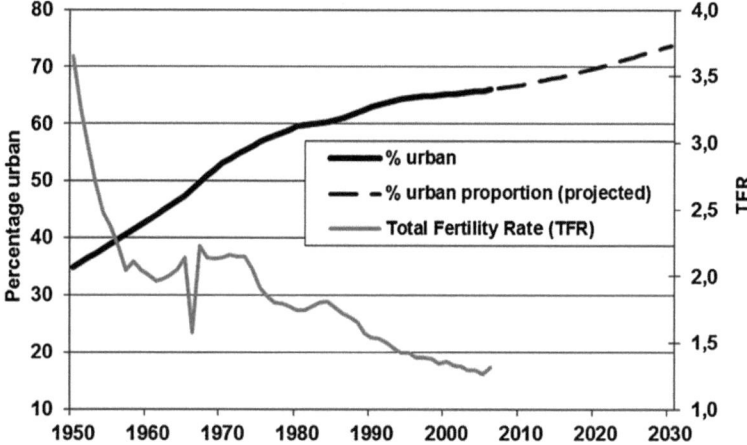

Fig. 5.18 Japan's urbanization and fertility decline since 1950 (Sources: United Nations (2006); Japan, Ministry of Health, Labour and Welfare (various years))

time. As assortative mating is common, having less than median education implies that one is less likely to attract a marriage partner with satisfactory social status and labor market prospects. By 2000, the school-leaving age of persons of median education was higher in Japan than in other low-fertility Asian countries, including Hong Kong, South Korea, and Singapore. The trend of older school-leaving ages may continue as a result of expected increases in education levels in the coming decades (Samir et al. 2008).

Growing urbanization is another factor that could imply lower fertility levels in the coming years (Fig. 5.18). In 1955, when the share of Japan's urban population reached 40 %, the total fertility rate fell to the replacement level; and as the proportion of urban inhabitants passed 55 % in the mid-1970s, the TFR sank below replacement. The share of urban population is projected to continue rising in future decades. The TFR varies across Japan according to the degree of urbanization, ranging from 1.87 births in the most fertile prefecture (Okinawa) to a low of 1.12 in the least fertile prefecture (Tokyo) in 2010 (Japan, Ministry of Health, Labour and Welfare 2011).

Urbanization is related to a number of factors that tend to depress fertility. These include a less family-oriented culture, greater employment and career opportunities, and increased focus on self-realization, individualism, and a single lifestyle. Kulu and Vikat (2007) observe that fertility is highest among couples in single-family houses and lowest among those in apartments, which are typically found in larger cities, with the variation remaining significant even after demographic and socioeconomic characteristics of women are controlled. Their results show elevated fertility levels after couples have changed their housing. Their study also reveals a relatively high probability of a third birth among couples living in single-family houses several years after the move, suggesting that living in spacious housing and in a family-friendly environment for a longer time may lead to higher fertility. Using data from Austria and Poland, Kulu (2006) has found that natives in urban areas in general, and in large cities in particular, have lower fertility than nonmigrants in rural areas, He also shows that people who move from one place to another adopt the dominant fertility behavior at the destination.

Using aggregate and individual-level registration data from Denmark, Finland, Norway, and Sweden, Kulu et al. (2007) show a significant variation in fertility level by settlement size in all four Nordic countries: the larger the settlement, the lower the fertility. They also report that the timing of childbearing varies across settlements: the larger the settlement, the later the peak of fertility. Socioeconomic characteristics of women account for only a small portion of fertility variation across settlements. Lutz et al. (2006b) suggest that the negative relation between population density and reproduction is universal. Fertility is shown to be density-dependent for a wide variety of other species; and evidence from 145 countries reveals a consistent and significant negative relationship between human fertility and fertility preferences on the one hand and population density on the other. Continued urbanization implies that in spite of a slow decline in population size, population density (particularly for younger adults, who are more likely to dwell in cities) can increase, and this could further lower fertility levels.

5.9 Implications of the Low-Fertility Trap

The future level of fertility in Japan is of utmost importance to that society's welfare. The consequences of aging will be more dramatic than currently assumed, should, despite a recent rebound, fertility resume a steady decline or even fall abruptly. But there is an even more immediate political issue that adds urgency to the question of whether the government should get actively involved in trying to raise the level of period fertility. Should the dynamic and self-reinforcing mechanisms assumed to be at work under the low-fertility trap hypothesis become a dominating force in determining Japan's future fertility, then steps to counteract those mechanisms will have a far greater chance of succeeding if they are taken soon. Once the assumed demographic regime change has advanced to the point at which ideal family size for the young generation falls well below the replacement level, as seems to be the case in Germany and Austria, it may be very difficult, if not impossible, to reverse it. Japan, in spite of its low fertility levels, has not yet reached below-fertility preference levels. If period fertility there and in the countries with very low fertility should increase in the near future—possibly through policies affecting the tempo of fertility rather than cohort fertility—this may still help to stop the "tanker" of family-size norms from making a 180° turn. It is through such immediate action that an irreversible demographic regime change may still be stopped by making children a part of normal life again. This will improve the chance that young people will see children as part of the life they wish to live, as seems to be the case in France and the Nordic countries.

In other words, if the low-fertility trap hypothesis has validity, then any attempt to reverse fertility decline in countries with already very low fertility is of great urgency. Governments should consider implementing, with priority and determination, polices that raise fertility. Conventional linear thinking that assumes that gradual fertility trends lead to gradual and reversible changes and consequences should be abandoned and replaced by a systems approach that includes the possibility of nonlinear responses and positive feedback loops. Such an approach allows for the possibility of tipping points and irreversible regime changes.

In the case in which the mechanisms assumed under the low-fertility trap hypothesis are not at work and the hypothesis can be falsified, governments can be more relaxed about the fertility trends and take the "wait and see" approach recommended by Van de Kaa (2006). In any case, an evaluation of the hypothesis is of critical political importance.

5.10 Discussion

In response to the question of whether the first mechanism described by the low-fertility trap hypothesis applies to Japan—that is, whether reproductive-age cohorts are shrinking—the answer is unambiguously *yes*. In response to the question of whether the second mechanism applies to Japan—that is, whether changing childbearing ideals and values have led to further fertility decline—the answer may also be *yes*. Although fertility ideals have not yet declined to below-replacement levels, we see evidence of a shift from a three-child to a two-child ideal and some evidence of a decline in ideal family size. Moreover, survey analyses reveal value changes, including more liberal views toward cohabitation and premarital sexual relations and increased tolerance of divorce. These factors could lead to a further decline and postponement of marriage and may exacerbate the downward trend in fertility levels.

As to whether the third mechanism of the low-fertility trap hypothesis applies to Japan—that is, whether relative economic conditions of the young have worsened—the answer is quite likely *yes*. Respondents to the National Survey on Work and Family cited the cost of children as a key reason for their low fertility. Young adults stated that a stable and sufficiently high income was the most important prerequisite for family formation. Yet economic stagnation and financial crises have particularly affected young Japanese, who have experienced a clear worsening of work conditions with more irregular jobs and lower pay compared with those of senior workers.

Other factors, including increased education, urbanization, delayed marriage and family formation, and expected growth in lifetime celibacy are depressing fertility levels. Continuously rising education levels (leading to postponed and depressed fertility) are an especially important factor. An increasingly higher level of education is required in order to stay at the same percentile in the education distribution, and this upward status spiral can lead to increasingly later and lower fertility. The strong trends underlying the rising proportion of unmarried—including changing ideals and values and rising education levels—will continue to grow in the coming decades and are likely to depress fertility further (Samir et al. 2008). Population density, another factor that discourages fertility, may increase due to growing urbanization, even as the size of Japan's population decreases.

There are, however, certain forces that could lead to somewhat higher fertility for Japan in the future. For instance a study by Myrskala et al. (2009) found that nations at the highest levels of development (measured as progress on the UN's Human Development Index) have somewhat higher fertility than less developed countries. Greater wealth or higher equity could raise fertility levels (Brewster and Rindfuss 2000). We also acknowledge that the relationship between the "new family forms" (e.g., rising levels of divorce or cohabitation) and fertility could potentially change over time (e.g., if out of wedlock childbearing became more acceptable), and contribute to an increase in fertility. Furthermore, a greater influence of women in political processes could potentially increase gender equality in institutions, which, in turn, could possibly raise fertility levels (McDonald, 2000).

Japan could through a variety of policies try to increase fertility. Whether policies aimed at reversing the downward trend in fertility would be accepted by a majority of the population and also effective is a question difficult to answer with the available data. However, policies that make it financially easier to marry and have children while continuing one's education and, hence, allow family formation to begin at a younger age deserve consideration (Lutz and Skirbekk 2005). An overview of recent Japanese fertility policies is given in Retherford and Ogawa (2006). These policies, which range from improved childcare subsidies to firm-specific measures to make family formation easier, may have been relatively unsuccessful so far. Another approach that the Japanese government should consider is reducing the costs of children's tertiary schooling, which are frequently mentioned as a hurdle to initiating childbearing (Ogawa et al. 2009). Also worth debating are policies that would favor the young to a larger extent in labor markets by increasing the share of stable, well paid jobs. With the availability of user-friendly and inexpensive telecommunications, shorter working days and more days working from home can reduce workloads, reduce job–family conflicts, and create a more child-friendly environment.

Although education is clearly related to lower realized fertility (Skirbekk 2008), more-educated women do not wish to have fewer children than less-educated women, and there may even be a positive relation between fertility and childbearing ideals (Noack and Lyngstad 2000; Symeonidou 2000; Testa and Grilli 2006; Van Peer 2002). Hence, policies that could narrow the gap between ideal and realized family size might focus on the more educated, particularly by making the combination of education, work, and family life easier. Lutz and Skirbekk (2005) offer an overview of some policies specifically aimed at allowing those with long periods of education to realize their fertility intentions.

Finally, it should be noted that the recent devastating earthquake and tsunami that struck Northeastern Japan and the ensuing nuclear disaster pose many new economic challenges to the country's policy-makers, given the need to channel funds to reconstruction efforts. Furthermore, population displacement and health concerns for pregnant women and young children caused by radiation leaks at the Fukushima Nuclear Power Plant may accelerate the currently mild decline in the ideal number of children.

References

Andersson, G. (2002). Fertility developments in Norway and Sweden since the early 1960s. *Demographic Research, 6*(4), 65–86.
Atoh, M. (2001, 23–28 June). *Why are cohabitation and extra marital births so few in Japan?* Paper presented at the Second Euresco Conference, The Second Demographic Transition in Europe, Bad Herrenalb, Germany.
Barber, J., & Axinn, W. G. (1998). The impact of parental pressure for grandchildren on young people's entry into cohabitation and marriage. *Population Studies, 52*(2), 129–144.
Brewster, K. L., & Rindfuss, R. R. (2000). Fertility and women's employment in industrialized nations. *Annual Review of Sociology, 26*, 271–296.
Chesnais, J.-C. (1992). *The demographic transition: Stages, patterns, and economic implications.* Oxford: Clarendon Press.
Clark, R., & Ogawa, N. (1992). Employment tenure and earnings profiles in Japan and the United States: Comments. *American Economic Review, 82*(1), 336–345.
Cleland, J. (2001). The effects of improved survival on fertility: A reassessment. In R. A. Bulatao & J. B. Casterline (Eds.), *The global fertility transition: Population and development review* (pp. 60–92, Supplement to Vol. 27). New York: Population Council.
Cleland, J., & Scott, C. (1987). *The world fertility survey—An assessment.* London: Oxford University Press.
Demeny, P. (2003). Population policy dilemmas in Europe at the dawn of the twenty-first century. *Population and Development Review, 29*(1), 1–28.
Easterlin, R. A. (1980). *Birth and fortune: The impact of numbers on personal welfare.* New York: Basic Books.
Global Entrepreneurship Monitor. (2004). *National team reports.* http://www.gemconsortium.org/. Accessed 13 June 2009.
Gottschalk, P. (2001). *What can we learn from the cohort size literature about the future demand for the graying baby boomers?* Manuscript, Roundtable on the Demand for Older Workers. Washington, DC: The Brookings Institution.
Inglehart, R., et al. (2010). *World values surveys and European values surveys.* Ann Arbor: Interuniversity Consortium for Political and Social Research (ICPSR).
Japan, Ministry of Education, Culture, Sports, Science and Technology (2009). *Monbu kagaku tokei yoran* (Statistical abstract). Tokyo: National Printing Bureau.
Japan, Ministry of Health, Labour and Welfare. (Various Years). *Jinko dotai tokei* (Vital statistics of Japan). Tokyo: Health and Welfare Statistics Association.
Japan, National Institute of Population and Social Security Research (2007). *Nihon no shorai suikei jinko: 2006–2055 nen, fu: sanko suikei 2056–2105 nen, heisei 18 nen 12 gatsu suikei* (Population projections for Japan: 2006–2055, with long-range population projections: 2056–2105, 2006 December projection). Tokyo: Health and Welfare Statistics Association.
Japan, Statistics Bureau, Management and Coordination Agency. (1996). *1995 population census of Japan.* Tokyo: Japan Statistical Association.
Japan, Statistics Bureau, Ministry of Internal Affairs and Communications. (2009). *Heisei 20 nen rodoryoku chosa nenpo* (2008 annual report on the Labor Force Survey). Tokyo: Japan Statistical Association.
Japanese Family Planning Association (2008). *Survey on sexual behaviour.* www.jfpa.or.jp. Accessed 22 Nov 2010.

Jimeno, J., & Rodríguez-Palenzuela, D. (2002). *Youth unemployment in the OECD: Demographic shifts, labor market institutions, and macroeconomic shocks* (ECB Working Paper 155). Frankfurt: European Central Bank.

Kaneko, R. (2007). Population prospects of the lowest fertility with the longest life: The new official population projections for Japan and their life course approaches. In *Proceedings of Joint Eurostat–UNECE Work Session on Demographic Projections, Bucharest, 10–12 Oct 2007, Eurostat* (pp. 117–194). Luxembourg: Office for Official Publications of the European Communities.

Kaneko, R., Sasai, T., Kamano, S., Iwasawa, M., Mita, F., & Moriizumi, R. (2008). Marriage process and fertility of Japanese married couples. *The Japanese Journal of Population, 6*(1), 24–50.

Kulu, H. (2006). Fertility of internal migrants: Comparison between Austria and Poland. *Population, Space and Place, 12*, 147–170.

Kulu, H., & Vikat, A. (2007). Fertility differences by housing type: The effect of housing conditions or of selective moves? *Demographic Research, 17*(26), 775–802.

Kulu, H., Vikat, A., & Andersson, G. (2007). Settlement size and fertility in the Nordic countries. *Population Studies, 61*(3), 265–285.

Lutz, W., & Skirbekk, V. (2005). Policies addressing the tempo effect in low-fertility countries. *Population and Development Review, 31*(4), 699–720.

Lutz, W., Skirbekk, V., & Testa, M. R. (2006a). The low fertility trap hypothesis: Forces that may lead to further postponement and fewer births in Europe. *Vienna Yearbook of Population Research, 4*, 167–192.

Lutz, W., Testa, M. R., & Penn, D. J. (2006b). Population density is a key factor in declining human fertility. *Population and Environment, 28*(2), 69–81.

Martin, L. G., & Ogawa, N. (1988). The effect of cohort size on relative wages in Japan. In R. D. Lee, W. B. Arthur, & G. Rodgers (Eds.), *Economics of changing age distributions in developed countries* (pp. 59–75). London: Oxford University Press.

Mason, A., Teh, Y.-Y., Ogawa, N., & Fukui, T. (1994). The intergenerational distribution of resources and income in Japan. In J. Ermisch & N. Ogawa (Eds.), *The family, the market, and the state in ageing societies* (pp. 158–197). Oxford: Clarendon Press.

Matsukura, R., Ogawa, N., & Clark, R. (2007). Analysis of employment patterns and the changing demographic structure of Japan. *The Japanese Economy, 34*(1), 82–153.

McDonald, P. (2000). Gender equity in theories of fertility transition. *Population and Development Review, 26*, 427–440.

Myrskylä, M., Kohler, H.-P., & Billari, F. C. (2009). Advances in development reverse fertility declines. *Nature, 460*(7256), 741–743.

Naito, T., & Gielen, U. P. (1992). Tatemae and honne: A study of moral relativism in Japanese culture. In U. P. Gielen, L. L. Adler, & N. A. Milgram (Eds.), *Psychology in international perspective: 50 years of the International Council of Psychologists* (pp. 161–172). Lisse: Swets & Zeitlinger.

Noack, T., & Lyngstad, T. H. (2000). Norske fruktbarhetsidealer 1977–1999: Idealene består. *Samfunnsspeilet, 3*, 30–34

OECD (Organisation for Economic Co-operation and Development). (2001). *Labor market statistics* [CD-ROM]. Paris: Organisation for Economic Co-operation and Development.

Ogawa, N. (2003). Japan's changing fertility mechanisms and its policy responses. *Journal of Population Research, 20*(1), 89–106.

Ogawa, N., & Retherford, R. D. (1993). The resumption of fertility decline in Japan: 1973–92. *Population and Development Review, 19*(4), 703–742.

Ogawa, N., Mason, A., Chawla, A., Matsukura, R., & Tung, A.-C. (2009). Declining fertility and the rising cost of children: What can NTA say about low fertility in Japan and other Asian countries? *Asian Population Studies, 5*(3), 289–307.

Oyama, M. (2006). Measuring cost of children using equivalence scale on Japanese panel data. *Applied Economics Letters, 13*(7), 409–415.

PEW Research Center. (2006). *Luxury or necessity? Things we can't live without: The list has grown in the past decade*. Washington, DC: PEW Research Center.
Population Reference Bureau. (2007). *Fertility rates for low birth-rate countries, 1995 to most recent year*. Washington, DC: Population Reference Bureau.
Reggy, H. (2008). East–West differences in attributions for company performance: A content analysis of Japanese and U.S. corporate annual reports. *Journal of Cross-Cultural Psychology, 39*(5), 618–629.
Retherford, R. D., & Ogawa, N. (2006). Japan's baby bust: Causes, implications, and policy responses. In F. Harris (Ed.), *The baby bust: Who will do the work? Who will pay the taxes?* (pp. 5–47). Lanham: Rowman & Littlefield.
Retherford, R. D., Ogawa, N., & Sakamoto, S. (1999). Values and fertility change in Japan. In R. Leete (Ed.), *Dynamics of values in fertility change* (pp. 121–147). Oxford: Oxford University Press.
Retherford, R. D., Ogawa, N., Matsukura, R., & Ihara, H. (2004). *Trends in fertility by education in Japan: 1966–2000*. Tokyo: Nihon University, Population Research Institute; and Statistical Research and Training Institute, Ministry of Public Management, Home Affairs, Posts and Telecommunications; and Honolulu: East–west Center.
Retherford, R. D., Ogawa, N., & Matsukura, R. (2008). Japan's declining fertility and policy responses. In G. Jones, P. T. Straughan, & A. Chan (Eds.), *Ultra-low fertility in Pacific Asia: Trends, causes and policy issues* (pp. 40–72). London/New York: Routledge.
Rindfuss, R., Choe, M. K., Bumpass, L. L., & Tsuya, N. O. (2004). Social networks and family change in Japan. *American Sociological Review, 69*(6), 838–861.
Samir, K. C., Barakat, B., Goujon, A., Lutz, W., & Skirbekk, V (2008). *Projection of populations by age, sex and level of educational attainment for 120 countries for 2005–2050* (Interim Report IR-08-038). Laxenburg: International Institute for Applied Systems Analysis
Sanderson, W. (2011). Low fertility and population aging in Germany and Japan: Prospects and policies. In N. Takayama & M. Werding (Eds.), *Fertility and public policy: How to reverse the trend of declining birth rates* (pp. 51–80). Cambridge, MA/London: MIT Press.
Shimer, R. (1998). Why is the US unemployment rate so much lower? *NBER Macroeconomics Annual, 13*(1), 11–61.
Shimer, R. (2001). The impact of young workers on the aggregate labor market. *Quarterly Journal of Economics, 116*(3), 969–1007.
Skans, O. N. (2005). Age effects in Swedish local labor markets. *Economics Letters, 86*(3), 419–426.
Skirbekk, V. (2008). Trends in fertility by social status. *Demographic Research, 18*(5), 145–180.
Skirbekk, V., & Samir, K. C. (2008). *Increased education and postponed fertility—The rising reproductive cost of attaining status*. Vienna: Mimeo, International Institute for Applied Systems Analysis.
Skirbekk, V., Kohler, H.-P., & Prskawetz, A. (2004). Birth month, school graduation, and the timing of births and marriages. *Demography, 41*(3), 547–568.
Sobotka, T. (2008). *Demographic data on the timing of first birth* (Demographic data sheet). Vienna: Vienna Institute of Demography, Austrian Academy of Sciences.
Stutzer, A. (2004). The role of income aspirations in individual happiness. *Journal of Economic Behavior and Organization, 54*(1), 89–109.
Symeonidou, H. (2000). Expected and actual family size in Greece: 1983–1997. *European Journal of Population, 16*(4), 335–352.
Tan, P. C., & Tey, N. P. (1994). Do fertility intentions predict subsequent behavior? Evidence from Peninsular Malaysia. *Studies in Family Planning, 25*(4), 222–231.
Testa, M. R., & Grilli, L. (2006). L'Influence des différences de fécondité dans les régions européennes sur la taille idéale de la famille (The influence of childbearing regional contexts on ideal family size in Europe: A multilevel analysis). *Population, 61*(1–2), 107–137
United Nations. (1973). *The determinants and consequences of population trends*. New York: United Nations.

United Nations. (2006). *World urbanization prospects: The 2005 revision*. New York: United Nations, Department of Economic and Social Affairs, Population Division.

United Nations. (2011). *World population prospects: The 2010 revision*. New York: United Nations, Department of Economic and Social Affairs, Population Division.

Van de Kaa, D. (2006). Temporarily new: On low fertility and the prospect of pro-natal policies. In *Vienna Yearbook of Population Research 2006* (pp. 193–211). Vienna: Austrian Academy of Sciences.

Van Peer, C. (2002). Desired and achieved fertility. In E. Klijzing & M. Corijn (Eds.), *Dynamics of fertility and partnership in Europe: Insights and lessons from comparative research* (Vol. 2, pp. 117–141). New York/Geneva: United Nations.

Westoff, C., & Bankole, A. (2002). *Reproductive preferences in developing countries at the turn of the century* (Comparative Reports (CR), Vol. 2). Calverton: Demographic and Health Surveys.

Yamada, M. (1996). *Kekkon no shakaigaku: Mikonka bankonka ha tsuzukunoka?* (The sociology of marriage: Will marriage continue to be delayed?). Tokyo: Maruzen Library.

Chapter 6
Low Fertility: Choice or Chance?

Paul F.A. Van Look

6.1 Introduction

The second half of the twentieth century saw remarkable declines in global fertility rates. Whereas for the world as a whole the average total fertility rate (TFR) in the 1950s was nearly five children per woman, today this number has been halved to 2.6 children (UN DESA Population Division 2009b: Vol. 1, Table A.24). The decline has been observed in all major regions of the world except Africa, where the average TFR currently still stands at 4.6 children per woman (as compared with 6.6 children in the early 1950s). (See Fig. 6.1.)

Within the African continent, however, subregional differences are substantial. Sub-Saharan Africa has shown the least progress, with fertility declining from 6.6 children per woman in the early 1950s to 5.1 in 2005–2010, as compared with, for instance, northern Africa, where the average fertility rate has dropped from 6.9 to 2.9 over the corresponding period. In many western European countries and in Canada and the US, where fertility was already low in the early 1950s (with rates around 2.5 children per woman), the downward trend has meant that most of those countries have slipped below the replacement fertility level of 2.1 children; that is, the number of children currently born to a woman is no longer sufficient for the population to replace itself from one generation to the next. According to United Nations data (UN DESA Population Division 2007b: 9), during 2005–10, 73 countries or areas (45 of them located in the more developed regions) had total fertility levels below 2.1 children per woman, whereas 122 countries or areas (all of which are located in the less developed regions) had total fertility levels at or above 2.1 children per woman. Among those 122 countries, 27 had total fertility levels at or above 5 children per

---

P.F.A. Van Look (✉)
Sexual and Reproductive Health, Route des Crosets 48, Case Postale 51,
CH-1873 Val-d'Illiez, Switzerland
e-mail: vanlookp@bluewin.ch

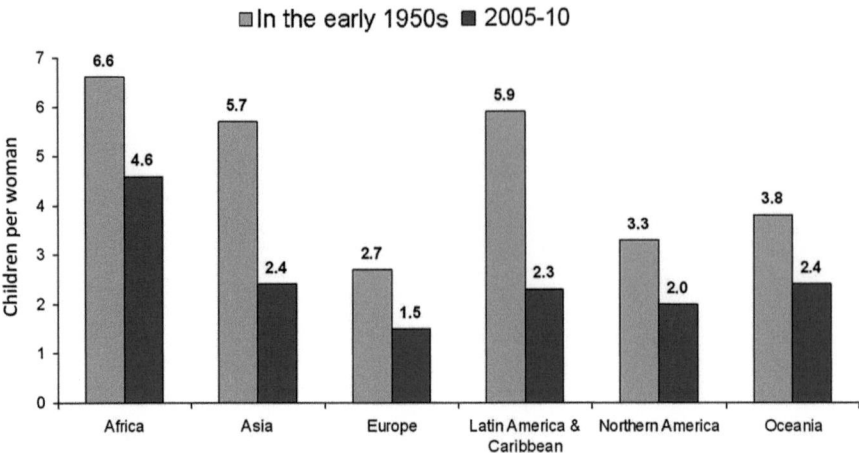

Fig. 6.1 Total fertility rates in the major world regions: in early 1950s and 2005–2010 (Source: UN DESA Population Division (2009b: Vol. 1, Table A.24))

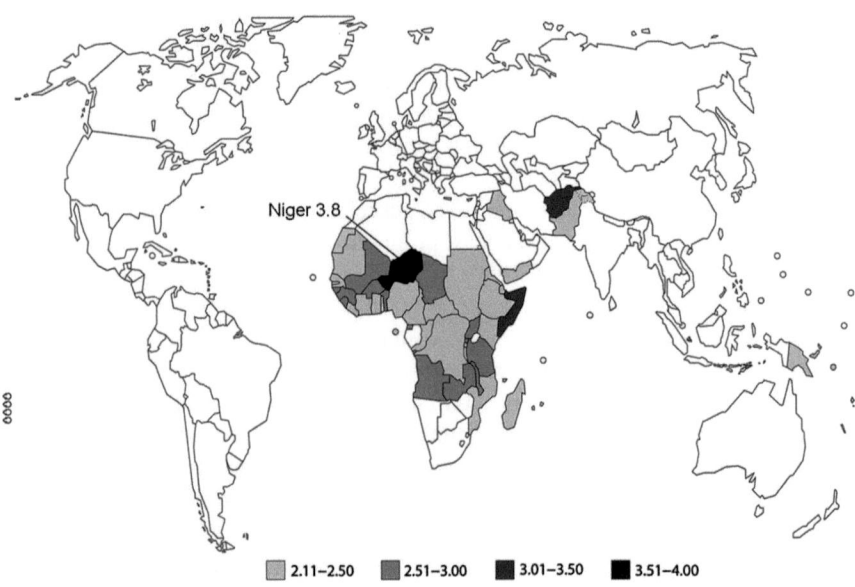

Fig. 6.2 Countries projected to have total fertility rates above replacement level in 2050 (Source: UN DESA Population Division (2009b: Vol. 1, Table A24))

woman; and 25 of those high-fertility nations are in the category of least developed. The United Nations projects that, by 2050, 49 countries and territories (out of a total of 196) will continue to have above-replacement fertility levels. Most of them will be in sub-Saharan Africa, and Niger will top the list with a TFR of 3.8 children per woman (UN DESA Population Division 2009b). (See Fig. 6.2.)

A second major demographic change that is shaping the makeup of societies worldwide, especially in East and Southeast Asia, is increasing life expectancy. For the world as a whole, life expectancy at birth has risen from some 47 years in the early 1950s to about 68 years today and, according to UN projections, will continue this upward trend to reach some 75 years by 2050 (UN DESA Population Division 2009b: Vol. 1, Table A.30). The rise in life expectancy is taking place in all major regions of the world, but differences between regions will continue to be substantial for several more decades. For instance, for 2050 the United Nations estimates a life expectancy at birth of about 83 years for the more developed regions but only 69 years for the least developed countries; in other words, the least developed countries will achieve only in 2050 the life expectancy that was reached by the more developed regions a century earlier, in 1950. Differences between individual countries are even more striking. For example, today's life expectancy of a girl born in Sierra Leone is only about half that of a girl born in Japan (45 years versus 86 years); and although this gap is expected to narrow over the next few decades, it is projected to still be nearly 30 years by 2050 (64 years versus 91 years).

This chapter covers but goes beyond the region of East Asia and provides a global overview in fertility and infertility and in related issues. In the sections that follow, I discuss some of the forces that are driving the global and regional fertility decline, specifically whether it is the result of deliberate behavioral choices made by couples or governments or, alternatively, due to biological "chance," defined here as factors outside a couple's control, in particular involuntary infertility. The potential role of assisted reproductive technology in addressing involuntary infertility will be discussed. Finally, I shall review briefly the impact of low fertility combined with increasing longevity on a population's age composition; the economic effects of a growing, "unproductive" older generation on a shrinking, economically productive young generation; and the epidemiologic transition, in which chronic, noncommunicable conditions rather than communicable diseases become the dominant problems challenging a country's health system.

6.2 Low Fertility Due to Choice

6.2.1 Individual Choice

Among the proximate determinants influencing fertility, use of contraception is by far the most significant. For instance, to lower the TFR from about 7 children per woman (a typical rate for a traditional society where prolonged breastfeeding is the main form of birth spacing) to the replacement level of 2.1 children, the World Bank (1984: Fig. 4.5) has calculated that "more use of contraception" contributes some 90 % to the reduction. Higher ages at marriage (about 25 %), more induced abortion (about 10 %), and other factors such as infanticide (a few percentage points) are much less important than contraceptive use. On the other hand, the reduced practice of prolonged breastfeeding in contemporary societies has the opposite effect on fertility, increasing the rate by some 25 % and thereby negating part of the reductions brought about by the other fertility determinants.

In light of the foregoing, it is clear that the worldwide decline in fertility rates is directly and causally related to the massive increase in the use of contraception, which could be rightly described as one of the public health successes of the twentieth century. For the developing countries as a whole, contraceptive prevalence increased from a mere 10 % in the early 1960s to some 62 % by 2007, a level approaching the 70 % rate in developed countries (UN DESA Population Division 2009a: Wall Chart). In fact, when only modern methods of contraception are considered, the prevalence rate in developing countries (56 %) is very close to that found in developed countries (59 %). As in so many areas of sexual and reproductive health, regional differences are considerable. Africa, particularly sub-Saharan Africa, trails well behind the other world regions. In 2007, for example, contraceptive prevalence of modern methods was 22 % for Africa as a whole and 15 % for sub-Saharan Africa, as compared with 61 % for Asia and 64 % for the Latin American and Caribbean region (UN DESA Population Division 2009a: Wall Chart).

The causes underlying the low use of contraception in sub-Saharan Africa are manifold and include, among others, problems of accessing services (due to geographical or financial barriers); personal, religious, or cultural objections to contraception; previous experience or fear of side effects associated with contraceptive use; and logistical failures resulting in product stock-outs. In addition, couples

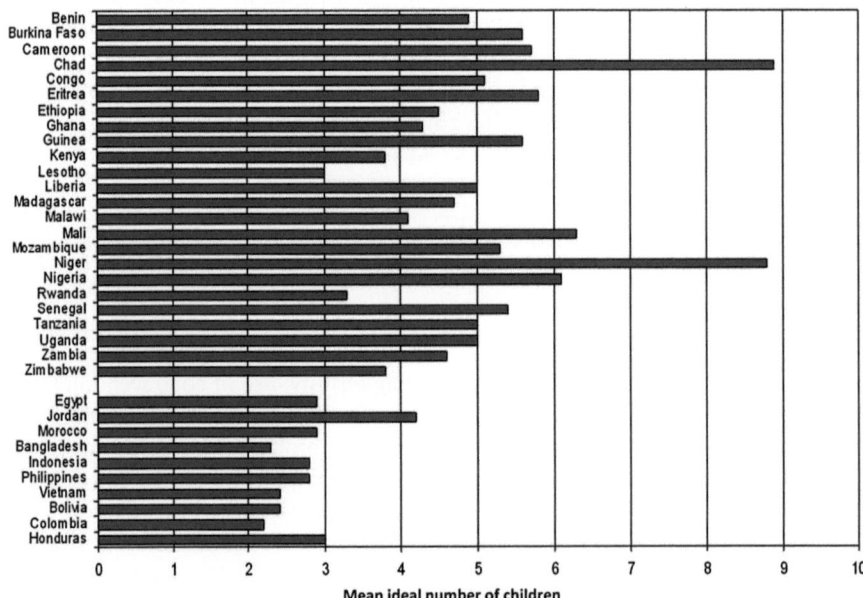

Fig. 6.3 Mean "ideal" number of children: selected countries (Source: Measure DHS (2011))

in most sub-Saharan African countries continue to desire larger families than in other areas of the world (Fig. 6.3). Nevertheless, unmet need for contraception as measured by the proportion of sexually active women who do not wish to become pregnant, yet are not using any form of contraception, is high, reaching some 25 % for sub-Saharan Africa as a whole (UN DESA 2010: 36).

Given this high level of unmet need, it is not surprising that unplanned pregnancies and abortion are frequent occurrences. Because induced abortion is legally restricted in nearly all African countries, most abortions that occur are unsafe and associated with a heavy toll of maternal mortality and of short-term and long-term morbidity. Of the 21.6 million unsafe abortions and 47,000 deaths related to unsafe abortions that were estimated to have occurred globally in 2008, 6.2 million (29 %) unsafe abortions and 27,500 (59 %) deaths, respectively, occurred in Africa (Shah and Åhman 2010: Table 1; WHO 2011: Tables 5 and 6). Among women surviving unsafe abortion, chronic, long-term pelvic infections leading to ectopic pregnancy and involuntary secondary infertility are well-documented sequelae.

6.2.2 Societal Choice

On rare occasions, a government may decide to limit the fertility of its citizens for "the societal good." When this happens, legitimate questions arise about the right of societies to take decisions that are in conflict with the human rights of their members, in particular the right to privacy or, as the US State Supreme Court justice Thomas Cooley of Michigan succinctly described it in 1888, "the right to be left alone." (Warren and Brandeis 1890: 195).

Throughout contraceptive history, incidents of coercive practices in family planning programs have made the headlines, from the mass sterilization camps in India in the mid-1970s and the forced sterilizations of indigenous people in rural areas of Peru under President Fujimori to the widespread practice of sterilization for the purpose of eugenics in such countries as Germany under the Nazi regime, Japan, the US, and several European countries. On a smaller, but no less publicized, scale are the ongoing debates about the abuse potential of some forms of contraception, such as implants or other long-acting methods, to achieve forced contraception in individuals judged incapable of looking after their children, or more children, because of their lifestyle or their history of abusing children.

Discussions about societal decisions to limit fertility inevitably turn to the People's Republic of China, which in 1979 introduced the one-child policy with the express purpose of limiting population growth. Although designated a "temporary measure," the policy remains largely in force today, some three decades after its establishment. The policy consists of a set of regulations governing the approved size of Chinese families. These regulations include restrictions on early marriage, family size, and close spacing of births in cases in which a second child is permitted. The National Population and Family Planning Commission sets overall targets and policy direction, whereas family planning committees at provincial and county levels formulate local strategies for implementation. Despite its name, the one-child rule applies only to a minority of the population. For urban residents and government employees the policy is strictly enforced, with few exceptions. The exceptions include families in which the first child has a disability or both parents work in high-risk occupations (such as mining) or, in some areas, are themselves from one-child families (Hesketh et al. 2005: 1171).

In rural areas, where approximately 70 % of the people live, a second child is generally allowed after 5 years, but this provision sometimes applies only if the first child is a girl—an unambiguous expression of the traditional preference for boys. A third child is allowed among some ethnic minorities and in remote, underpopulated areas. The policy is underpinned by a system of rewards and penalties, which are largely decided by local officials and hence vary widely. They include economic incentives for compliance and substantial fines, confiscation of belongings, and dismissal from work for noncompliance. Pressure to abort a nonauthorized pregnancy and forced sterilization have been said to occur, but the central authorities have generally denied such claims or have blamed local officials for "misunderstanding" or "overinterpretation" of the policy directives or for "overzealous pursuance" of family planning targets. (See Hesketh et al. 2005 for a discussion of the Chinese government's policy.)

China's fertility rate at the time of introducing the one-child policy in 1979 was about 2.8 children per woman; it has declined since then to the current level of 1.8. It should be noted, however, that the rate had already been halved prior to 1979, in the period following the 1965 launch of the Cultural Revolution, when it stood at about 6 (UN DESA Population Division 2009b: Table A.24). The one-child policy has been estimated to have reduced population growth in China by as much as 300 million people over its first 20 years and is credited with having contributed significantly to China's emergence as a major economic power. In the absence of a valid comparison it is difficult to judge, however, how much of the fertility decline was due to the introduction of the one-child policy and how much of it was a reflection of the declining trend in fertility occurring worldwide in the last few decades. That the one-child policy did not accelerate the ongoing decline of China's fertility rate after its introduction suggests that the policy as a societal "choice" may have benefited from an already ongoing evolution in personal preference for smaller families. This assumption is supported in some measure by survey findings indicating that Chinese women, like many of their Western counterparts, prefer to have fewer than two children (Table 6.1)—although caution must be exercised in interpreting these data, since respondents may have expressed an official position rather than a personal opinion.

Data about the sex of babies born to mothers interviewed in the above-cited survey are likely to be more solid. The data confirm the severe distortion of the sex ratio in China, where the overall value is 1.15 (i.e., 115 male babies born for every 100 girls), as compared with the global average of 1.05 (Table 6.2). Whereas the sex ratio for first births is about normal, a rising trend is clearly discernable for second, third, and higher-order births and is an almost sure sign of female feticide as couples try to ensure the birth of a male heir. The rise in the sex ratio with birth

Table 6.1 Mean preferred number of children among 39,344 women interviewed in the Chinese National Family Planning and Reproductive Health Survey, 2001

Mother's characteristics	Mean preferred number of children
Age (years)	
15–19	1.45
20–29	1.65
30–39	1.76
40–49	1.83
Area of residence	
Urban	1.42
Rural	1.77
Education	
Illiterate or semi-literate	1.98
Primary school	1.84
Secondary school	1.50
College	1.43
All women	1.71

Source: Adapted from Ding and Hesketh (2006: Table 3)

Table 6.2 Sex ratio among 56,830 babies born to women interviewed in the Chinese National Family Planning and Reproductive Health Survey, 2001

	Sex ratio		
Birth order	All areas	Urban areas	Rural areas
1st	1.06	1.13	1.05
2nd	1.24	1.30	1.23
3rd	1.28	1.19	1.29
≥4th	1.31	1.19	1.32
All birth orders	1.15	1.16	1.15

Source: Adapted from Ding and Hesketh (2006: Table 1).

order for all births closely follows that in rural areas, reflecting the predominantly rural distribution of China's population. By contrast, in urban areas, where the one-child policy is more strictly implemented and access to ultrasound for determining the sex of the fetus is easier, the sex ratio is already markedly distorted among first births and becomes even more so among second births, which may be couples' last chance of having a boy.

6.3 Low Fertility Due to Chance

6.3.1 Magnitude and Causes of Infertility

Infertility, i.e., failure to bear children, is without doubt the single greatest cause of a couple's inability to attain their desired family size. Both clinicians and demographers distinguish between primary and secondary infertility, but they differ in the criteria they use to define these terms. Demographers usually define primary infertility as the inability of a woman to bear any children, due either to the inability to conceive or to the inability to bear a live child, whereas secondary infertility denotes a woman's inability to bear a child after having had a previous child. Clinicians, on the other hand, define infertility as the inability of a couple to conceive a pregnancy rather than the inability to deliver a child. Clinicians and demographers also differ in the time dimension: clinicians generally consider a couple infertile if no pregnancy has resulted from 12 months' exposure to unprotected sexual intercourse, whereas demographers usually use a longer time frame, such as 5 years.

Global data on the number of infertile couples are not available. Infertility is not a notifiable condition and no national registries are kept. Information needs to be gathered, therefore, from population-based surveys, such as the Demographic and Health Surveys (DHS), which have been conducted in developing countries since the mid-1980s. Rutstein and Shah (2004) used DHS data from 47 developing countries (excluding the People's Republic of China) and including some 497,000 women to estimate the prevalence of infertility. They reported that in 2002 more than 186 million ever-married women of reproductive age (15–49 years) in those countries were involuntarily infertile (according to the demographic definition of having had no live birth within the last 5 years) because of primary infertility (18 million) or secondary infertility (168 million). This prevalence represented more than one fourth of all ever-married women of reproductive age in those countries at that time (Rutstein and Shah 2004: 24).

A much lower prevalence of infertility was estimated by Boivin et al. (2007, 2009), based on an analysis of 25 population surveys sampling some 172,000 women in both more developed and less developed countries. The authors found a 12-month prevalence rate ranging from 3.5 to 16.7 % in more developed countries and from 6.9 to 9.3 % in less developed countries, with an estimated overall median prevalence of 9 % (5–15 %). In absolute terms this prevalence was calculated to represent a global total of 72 million (40–120 million) infertile women aged 20–44 in marital or consensual unions (Boivin et al. 2007: 1506). Of these, some 56 % (30–75 %) of couples (42–76 % in 12 studies in more developed countries, 27–74 % in five studies in less developed countries) had sought infertility medical care; they represented about 41 million (12–90 million) couples. Not all of these couples received medical treatment for their infertility, however. Boivin et al. (2007: 1506) estimated that only some 22 % of couples seeking medical care actually received treatment, but this estimate was based on a small sample of only six studies (five in more developed countries and one in a less developed country) involving about 1,350 couples.

A recent study by Mascarenhas et al. (2012: e1001356), covering 190 countries and territories, shows that globally in 2010, 1.9 % of couples who were exposed to the risk of pregnancy and wanted to have a live birth were unable to have one (defined by authors as *primary infertility*) and 10.5 % were unable to have another child after having had a live birth (defined by authors as *secondary infertility*). From 1990 to 2010, primary infertility did not change in China and Japan (1.3 % in each country in each year), Hong Kong and in Taiwan (1.8 % in each country in each year), South Korea (1.1 % vs. 1.0 %), Singapore (1.4 % vs. 1.3 %), Thailand (2.3 %

in each year), and slightly increased in Mongolia from 1.6 % in 1990 to 2 % in 2010. However, secondary infertility increased somewhat in all countries, except in Japan where it was 8 % in 1990 and 8.4 % in 2010. The greatest increase was in Mongolia (11.6 % in 1990 vs. 15.2 % in 2010). In other countries, secondary infertility rose from 1990 to 2010 as follows: South Korea 5.5 % vs. 7.4 %, Taiwan 8.8 % vs. 11.4 %, Singapore 6.5 % vs. 8.6 % and in Thailand it rose from 8.4 % in 1990 to 11.1 % in 2010 (Mascarenhas et al. 2012: e1001356, supporting dataset S2). No estimate of secondary infertility was made for China because of its one-child policy.

In the absence of firm data on the number of infertile couples receiving treatment, and since no data are available on the effectiveness of infertility treatment (all types) worldwide, no estimate can be made of the positive contribution, if any, of infertility treatment to raising fertility rates.

The causes of subfertility or infertility are multiple. They include genetic factors (e.g., immotile cilia syndrome), developmental factors (e.g., congenital anomalies of the genital tract), anatomical factors (e.g., fibroids, varicocele), endocrinological factors (e.g., hypothalamic-pituitary-ovarian dysfunction), infectious disease, iatrogenic factors (e.g., pelvic surgery), behavior (e.g., late marriage), drug exposure (e.g., chemotherapy), trauma (e.g., spinal cord injury), illness (e.g., AIDS), environmental hazards (e.g., tobacco use), and idiopathic factors. In some cases, more than one factor may be responsible.

Using a standard approach, the World Health Organization carried out a systematic investigation into the causes of infertility in 33 medical centers in 25 countries throughout the developed and developing world between 1979 and 1984. Over 5,800 couples completed the investigation (Cates et al. 1985). The study revealed a pattern of infertility that was different in African centers from that in centers in other developing regions or the developed countries. In particular, African couples were more likely to have secondary infertility or infertility of longer duration, to have a history of pregnancy complications or sexually transmitted infections, and to have infertility diagnoses, such as bilateral tubal occlusion or pelvic adhesions, suggestive of previous genital infections. This preponderance of infection-related conditions has wide-ranging implications for treatment prospects since the management of such patients generally requires either pelvic surgery or some form of assisted reproductive technology—neither of which is affordable within public health care budgets of almost all developing countries. Besides, as will be discussed below, the potential effect of wider use of assisted reproductive technology (ART) on fertility rates, even at "maximum" access levels, is small.

6.3.2 *The Potential Effect of Wider Use of ART on Fertility Rates*

Since the birth of Louise Brown in 1978 following the successful *in vitro* fertilization of a human egg by a human spermatozoon, some five million children have been born as a result of the use of this and related ART procedures. Systematic data collection by the International Committee Monitoring Assisted Reproductive Technologies (ICMART) has revealed huge variations in the availability of ART treatments and their success rates across countries. In the Committee's last world report, which analyzes ART practice and results for the year 2004 from 2,184 clinics in 52 countries, availability was stated to be at its highest level in Israel, which provided 3,844 ART cycles per million population, followed by Denmark (2,073 cycles per million), Spain (2,051 cycles per million), and Belgium (1,911 cycles per million) (ICMART 2013: Table 1). In 2004, Denmark also had the greatest proportion of ART births among all births, at 4.1 %, closely followed by Israel (4 %) and Spain (3.7 %). In Japan, the proportion of ART births among all births rose from 1.6 % in 2004 to 2 % in 2008 (Ooki 2011: 10.1155). In South Korea, 2.2 % of all births in 2004 resulted from ART treatment. In Latin American countries there tended to be fewer than 100 cycles provided per million population, and ART births represented less than 0.1 % of all births. In 2004, Japan accounted for 16 % of all recorded ART treatment cycles. One in three cycles reported took place in just two countries—the US and Japan. As of 2009, the total number of babies born through ART treatment in Japan was estimated at 242,435 (Study Group of Reproductive Technology and Health Care, 2013: 1). The number of treatment cycles provided by 627 clinics in Japan rose by 15 % from 2007 to 2008 (Japan Society of Obstetrics and Gynecology 2008: 3).

Within European countries, people in the UK were among the least likely to receive ART treatment. In a 2003 survey, the UK was 12th out of the 15 European countries that provided data, with only Macedonia, Croatia, and Austria performing fewer cycles of treatment per head of population (Fig. 6.4) (Ziebe and Devroey (2008: Fig. 3A).

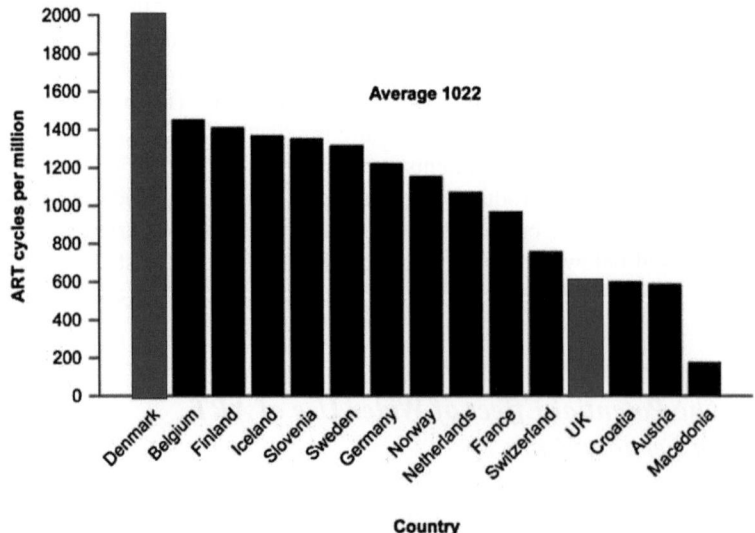

Fig. 6.4 Access to assisted reproductive technologies: selected European countries (Source: Reproduced with permission from Ziebe and Devroey (2008: Table 3A))

6 Low Fertility: Choice or Chance?

Table 6.3 The total fertility rate (TFR) with and without access to assisted reproductive technologies (ART): Denmark and the UK

Scenario	Denmark	UK
TFR without ART	1.65	1.62
Observed TFR with ART, 2002	1.72	1.64
TFR with access to ART at 2002 Danish level	1.72	1.68
Maximum TFR with ART	1.89	1.84

Source: Adapted from Hoorens et al. (2007: Table 2).

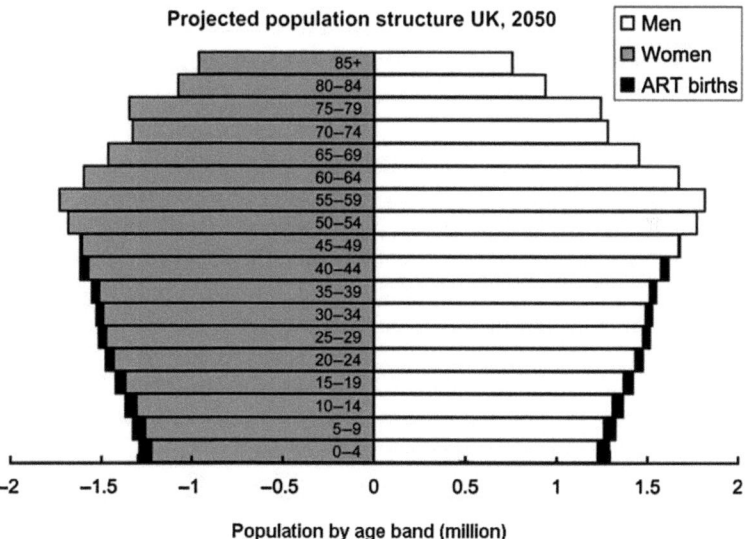

Fig. 6.5 Projected effect of assisted reproductive technologies (ART) on age structure in the UK in 2050 (Source: Reproduced with permission from Hoorens et al. (2007: Fig. 2))

Hoorens et al. (2007) developed a deterministic model to quantify the effect of ART policies on the total fertility rate. Using data from Denmark and the UK, they calculated that the TFR in the UK would increase by 0.04, from 1.64 to 1.68, if access to ART were increased to the level found in Denmark (Table 6.3).

The projected cumulative effect of ART on the population structure of the UK in the year 2050 is shown in Fig. 6.5. Altogether, this slight broadening of the base of the population pyramid would result in a very modest decrease by 1.7 % of the old-age dependency ratio, defined as the proportion of older persons (persons aged 65 years and over) to the proportion of persons in the working ages, that is those aged 15–64 years.

According to Hoorens et al. (2007), the direct cost associated with adopting ART as a population policy would be comparable to that of existing pronatalist policies often used by governments to encourage larger family size. As the authors acknowledge, however, the mathematical models do not include behavioral components, which are often critical to the success or failure of policies affecting the sexual and reproductive health and the rights of individuals. As shown in Table 6.3, ART could theoretically lead to more substantial increases in the TFR ("maximum TFR with ART") in both Denmark and the UK, but such levels are unlikely to be achieved since this scenario assumes that all ART-treated women achieve the fertility rate of fertile women. Also, one may note that the percentage of all births which are due to ART treatment in East Asia continues to be low (2 % or less) despite an increasing use of this technology.

6.4 Population Aging and Some of Its Consequences

Declining fertility coupled with increasing life expectancy is having a profound effect on the age structure of societies and significant implications for pensions and other social-benefit schemes for older people, as well as for health care systems. The "graying" of populations, i.e., the progressive rise in the proportion of older people in a society, is a demographic reality generally thought to be associated with developed nations. This view is no longer valid, however, since many developing countries are experiencing the same phenomenon and, in fact, have populations that are aging at a much faster rate than that seen in most developed countries, the exception being Japan (Population Reference Bureau 2006). For instance, in European countries, the US, and Canada, it took 45 years or more (and even up to 115 years in the case of France) for the population aged 65 years and older to double from 7 to 14 % of the total population. In contrast, many of the middle-income developing countries will go through the same process two to three times faster, with the elder population generally doubling from 7 to 14 % in just 20–30 years. Among developed countries, only Japan witnessed a similarly rapid aging process, with its older population increasing from 7 to 14 % within 26 years between 1970 and 1996. Figure 6.6 illustrates the remarkable impact of this continuing graying process on

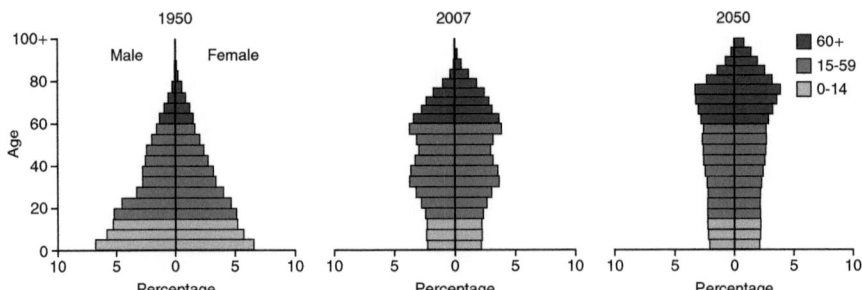

Fig. 6.6 Population pyramid of Japan: 1950, 2007, and projection for 2050 (Source: UN DESA Population Division (2007a: 311))

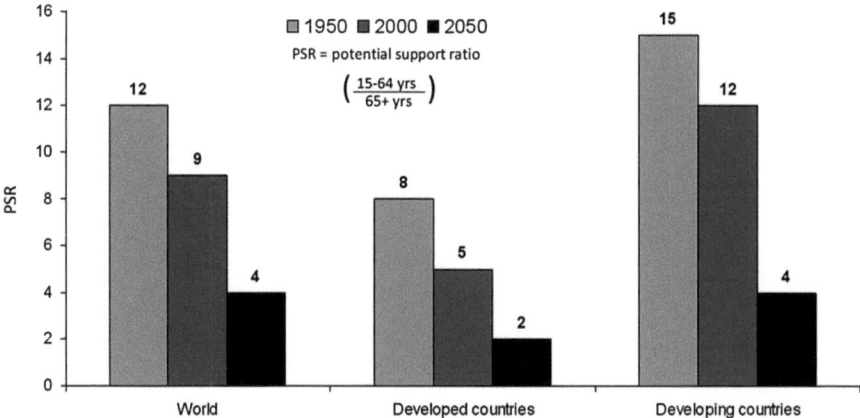

Fig. 6.7 Potential support ratios (PSR) for the world, developed countries, and developing countries: 1950, 2000, and projection for 2050 (Source: UN DESA Population Division (2007a: Fig. 20))

the age structure of Japan's population in 2007 and the 2050 projection. Developing countries with similar rates of demographic transition can expect to follow Japan's path.

The aging of populations creates a multitude of challenges for individuals, families, and societies. A comprehensive discussion of them is outside the scope of this chapter, but two aspects will be briefly mentioned. First, a growing population of older people who are dependent for their pensions and other social benefits on a shrinking number of economically productive members in a society represents a potential source of social unrest, as witnessed recently in some European countries where governments have proposed raising the age of retirement. In developed countries in the year 2000, the potential support ratio—that is, the number of people in the economically productive age group of 15–64 years who support one "unproductive" individual aged 65 years or more—was 5 (UN DESA Population Division 2007b: Fig. 20). (See Fig. 6.7.) By the year 2050 the ratio is projected to decrease to 2. In contrast, for the developing countries as a group, the corresponding ratios are 12 and 4, a drop of 8 "workers" for every one "pensioner." Given that the economic situation in the majority of developing countries remains fragile and many older people must rely on informal family support in the absence of centrally organized social security systems, the rapid demographic aging in these countries over the next few decades will require concerted effort by both the countries concerned and their development partners to establish sound, equitable, and sustainable social policies if major social upheavals are to be avoided.

A second challenge for governments faced with an aging population is to develop and strengthen their health care systems, to make them capable of coping with an increasing caseload of chronic, noncommunicable diseases, including cardiovascular degeneration, chronic respiratory diseases, cancer, diabetes, and

Table 6.4 The ten major risk factors to health in 2000 and projection to 2020, ranked by estimated attributable and avoidable disability-adjusted life-years (DALYs) burden

Rank	2000	2020	Change in rank, 2020–2000
1	Underweight	Unsafe sex	−1
2	Unsafe sex	Blood pressure	−1
3	Blood pressure	Tobacco	−1
4	Tobacco	Cholesterol	−3
5	Alcohol	Underweight	+4
6	Unsafe water sanitation and hygiene	Alcohol	+1
7	Cholesterol	Overweight	−3
8	Indoor smoke from solid fuels	Low fruit and vegetable intake	−4
9	Iron deficiency	Iron deficiency	0
10	Overweight	Physical inactivity	−4

Source: Adapted from WHO (2002: Table 4.11)

such mental health problems as dementias. As shown in Table 6.4, several of the risk factors to health traditionally associated with the developing countries and responsible for much of their health care burden, such as unsafe water sanitation and hygiene, underweight, and exposure to smoke from indoor fuels, are expected to be less significant by the year 2020. Their place, in this epidemiologic transition from communicable to noncommunicable diseases, will be taken by an increasing role for tobacco consumption and other adverse lifestyle factors such as physical inactivity, high consumption of fats, and low consumption of fruits and vegetables, producing concomitant risks of high blood cholesterol levels and being overweight.

The strain this shifting pattern of health burden is likely to place on the health systems of developing countries, many of which are still struggling to prevail over the infectious illnesses that decimate their societies, is likely to be enormous. In any event, it will require a stronger political commitment to providing resources to the health sector than is currently the case in many developing countries.

6.5 Conclusion

Fertility rates are declining worldwide, albeit more slowly in least developed countries than elsewhere, and the number of nations with fertility rates below the replacement level of about 2.1 children per woman is constantly growing. Individual choice, expressed primarily through more widespread use of contraception, is the primary determinant of reduced fertility. An increased prevalence of infertility does not appear to play a role in this phenomenon. In fact, levels of infertility appear to have declined during the last two decades of the twentieth century, as judged from a comparison of data collected by the World Fertility Survey (WFS) program in the 1970s and 1980s with data on infertility collected by the DHS program some

20 years later in the same countries (Rutstein and Shah 2004: 53). Within-country comparison of infertility rates for countries that had more than one DHS leads to the same conclusion, even though the interval between the DHS surveys being compared is shorter (generally less than ten years) than when WFS and DHS data are compared. Thus "choice" rather than "chance" appears to be the driving force behind the worldwide demographic shift toward smaller family size.

Acknowledgment I thank Svetlin Kolev for preparing the figures and tables for this chapter.

References

Boivin, J., Bunting, L., Collins, J. A., & Nygren, K. G. (2007). International estimates of infertility prevalence and treatment-seeking: Potential need and demand for infertility medical care. *Human Reproduction, 22*, 1506–1512.

Boivin, J., Bunting, L., Collins, J. A., & Nygren, K. G. (2009). Reply: International estimates on infertility prevalence and treatment-seeking: Potential need and demand for infertility medical care. *Human Reproduction, 24*, 2380–2383.

Cates, W., Farley, T. M. M., & Rowe, P. J. (1985). Worldwide patterns of infertility: Is Africa different? *Lancet, 2*(8455), 596–598.

Ding, Q. J., & Hesketh, T. (2006). Family size, fertility preferences, and sex ratio in China in the era of the one child family policy: Results from National Family Planning and Reproductive Health Survey. *British Medical Journal, 333*, 371–373.

Hesketh, T., Lu, L., & Xing, Z. W. (2005). The effect of China's one-child family policy after 25 years. *New England Journal of Medicine, 353*, 1171–1176.

Hoorens, S., Gallo, F., Cave, J. A. K., & Grant, J. C. (2007). Can assisted reproductive technologies help to offset population ageing? An assessment of the demographic and economic impact of ART in Denmark and UK. *Human Reproduction, 22*, 2471–2475.

ICMART [International Committee for Monitoring Assisted Reproductive Technology], Sullivan, E., Zegers-Hochschild, F., Mansour, R., Ishihara, O., de Mouzon, J., Nygren, K. G., & Adamson, D. (2013). World report: Assisted reproductive technology, 2004. *Human Reproduction, 28*, 1375–1390.

Japan Society of Obstetrics and Gynecology (JSOG). (2008). ART registry of Japan, 2008. http://www.jsog.or.jp/english/img/art%20registry%20of%20japan%202008.pdf. Accessed 10 Nov 2013.

Mascarenhas, M. N., Flaxman, S. R., Boerma, T., Vanderpoel, S., & Stevens, G. A. (2012). National, regional, and global trends in infertility prevalence since 1990: A systematic analysis of 277 Health Surveys. *PLoS Medicine, 9*(12), e10.1371/journal.pmed.1001356.

Measure, DHS. (2011). *STATcompiler*. http://www.statcompiler.com. Accessed 30 Jan 2011.

Ooki, S. (2011). Birth defects in singleton versus multiple ART births in Japan (2004–2008). *Journal of Pregnancy*. doi:10.1155/2011/285706.

Population Reference Bureau. (2006). Speed of population aging in selected countries. *Graphics Bank: Aging*. http://www.prb.org/Home/Publications/GraphicsBank/Aging.aspx. Accessed 29 Jan 2011.

Rutstein, S. O., & Shah, I. H. (2004). *Infecundity, infertility and childlessness in developing countries*. DHS Comparative Reports, No. 9. Calverton: ORC Macro; Geneva: World Health Organization.

Shah, I., & Åhman, E. (2010). Unsafe abortion in 2008: Global and regional levels and trends. *Reproductive Health Matters, 18*(36), 90–101.

Study Group of Reproductive Technology and Health Care (SGRH). *Assisted reproductive technology in Japan.* http://saisentan.w3.kanazawa-u.ac.jp/image/ART%20in%20Japan_20130626. pdf. Accessed 10 Nov 2013.

UN [United Nations], & DESA [Department of Economic and Social Affairs]. (2010). *The millennium development goals report 2010*. New York: United Nations.

UN [United Nations], DESA [Department of Economic and Social Affairs], Population Division. (2007a). *World population ageing 2007*. New York: United Nations.

UN [United Nations], DESA [Department of Economic and Social Affairs], Population Division. (2007b). *World population prospects: The 2006 revision*. New York: United Nations.

UN [United Nations], DESA [Department of Economic and Social Affairs], Population Division. (2009a). *World contraceptive use 2009*. New York: United Nations.

UN [United Nations], DESA [Department of Economic and Social Affairs], Population Division. (2009b). *World population prospects: The 2008 revision*. New York: United Nations.

Warren, S. D., & Brandeis, L. D. (1890). The right to privacy. *Harvard Law Review, 4*(5), 193–220.

WHO [World Health Organization] (2002). *The world health report 2002: Reducing risks, promoting healthy life*. Geneva: WHO.

WHO [World Health Organization]. (2011). *Unsafe abortion: Global and regional estimates of the incidence of unsafe abortion and associated mortality in 2008*. Geneva: WHO.

World Bank. (1984). *World development report 1984*. New York: Oxford University Press for the World Bank.

Ziebe, S., & Devroey, P. (on behalf of the State of the ART Workshop Group). (2008). Assisted reproductive technologies are an integrated part of national strategies addressing demographic and reproductive challenges. *Human Reproduction Update, 14,* 583–592.

Chapter 7
Trends in Male Reproductive Health and Decreasing Fertility: Possible Influence of Endocrine Disrupters

Tina Harmer Lassen, Teruaki Iwamoto, Tina Kold Jensen, and Niels E. Skakkebæk

7.1 Introduction

In most European countries and in many parts of East and Southeast Asia, fertility rates have declined drastically and are now below replacement level (Lutz 2006; UN 2007). The decline is, beyond doubt, due primarily to changes in social and economic conditions, such as the use of more effective contraception, women's entrance into the labor force, and the postponement of childbirth (Lutz 2006). Nevertheless, the declining fertility rates may also be partly due to a decrease in the ability to conceive. In many countries, demand has been increasing for assisted reproductive techniques (ART) (Andersen and Erb 2006; Andersen et al. 2008a); and a growing body of evidence points toward adverse trends in male reproductive health, including reduced semen quality, increased incidence of testicular cancer, and congenital malformations (cryptorchidism and hypospadias) (Skakkebæk et al. 2001). In this chapter we focus on deteriorating male reproductive health in relation to the declining fertility rates and on the possible influence of endocrine disrupters and lifestyle.

T.H. Lassen • N.E. Skakkebæk (✉)
University Department of Growth and Reproduction, Rigshospitalet, Copenhagen, Denmark
e-mail: nes@rh.dk

T. Iwamoto
Division of Male Infertility, Center for Infertility and IVF, International University of Health and Welfare Hospital, Nasushiobara, Tochigi, Japan

T.K. Jensen
University Department of Growth and Reproduction, Rigshospitalet, Copenhagen, Denmark
Department of Environmental Medicine, University of Southern Denmark, Odense, Denmark

7.2 Declining Semen Quality

Several studies indicate that semen quality has been declining during the past half-century in the industrialized countries (Carlsen et al. 1992; Swan et al. 2000). A meta-analysis by Carlsen et al. (1992), which included 61 papers from all regions of the world published between 1938 and 1990, showed a significant decrease in sperm quality. During the study period a reduction of almost 50 % in mean sperm count (from 113×10^6/ml in 1940 to 66×10^6/ml in 1990) was reported. That study has been criticized for not controlling for differences in period of abstinence or differences in methods used to analyze the semen samples. Moreover, geographical variations in semen quality could have also biased the results (see the review by Jouannet et al. 2001 for more detailed information on the controversy). Because of the controversy, Swan et al. (1997) reanalyzed the data used by Carlsen et al. stratified the analysis by geographic region, and took into account the period of abstinence. The reanalysis confirmed the declining trend in sperm quality, and similar results were found a few years later in a study expanding the data to a total of 101 papers (Swan et al. 2000) (Figs. 7.1 and 7.2). The question of temporal changes in semen quality, however, remains controversial (Jouannet et al. 2001). Recent investigations have found, in accordance with the reported adverse trend, remarkably poor semen quality among young men from general populations in Northern Europe (Andersen et al. 2000; Jørgensen et al. 2002, 2012). A slight increase in median sperm concentration was seen among young Danish men during the period 1996–2010; but approximately 15 % of young Danish men had a sperm concentration below the most recent World Health Organization reference level of 15 mill/ml (WHO 2010), and more than 40 % of the men had a sperm concentration below 40 mill/ml (Jørgensen et al. 2012), which have been associated with a reduced chance of conceiving during a partner's menstrual cycle (Bonde et al. 1998) (Fig. 7.3).

Worldwide studies of fertile men using standardized protocols have shown significant regional differences in semen quality (Iwamoto et al. 2006; Jørgensen et al. 2001; Swan et al. 2003). Finnish (Turku) men had a 35 % higher sperm

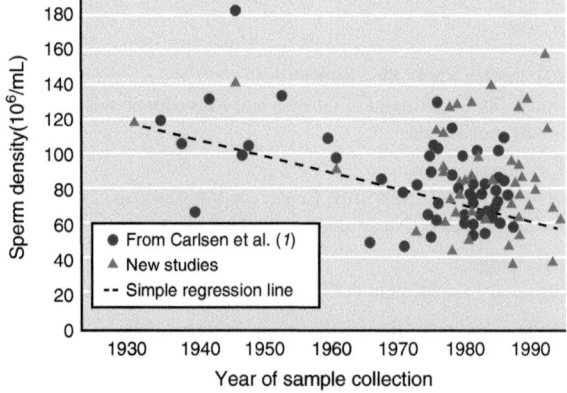

Fig. 7.1 Mean sperm density in 101 studies published 1934–1996 and simple regression line (Source: Swan et al. (2000: Fig. 1) with permission)

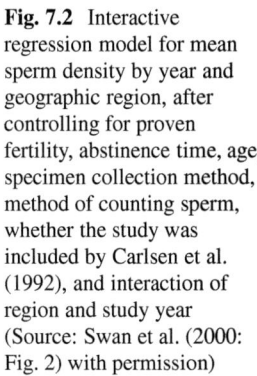
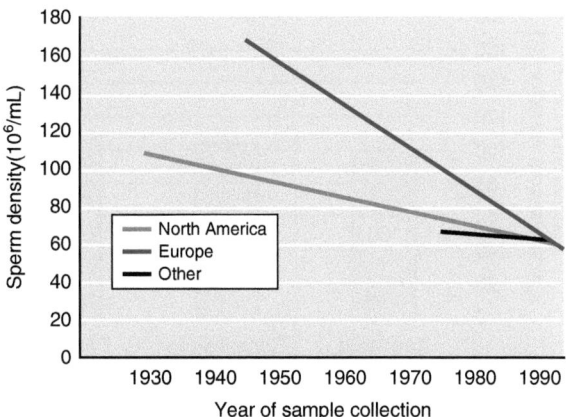

Fig. 7.2 Interactive regression model for mean sperm density by year and geographic region, after controlling for proven fertility, abstinence time, age, specimen collection method, method of counting sperm, whether the study was included by Carlsen et al. (1992), and interaction of region and study year (Source: Swan et al. (2000: Fig. 2) with permission)

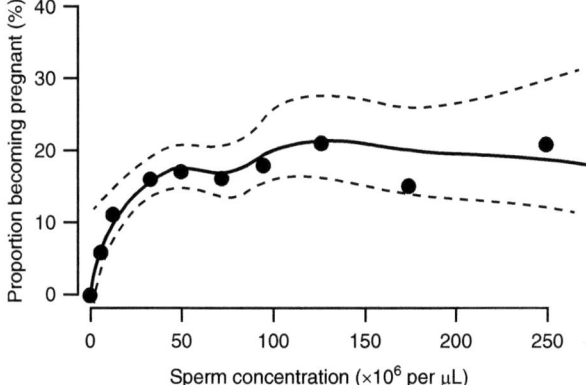

Fig. 7.3 Probability of pregnancy in a menstrual cycle (Source: Bonde et al. (1998: Fig. 1) with permission. Note: The association between semen quality and the probability of conception in a single menstrual cycle was examined in 430 Danish couples with no previous reproductive experience. The couples stopped use of contraception and they were hereafter followed up for six menstrual cycles or until verification of a pregnancy within that period. Semen samples were collected at enrolment. The probability of conception in a menstrual cycle increased with increasing sperm concentration up to 40 mill/ml. There was no additional likelihood of pregnancy associated with any higher sperm concentration.)

concentration than the Danish (Copenhagen) men, while Scottish (Edinburgh) and French (Paris) men had counts in between (Jørgensen et al. 2001). Similar regional differences in semen quality were found between fertile men from four US cities. The median unadjusted sperm concentration was lowest (53.5 mill/ml) among men from Columbia (Missouri), while corresponding estimates were 64.8 mill/ml among men from Los Angeles (California), 81.8 mill/ml among men from Minneapolis (Minnesota), and 88.5 mill/ml among men from New York (New York) (Swan et al. 2003). Japanese fertile men from Kawasaki had a sperm concentration at the same low level as the Danish men (Iwamoto et al. 2006) (Fig. 7.4), which is in line with

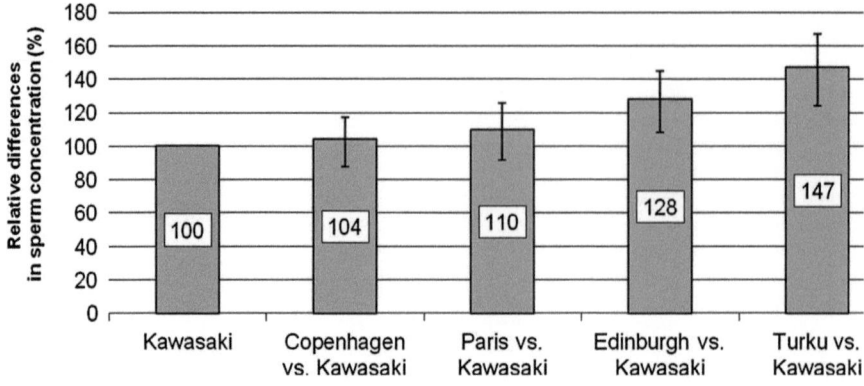

Fig. 7.4 Relative differences (%) in sperm concentration between fertile men from Kawasaki (Japan) and four European cities after adjustment for ejaculation abstinence period and other potential confounders (Source: Adapted from Iwamoto et al. (2006: Table IV) with permission. Note: The reference city is Kawasaki. The European cities are Copenhagen (Denmark), Paris (France), Edinburgh (Scotland), and Turku (Finland). The relative difference of 104 % between Copenhagen and Kawasaki, for example, shows that fertile men from Copenhagen had a 4 % higher sperm concentration than the fertile men from Kawasaki)

another study showing low sperm concentrations among Asian men (Chia et al. 1998). More studies are needed, however, to elucidate whether Asian men in general have low sperm concentrations.

The reasons for these significant geographical differences in semen quality are largely unknown. However, similar regional differences in other disorders of the male reproductive system have been observed, including testicular cancer (TC) and congenital malformations in the male reproductive tract.

7.3 Increase in Testicular Cancer

Testicular cancer is the most common cancer in young men in many countries. The etiology of TC is unknown, but it has been suggested that cancer *in situ* (CIS) of the testis, which is a precursor of testicular germ cell tumors, is generated during fetal development and that the disease therefore has a prenatal origin (Skakkebæk et al. 1987; Rajpert-De Meyts 2006). Testicular cancer is associated with impaired semen quality (Jacobsen et al. 2000) and lower fertility rates even prior to development of the cancer (Fig. 7.5) (Møller and Skakkebæk 1999). The incidence of testicular cancer has been increasing over the past 40–50 years in most of the industrialized countries (Huyghe et al. 2003, 2007) synchronically with the apparent decline in semen quality. The regional differences in testicular cancer follow the same patterns as observed for semen quality, as semen quality in high-risk testicular cancer areas is lower than in low-risk testicular cancer areas (Jørgensen et al. 2006). The age-standardized incidence rate of testicular cancer is thus considerably

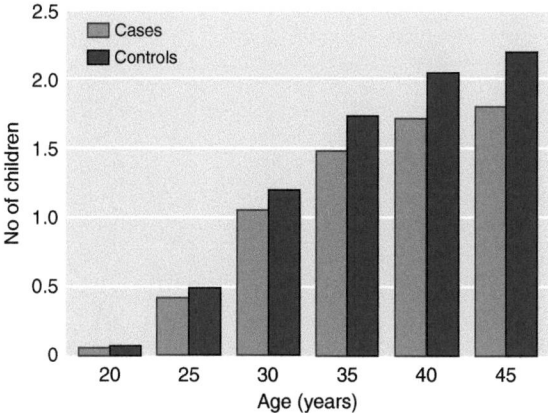

Fig. 7.5 Mean cumulative age-specific fertilities of men with testicular cancer and of control men (Source: Møller and Skakkebæk (1999: Fig. 1) with permission. Note: In a population-based case-control study the association between subfertility in Danish men and the subsequent risk of testicular cancer was evaluated. Five hundred and fourteen men with cancer identified in the Danish Cancer Registry and 720 controls randomly selected from the Danish population participated. In the analysis only children born two or more years before the year of diagnosis were considered. In the control group the men were randomly assigned a "date of diagnosis.")

higher in Denmark than in Finland, following the pattern of lower semen quality among Danish than among Finnish men (Jørgensen et al. 2001, 2002; Richiardi et al. 2004). A different pattern is seen among Asian men, however. Japanese fertile men have a sperm concentration at the same low level as the fertile Danish men, but a considerably lower age-standardized testicular cancer incidence rate (Matsuda and Saika 2008)—e.g., 3.2 per 10^5 in 1994 in the Gunna region in eastern Japan (Huyghe et al. 2003). In addition, two Chinese registries have reported age-standardized incidence rates of testicular cancer of less than 2 per 10^5 during the period 1974–1997 (Matsuda and Saika 2008). The reason for this discrepancy is not known, but it could be due to genetic factors.

7.4 Increase in Congenital Malformations of the Male Reproductive Tract

Cryptorchidism (undescended testis) and hypospadias (incomplete fusion of the urethral folds that form the penis) are among the most common congenital malformations in boys. These two congenital abnormalities share common risk factors (Akre et al. 1999; Weidner et al. 1999), and both are associated with reduced fertility (Lee and Coughlin 2001; Asklund et al. 2010). Cryptorchidism is also associated with poor semen quality (Lee and Coughlin 2001) and an increased risk of testicular cancer (Prener et al. 1996). The incidence of theses malformations seems to have

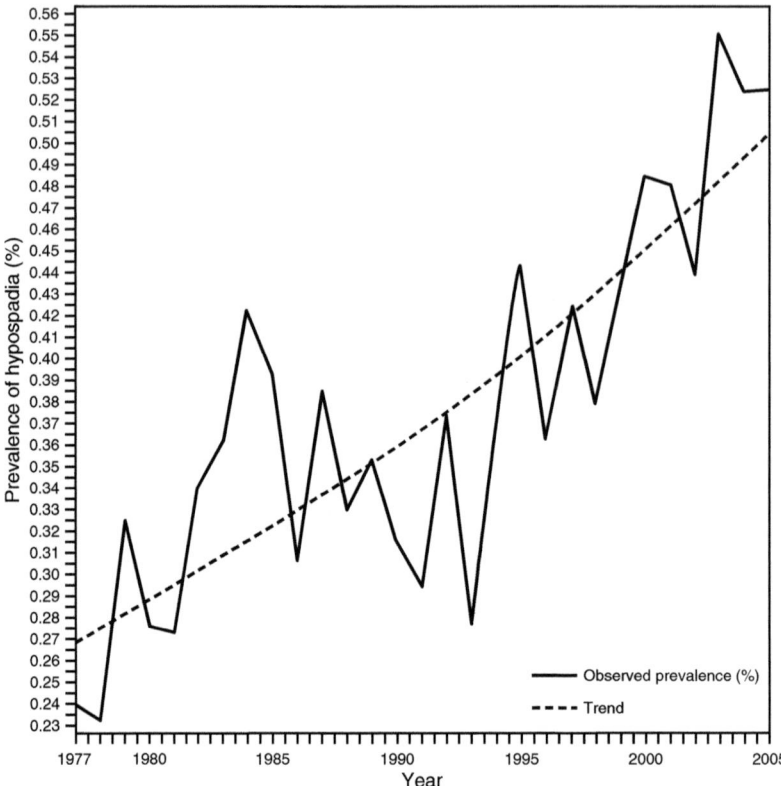

Fig. 7.6 Observed prevalence and trend of hypospadias among newborn Danish boys, 1977–2005 (Source: Lund et al. (2009: Fig. 1) with permission. Note: The mean annual increase was 2.40 %)

been increasing in Western countries during recent decades, although hypospadias apparently leveled off in most European countries during the 1980s (Toppari et al. 2001). In Denmark an annual increase of 2.4 % in the prevalence of hypospadias has been observed among newborn Danish boys born between 1977 and 2005 (Lund et al. 2009) (Fig. 7.6). Interestingly, large geographical variations have been observed in cryptorchidism, mirroring the pattern for testicular cancer and semen quality, with higher prevalence among Danish than among Finnish boys (Boisen et al. 2004). Lower rates of hypospadias have also been observed in China and Japan than in Denmark (Paulozzi 1999).

7.5 Fertility and Fecundity

The crucial question is whether the semen quality among young men in the industrialized countries is now so low that it has reached a tipping point at which fertility rates may be affected (Andersson et al. 2008). In recent studies, Jensen et al. (2008)

and Lassen et al. (2012) examined trends in pregnancy rates among native Danish women born between 1960 and 1984. A "rate of natural conceptions" (RNC) was defined as including the total number of births and induced abortions but excluding births occurring after the use of assisted reproductive techniques (ART). Among younger cohorts who had not finished their reproductive careers, projections were used to estimate their future RNC. The RNC gradually declined among women born from 1960 to 1979 and stabilized among the youngest cohorts. Their use of ART increased substantially, which partly compensated for the decline in RNC (Lassen et al. 2012) (Fig. 7.7). Among men born from 1945 to 1960, Priskorn et al. (2012) found increasing trends in childlessness with increasing birth cohorts. Socioeconomic changes and the introduction of modern contraception are without doubt the main explanations for these trends among Danish men and women, but a temporal change in fecundity (ability to conceive) may also be contributing.

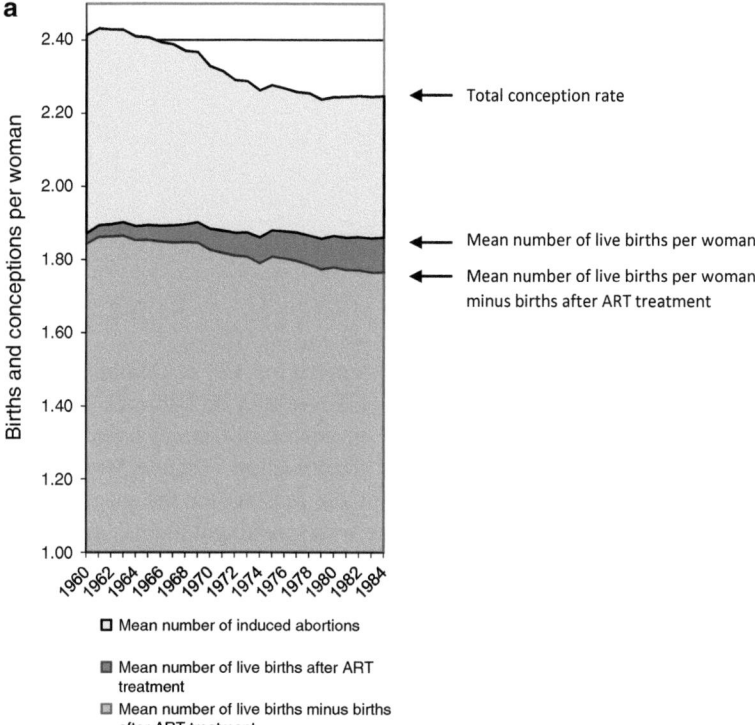

Fig. 7.7 The total conception rate, induced abortion rate (mean number of induced abortions per woman), completed fertility rate (mean number of live births per woman), completed fertility rate minus births after ART treatment (mean number of live births per woman minus births after ART treatment) and fertility rate after ART treatment (mean number of live births after ART treatment per woman) for the cohorts of native Danish women born from 1960 to 1984. The rates are based on observed data until 2007 and projections for the following years. Births after ART treatments are excluded in (**b**) (Source: Lassen et al. (2012: Fig. 1) with permission)

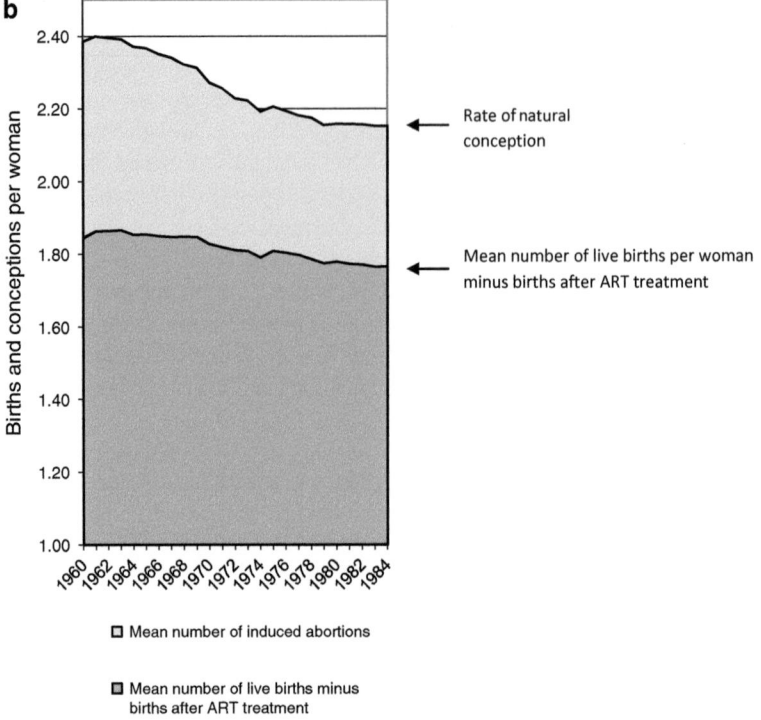

Fig. 7.7 (continued)

The findings are consistent with a growing demand for ART in Denmark. It has been estimated that approximately 8 % of all children born in Denmark in 2007 were conceived by use of ART, which include in vitro fertilization, intracytoplasmatic sperm injection (ICSI), and intrauterine insemination (Danish Fertility Society 2010). Poor semen quality may be one of the reasons for the increasing use of ART, a hypothesis that is supported by the widespread and increasing use of ICSI (Andersen et al. 2008a).

7.6 Testicular Dysgenesis Syndrome (TDS)

We have witnessed synchronically increasing trends in testis cancer and congenital malformations in the male reproductive tract along with a trend toward poorer semen quality. In addition, most of these disorders share common risk factors and are risk factors for each other. Skakkebæk et al. (2001) have proposed that these conditions may represent a syndrome of disorders, called testicular dysgenesis syndrome (TDS), that is caused by a common underlying entity, which results in a disturbance of the development of the testes during fetal life. The etiology of TDS is unclear, but the apparent rapid increase in male reproductive health problems during a short span of generations suggests changes in lifestyle and environmental factors rather than genetic factors as likely causes (Skakkebæk et al. 2001). Scientific attention has focused in particular on endocrine-disrupting chemicals as factors possibly contributing to the rise in the incidence of TDS disorders (Toppari et al. 1996).

7.7 Endocrine-Disrupting Chemicals

Endocrine-disrupting chemicals have the potential capability of interfering with sex differentiation during fetal life. The process by which a fetus develops into a male takes place in a cascade of events. Sex-determining genes initially activate the process of testis formation, which is a hormone-independent process. Subsequent steps in masculinization, which include the formation of external genitalia and the descent of the testicles into the scrotum, are hormone-dependent (Welsh et al. 2008). The hormones testosterone, insulin-like factor 3, and Anti-Müllerian hormone regulate the early stages of development. This masculinization of the external genital organs takes place during the first trimester of pregnancy, and the timing of hormonal secretion is critical for normal development of the reproductive organs (Welsh et al. 2008). An impairment in the action of male hormones in a male fetus leads to under-masculinization, whereas exposure of a female fetus to male hormones will cause masculinization (Toppari 2008). Endocrine-disrupting chemicals with estrogenic or antiandrogenic properties may therefore potentially disturb the development of reproductive organs during fetal life (Fig. 7.8).

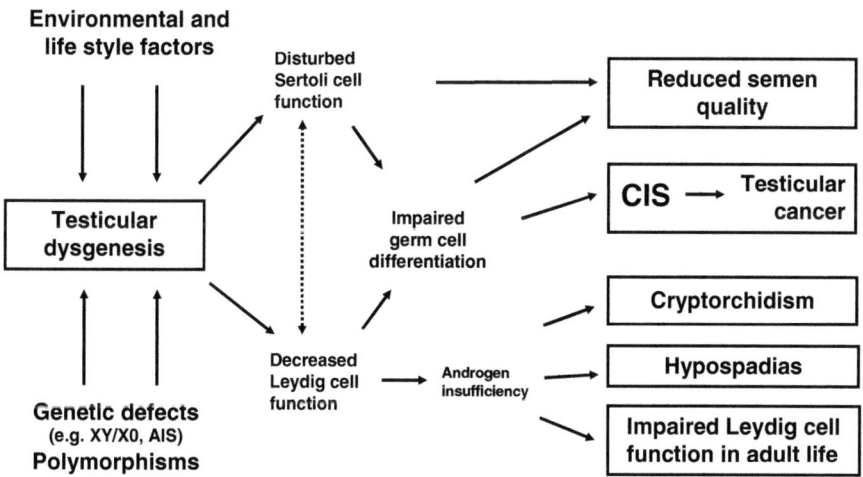

Fig. 7.8 Schematic representation of pathogenetic links between the components of testicular dysgenesis syndrome (Source: Modified from Skakkebæk et al. (2001: Fig. 1) with permission)

Animal experiments have disclosed that certain endocrine-disrupting chemicals can cause adverse effects in the male reproductive system resembling the symptoms described in human TDS, except for testicular cancer (Fisher et al. 2003). Wildlife exposed to environmental contaminants also exhibit abnormal reproductive development (Edwards et al. 2006).

The list of chemicals that have been identified in animal and experimental studies as having endocrine-disrupting properties is growing and contains numerous substances found in household and consumer products, including phthalates in cosmetics, shampoos, and food wrapping (Fisher et al. 2003; Foster 2006; Schettler 2006); dioxin in fish and milk products (Birnbaum and Tuomisto 2000); bisphenol A in water and baby formulas (Welshons et al. 2006; Richter et al. 2007); UV filters in sunscreens (Schlumpf et al. 2004; Morohoshi et al. 2005; Suzuki et al. 2005); polychlorinated biphenyls in paint, carbonless copy paper, and fish (Lundkvist 1990; Bonefeld-Jørgensen et al. 2001); and various pesticides and other agrochemicals (e.g., DDT, DDE, and vinclozolin) (Gray et al. 2006), to which humans are exposed through contaminated food.

The mechanisms by which synthetic chemicals cause hormonal alterations are known for only relatively few compounds. Some substances have been identified as antiandrogenic—e.g., p,p'-DDE, which is a metabolite of the pesticide DDT, and the fungicide vinclozolin. They exert effects by blocking the androgen receptors (Kelce and Wilson 1997), whereas the phthalates esters diethylhexyl phthalate and di-n-butyl phthalate interfere with androgen biosynthesis, causing antiandrogenic effects (Toppari 2008). Other chemicals exhibit estrogenic activity, and the adverse effects of estrogens in males are similar to those of antiandrogens (Toppari 2008). An example of an estrogenic chemical is bisphenol A, which in the 1930s was identified as a synthetic estrogen (Dodds and Lawson 1936). Bisphenol A exerts estrogenic effects by binding to estrogen receptors (Welshons et al. 2006). In addition, some chemicals can act through multiple mechanisms—for example, the fungicide prochloraz, which acts both by blocking the androgen receptor and by inhibiting fetal steroidogenesis, i.e., production of testosterone (Vinggaard et al. 2006).

For a wide range of endocrine-disrupting chemicals the mechanisms of action are still poorly understood. Moreover, humans are exposed to mixtures of chemicals, a situation that makes their effects unpredictable. In a study of rats, exposure to a mixture of three chemicals with antiandrogen properties increased the risk of hypospadias, although exposure to the individual chemicals at doses present in the mixture did not seem to induce hypospadias (Christiansen et al. 2008). It could be assumed that similar additive effects can occur in humans. If that is the case, it introduces enormous complexity to identifying the causal contribution of individual chemicals to TDS disorders, if any, as humans are exposed to a complex cocktail of environmental chemicals. The regulation of such chemicals presents similar complexity.

Human research on the effects of endocrine disrupters on male reproductive health is still sparse, but emerging epidemiological studies point to an association between those chemicals and the four components of TDS in humans. In the remainder of this section we discuss human studies with biomarkers of exposure to putative endocrine-disrupting chemicals in relation to TDS components.

A number of human studies have found associations between exposure to endocrine-disrupting chemicals and malformations of the male urogenital tract. Higher concentrations of persistent pesticides (Damgaard et al. 2006) and flame retardants (Main et al. 2007) in human breast milk (used as a proxy for fetal exposure) were seen in mothers of boys with cryptorchidism than in controls. Maternal occupational pesticide exposure in pregnancy, determined not by biomarkers, but through thorough evaluation of working conditions done by toxicologists, has also been found to be related to increased risk of cryptorchidism among the offspring (Andersen et al. 2008b). Furthermore, increased levels of phthalates in maternal urine samples collected during pregnancy were related to a shorter anogenital distance (AGD) in the sons (Swan et al. 2005). AGD has been identified in animal studies as a marker of prenatal antiandrogen exposure. A case-control study reported an association between a combination of various environmental estrogens measured in the placenta and increased risk of cryptorchidism or hypospadias, or both (Fernandez et al. 2007). A small study from the Faroe Islands, however, did not find an association between prenatal exposure to PCB in umbilical-cord blood and cryptorchidism among boys at 14 years of age (Mol et al. 2002).

Few human studies have examined the effects of prenatal exposure to endocrine disrupters on future semen quality or the risk of testicular cancer, probably because of the challenging lag time between exposures and the occurrence of these disorders, which do not manifest themselves until after puberty. Two studies in human populations that were accidentally exposed to high levels of polychlorinated biphenyls (PCB) and dibenzofurans during fetal life (Guo et al. 2000) and dioxin during infancy (Mocarelli et al. 2008), respectively, found adverse effects on semen quality. Another study found that mothers of sons with testicular cancer had higher PCB levels in serum at the time of diagnosis than did age-matched control mothers. Although not measured during the relevant exposure window, current maternal levels may reflect prenatal exposure, owing to the long half-life of PCBs (Hardell et al. 2004). Higher prediagnostic levels of the compound p,p'-DDE have also been found among testis cancer patients than among controls (McGlynn et al. 2008).

Interestingly, Danish mothers have higher concentrations of several chemicals in their breast milk than do Finnish mothers (Shen et al. 2008; Krysiak-Baltyn et al. 2010). This indicates a higher exposure of those chemicals among Danish fetuses and infants, which match the differences in male reproductive disorders between the two countries.

Besides the potential influence of prenatal exposure to endocrine-disrupting chemicals on TDS disorders, current exposure may also be important. The human epidemiological evidence of current exposure to endocrine-disrupting chemicals on semen quality is still sparse, however (Hauser 2006; Phillips and Tanphaichitr 2008). Several studies have found associations between PCBs and reduced semen quality (Hauser 2006; Phillips and Tanphaichitr 2008), including a study of young Swedish men from the general population, which found an inverse association between PCB levels and sperm motility (Richthoff et al. 2003). Firm conclusions cannot be drawn on the basis of the few studies, however. Moreover, evidence of the effects of adult exposure to phthalates and pesticides on sperm quality is still inconclusive (Hauser 2006).

In summary, the human studies indicate that the increasing male reproductive health problems could be due, at least in part, to exposure to endocrine disrupters. However, there are relatively few studies and the results are limited to associations. Firm conclusions about causal relations can therefore not be drawn from these studies, and more research is urgently needed. In addition, the current evidence does not provide grounds for concluding that exposure to endocrine-disrupting chemicals is the sole cause of the increased incidence of male reproductive health problems.

7.8 Lifestyle Factors

Lifestyle factors may also contribute to the observed adverse trends in male reproductive health. Huge changes in Western lifestyle have occurred during the past 50 years. Obesity is reaching epidemic proportions worldwide (Mokdad et al. 2001; Caballero 2007), and the prevalence of smokers is high in many Western countries (Molarius et al. 2001). Several studies of men from the general population (Jensen et al. 2004a) and of infertile men (Koloszar et al. 2005; Magnusdottir et al. 2005; Kort et al. 2006; Hammoud et al. 2008) have shown that obesity is associated with reduced semen quality. Smoking has also been found to impair semen quality. A meta-analysis published in 1994, based on 20 study populations (Vine et al. 1994), found that smokers had significantly lower sperm density than nonsmokers; and a recent Danish study among men from the general population found a dose-response relationship between smoking on the one hand and sperm motility and total sperm count on the other (Ramlau-Hansen et al. 2007a). Recently, maternal smoking during pregnancy has been found to have a negative impact on semen quality among male offspring, indicating that prenatal exposure is also important (Storgaard et al. 2003; Jensen et al. 2004b; Ramlau-Hansen et al. 2007b). In contrast, a meta-analysis has shown that maternal smoking during pregnancy is not associated with increased risk of testicular cancer in sons (Tuomisto et al. 2009). Studies on the association between caffeine intake and semen quality have been inconclusive (Marshburn et al. 1989; Oldereid et al. 1992; Vine et al. 1997; Sobreiro et al. 2005), partly because they were conducted on highly selected groups of either infertile men (Marshburn et al. 1989; Oldereid et al. 1992) or fertile men undergoing vasectomy (Sobreiro et al. 2005). Only a few studies have investigated the association between alcohol intake and semen quality, and the results are contradictory (Dunphy et al. 1991; Oldereid et al. 1992; Martini et al. 2004; Muthusami and Chinnaswamy 2005).

7.9 Genetic Factors

Male reproductive disorders may also be caused by genetic factors (Giwercman et al. 2000; McElreavey and Quintana-Murci 2003). The observed familial aggregations of TDS disorders indicate that genetic factors may be involved in the etiology. The risk of developing testicular cancer is markedly increased among brothers and sons of patients with testicular cancer (Lutke Holzik et al. 2004), and likewise cryptorchidism as well as hypospadias aggregates among male twins and among first-, second-, and third-degree relatives (Schnack et al. 2008a, b). Besides rare point mutations (e.g., SRY mutation) and abnormal chromosome constitutions (e.g., 45X/46,XY), which are associated with increased risk of testis cancer, little is known about the role that genes play in the etiology of TDS disorders. Specific gene-mutations, which are mutations in the AR gene or in the gene encoding for the 5-α-reductase type II enzyme, are associated with cryptorchidism and hypospadias; but these mutations are extremely rare. Furthermore, to date there is virtually no evidence that specific genotypes predispose males to adverse effects of environmental or lifestyle factors (Giwercman et al. 2006). Racial differences in TDS, however, indicate a genetic component. US white men exhibit a markedly higher incidence of testicular cancer than do African American and other nonwhite US men (Shah et al. 2007). In theory, geographical differences in TDS—e.g., between Danish and Finnish men—may be due to both genetic differences and differences in exposure to environmental factors. However, a Scandinavian study has shown that the incidence of testicular cancer among Finnish first-generation immigrants to Sweden mirrors that of the country of origin, whereas among second-generation immigrants it resembles that of the host country (Hemminki and Li 2002), suggesting environmental rather than genetic causes (Hemminki and Li 2002; Myrup et al. 2008).

7.10 Conclusions

During recent years we have witnessed significant adverse trends in male reproductive health problems with large geographical variations. In some Western countries, at least 15 % of young men exhibit sperm concentrations below the World Health Organization's reference level. The increasing use of assisted reproductive techniques also indicates that infertility is a growing problem. The widespread male reproductive health problems may—besides obvious social and economic factors—contribute to decreasing fertility rates. We have proposed that a significant proportion of men with testicular cancer, poor semen quality, cryptorchidism, and hypospadias may have a testicular dysgenesis syndrome of prenatal origin. The rapid increase in the disorders included in the TDS strongly indicates that some of the male reproductive health problems are caused by environmental exposure, changes in lifestyle, or both, rather than genetic factors. More human studies are needed that examine the effects of endocrine-disrupting chemicals on human reproduction functioning, and social scientists and demographers are encouraged to collaborate with medical scientists working in reproductive medicine to delineate the role of increasing infertility in the current low fertility rates.

References

Akre, O., Lipworth, L., Cnattingius, S., Sparen, P., & Ekbom, A. (1999). Risk factor patterns for cryptorchidism and hypospadias. *Epidemiology, 10*(4), 364–369.

Andersen, A. N., & Erb, K. (2006). Register data on assisted reproductive technology (ART) in Europe including a detailed description of ART in Denmark. *International Journal of Andrology, 29*(1), 12–16.

Andersen, A. G., Jensen, T. K., Carlsen, E., Jørgensen, N., Andersson, A. M., Krarup, T., et al. (2000). High frequency of sub-optimal semen quality in an unselected population of young men. *Human Reproduction, 15*(2), 366–372.

Andersen, A. N., Carlsen, E., & Loft, A. (2008a). Trends in the use of intracytoplasmatic sperm injection marked variability between countries. *Human Reproduction Update, 14*(6), 593–604.

Andersen, H. R., Schmidt, I. M., Grandjean, P., Jensen, T. K., Budtz-Jørgensen, E., Kjaerstad, M. B., et al. (2008b). Impaired reproductive development in sons of women occupationally exposed to pesticides during pregnancy. *Environmental Health Perspectives, 116*(4), 566–572.

Andersson, A. M., Jørgensen, N., Main, K. M., Toppari, J., Rajpert-De Meyts, E., Leffers, H., et al. (2008). Adverse trends in male reproductive health: We may have reached a crucial 'tipping point'. *International Journal of Andrology, 31*(2), 74–80.

Asklund, C., Jensen, T. K., Main, K. M., Sobotka, T., Skakkebæk, N. E., & Jørgensen, N. (2010). Semen quality, reproductive hormones and fertility of men operated for hypospadias. *International Journal of Andrology, 33*(1), 80–87.

Birnbaum, L. S., & Tuomisto, J. (2000). Non-carcinogenic effects of TCDD in animals. *Food Additives & Contaminants, 17*(4), 275–288.

Boisen, K. A., Kaleva, M., Main, K. M., Virtanen, H. E., Haavisto, A. M., Schmidt, I. M., et al. (2004). Difference in prevalence of congenital cryptorchidism in infants between two Nordic countries. *Lancet, 363*(9417), 1264–1269.

Bonde, J. P., Ernst, E., Jensen, T. K., Hjollund, N. H., Kolstad, H., Henriksen, T. B., et al. (1998). Relation between semen quality and fertility: A population-based study of 430 first-pregnancy planners. *Lancet, 352*(9135), 1172–1177.

Bonefeld-Jørgensen, E. C., Andersen, H. R., Rasmussen, T. H., & Vinggaard, A. M. (2001). Effect of highly bioaccumulated polychlorinated biphenyl congeners on estrogen and androgen receptor activity. *Toxicology, 158*(3), 141–153.

Caballero, B. (2007). The global epidemic of obesity: An overview. *Epidemiologic Reviews, 29*, 1–5.

Carlsen, E., Giwercman, A., Keiding, N., & Skakkebæk, N. E. (1992). Evidence for decreasing quality of semen during past 50 years. *British Medical Journal, 305*(6854), 609–613.

Chia, S. E., Tay, S. K., & Lim, S. T. (1998). What constitutes a normal seminal analysis? semen parameters of 243 fertile men. *Human Reproduction, 13*(12), 3394–3398.

Christiansen, S., Scholze, M., Axelstad, M., Boberg, J., Kortenkamp, A., & Hass, U. (2008). Combined exposure to anti-androgens causes markedly increased frequencies of hypospadias in the rat. *International Journal of Andrology, 31*(2), 241–248.

Damgaard, I. N., Skakkebæk, N. E., Toppari, J., Virtanen, H. E., Shen, H., Schramm, K. W., et al. (2006). Persistent pesticides in human breast milk and cryptorchidism. *Environmental Health Perspectives, 114*(7), 1133–1138.

Danish Fertility Society. (2010). www.fertilitetsselskab.dk. Accessed 6 Sept 2010.

Dodds, E. C., & Lawson, W. (1936). Synthetic oestrogenic agents without the phenanthrene nucleus. *Nature, 137,* 996.

Dunphy, B. C., Barratt, C. L., & Cooke, I. D. (1991). Male alcohol consumption and fecundity in couples attending an infertility clinic. *Andrologia, 23*(3), 219–221.

Edwards, T. M., Moore, B. C., & Guillette, L. J., Jr. (2006). Reproductive dysgenesis in wildlife: A comparative view. *International Journal of Andrology, 29*(1), 109–121.

Fernandez, M. F., Olmos, B., Granada, A., Lopez-Espinosa, M. J., Molina-Molina, J. M., Fernandez, J. M., et al. (2007). Human exposure to endocrine-disrupting chemicals and prenatal risk factors for cryptorchidism and hypospadias: A nested case-control study. *Environmental Health Perspectives, 115*(Suppl 1), 8–14.

Fisher, J. S., Macpherson, S., Marchetti, N., & Sharpe, R. M. (2003). Human 'testicular dysgenesis syndrome': A possible model using in-utero exposure of the rat to dibutyl phthalate. *Human Reproduction, 18*(7), 1383–1394.

Foster, P. M. (2006). Disruption of reproductive development in male rat offspring following in utero exposure to phthalate esters. *International Journal of Andrology, 29*(1), 140–147.

Giwercman, A., Kledal, T., Schwartz, M., Giwercman, Y. L., Leffers, H., Zazzi, H., et al. (2000). Preserved male fertility despite decreased androgen sensitivity caused by a mutation in the ligand-binding domain of the androgen receptor gene. *Journal of Clinical Endocrinology and Metabolism, 85*(6), 2253–2259.

Giwercman, A., Rylander, L., Hagmar, L., & Giwercman, Y. L. (2006). Ethnic differences in occurrence of TDS—genetics and/or environment? *International Journal of Andrology, 29*(1), 291–297.

Gray, L. E., Jr., Wilson, V. S., Stoker, T., Lambright, C., Furr, J., Noriega, N., et al. (2006). Adverse effects of environmental antiandrogens and androgens on reproductive development in mammals. *International Journal of Andrology, 29*(1), 96–104.

Guo, Y. L., Hsu, P. C., Hsu, C. C., & Lambert, G. H. (2000). Semen quality after prenatal exposure to polychlorinated biphenyls and dibenzofurans. *Lancet, 356*(9237), 1240–1241.

Hammoud, A. O., Wilde, N., Gibson, M., Parks, A., Carrell, D. T., & Meikle, A. W. (2008). Male obesity and alteration in sperm parameters. *Fertility and Sterility, 90*(6), 2222–2225.

Hardell, L., Van Bavel, B., Lindstrom, G., Carlberg, M., Eriksson, M., Dreifaldt, A. C., et al. (2004). Concentrations of polychlorinated biphenyls in blood and the risk for testicular cancer. *International Journal of Andrology, 27*(5), 282–290.

Hauser, R. (2006). The environment and male fertility: Recent research on emerging chemicals and semen quality. *Seminars in Reproductive Medicine, 24*(3), 156–167.

Hemminki, K., & Li, X. (2002). Cancer risks in Nordic immigrants and their offspring in Sweden. *European Journal of Cancer, 38*(18), 2428–2434.

Huyghe, E., Matsuda, T., & Thonneau, P. (2003). Increasing incidence of testicular cancer worldwide: A review. *Journal of Urology, 170*(1), 5–11.

Huyghe, E., Plante, P., & Thonneau, P. F. (2007). Testicular cancer variations in time and space in Europe. *European Urology, 51*(3), 621–628.

Iwamoto, T., Nozawa, S., Yoshiike, M., Hoshino, T., Baba, K., Matsushita, T., et al. (2006). Semen quality of 324 fertile Japanese men. *Human Reproduction, 21*(3), 760–765.

Jacobsen, R., Bostofte, E., Engholm, G., Hansen, J., Olsen, J. H., Skakkebæk, N. E., et al. (2000). Risk of testicular cancer in men with abnormal semen characteristics: Cohort study. *British Medical Journal, 321*(7264), 789–792.

Jensen, T. K., Andersson, A. M., Jørgensen, N., Andersen, A. G., Carlsen, E., Petersen, J. H., et al. (2004a). Body mass index in relation to semen quality and reproductive hormones among 1,558 Danish men. *Fertility and Sterility, 82*(4), 863–870.

Jensen, T. K., Jørgensen, N., Punab, M., Haugen, T. B., Suominen, J., Zilaitiene, B., et al. (2004b). Association of in utero exposure to maternal smoking with reduced semen quality and testis size in adulthood: A cross-sectional study of 1,770 young men from the general population in five European countries. *American Journal of Epidemiology, 159*(1), 49–58.

Jensen, T. K., Sobotka, T., Hansen, M. A., Pedersen, A. T., Lutz, W., & Skakkebæk, N. E. (2008). Declining trends in conception rates in recent birth cohorts of native Danish women: A possible role of deteriorating male reproductive health. *International Journal of Andrology, 31*(2), 81–92.

Jørgensen, N., Andersen, A. G., Eustache, F., Irvine, D. S., Suominen, J., Petersen, J. H., et al. (2001). Regional differences in semen quality in Europe. *Human Reproduction, 16*(5), 1012–1019.

Jørgensen, N., Carlsen, E., Nermoen, I., Punab, M., Suominen, J., Andersen, A. G., et al. (2002). East–west gradient in semen quality in the Nordic-Baltic area: A study of men from the general population in Denmark, Norway, Estonia and Finland. *Human Reproduction, 17*(8), 2199–2208.

Jørgensen, N., Asklund, C., Carlsen, E., & Skakkebæk, N. E. (2006). Coordinated European investigations of semen quality: Results from studies of Scandinavian young men is a matter of concern. *International Journal of Andrology, 29*(1), 54–61.

Jørgensen, N., Joensen, U. N., Jensen, T. K., Jensen, M. B., Almstrup, K., Olesen, I. A., Juul, A., Andersson, A.-M., Carlsen, E., Petersen, J. H., Toppari, J., & Skakkebæk, N. E. (2012). Human semen quality in the new millennium: A prospective cross-sectional population-based study of 4867 men. *BMJ Open, 2*, e000990.

Jouannet, P., Wang, C., Eustache, F., Kold-Jensen, T., & Auger, J. (2001). Semen quality and male reproductive health: The controversy about human sperm concentration decline. *Acta Pathologica, Microbiologica et Immunologica Scandinavica, 109*(5), 333–344.

Kelce, W. R., & Wilson, E. M. (1997). Environmental antiandrogens: Developmental effects, molecular mechanisms, and clinical implications. *Journal of Molecular Medicine, 75*(3), 198–207.

Koloszar, S., Fejes, I., Zavaczki, Z., Daru, J., Szollosi, J., & Pal, A. (2005). Effect of body weight on sperm concentration in normozoospermic males. *Archives of Andrology, 51*(4), 299–304.

Kort, H. I., Massey, J. B., Elsner, C. W., Mitchell-Leef, D., Shapiro, D. B., Witt, M. A., et al. (2006). Impact of body mass index values on sperm quantity and quality. *Journal of Andrology, 27*(3), 450–452.

Krysiak-Baltyn, K., Toppari, J., Skakkebæk, N. E., Jensen, T. S., Virtanen, H. E., Schramm, K. W., et al. (2010). Country-specific chemical signatures of persistent environmental compounds in breast milk. *International Journal of Andrology, 33*(2), 270–278.

Lassen, T. H., Sobotka, T., Jensen, T. K., Jacobsen, R., Erb, K., & Skakkebæk, N. E. (2012). Trends in rates of natural conceptions among Danish women born during 1960–1984. *Human Reproduction, 27*, 2815–2822.

Lee, P. A., & Coughlin, M. T. (2001). Fertility after bilateral cryptorchidism: Evaluation by paternity, hormone, and semen data. *Hormone Research, 55*(1), 28–32.

Lund, L., Engebjerg, M. C., Pedersen, L., Ehrenstein, V., Nørgaard, M., & Sørensen, H. T. (2009). Prevalence of hypospadias in Danish boys: A longitudinal study, 1977–2005. *European Urology, 55*(5), 1022–1026.

Lundkvist, U. (1990). Clinical and reproductive effects of clophen A50 (PCB) administered during gestation on pregnant guinea pigs and their offspring. *Toxicology, 61*(3), 249–257.

Lutke Holzik, M. F., Rapley, E. A., Hoekstra, H. J., Sleijfer, D. T., Nolte, I. M., & Sijmons, R. H. (2004). Genetic predisposition to testicular germ-cell tumours. *Lancet Oncology, 5*(6), 363–371.

Lutz, W. (2006). Fertility rates and future population trends: Will Europe's birth rate recover or continue to decline? *International Journal of Andrology, 29*(1), 25–33.

Magnusdottir, E. V., Thorsteinsson, T., Thorsteinsdottir, S., Heimisdottir, M., & Olafsdottir, K. (2005). Persistent organochlorines, sedentary occupation, obesity and human male subfertility. *Human Reproduction, 20*(1), 208–215.

Main, K. M., Kiviranta, H., Virtanen, H. E., Sundqvist, E., Tuomisto, J. T., Tuomisto, J., et al. (2007). Flame retardants in placenta and breast milk and cryptorchidism in newborn boys. *Environmental Health Perspectives, 115*(10), 1519–1526.

Marshburn, P. B., Sloan, C. S., & Hammond, M. G. (1989). Semen quality and association with coffee drinking, cigarette smoking, and ethanol consumption. *Fertility and Sterility, 52*(1), 162–165.

Martíni, A. C., Molina, R. I., Estofan, D., Senestrari, D., Fiol, D. C. M., & Ruiz, R. D. (2004). Effects of alcohol and cigarette consumption on human seminal quality. *Fertility and Sterility, 82*(2), 374–377.

Matsuda, T., & Saika, K. (2008). Comparison of time trends in testicular cancer incidence (1973–97) in East Asia, Europe and USA, from *cancer incidence in five continents,* vols. IV–VIII. *Japanese Journal of Clinical Oncology, 38*(8), 578–579.

McElreavey, K., & Quintana-Murci, L. (2003). Y chromosome haplogroups: A correlation with testicular dysgenesis syndrome? *Acta Pathologica Microbiologica et Immunologica Scandinavica, 111*(1), 106–113.

McGlynn, K. A., Quraishi, S. M., Graubard, B. I., Weber, J. P., Rubertone, M. V., & Erickson, R. L. (2008). Persistent organochlorine pesticides and risk of testicular germ cell tumors. *Journal of the National Cancer Institute, 100*(9), 663–671.

Mocarelli, P., Gerthoux, P. M., Patterson, D. G., Jr., Milani, S., Limonta, G., Bertona, M., et al. (2008). Dioxin exposure, from infancy through puberty, produces endocrine disruption and affects human semen quality. *Environmental Health Perspectives, 116*(1), 70–77.

Mokdad, A. H., Bowman, B. A., Ford, E. S., Vinicor, F., Marks, J. S., & Koplan, J. P. (2001). The continuing epidemics of obesity and diabetes in the United States. *Journal of the American Medical Association, 286*(10), 1195–1200.

Mol, N. M., Sorensen, N., Weihe, P., Andersson, A. M., Jørgensen, N., Skakkebæk, N. E., et al. (2002). Spermaturia and serum hormone concentrations at the age of puberty in boys prenatally exposed to polychlorinated biphenyls. *European Journal of Endocrinology, 146*(3), 357–363.

Molarius, A., Parsons, R. W., Dobson, A. J., Evans, A., Fortmann, S. P., Jamrozik, K., et al. (2001). Trends in cigarette smoking in 36 populations from the early 1980s to the mid-1990s: Findings from the WHO MONICA Project. *American Journal of Public Health, 91*(2), 206–212.

Møller, H., & Skakkebæk, N. E. (1999). Risk of testicular cancer in subfertile men: Case-control study. *British Medical Journal, 318*(7183), 559–562.

Morohoshi, K., Yamamoto, H., Kamata, R., Shiraishi, F., Koda, T., & Morita, M. (2005). Estrogenic activity of 37 components of commercial sunscreen lotions evaluated by in vitro assays. *Toxicology in Vitro, 19*(4), 457–469.

Muthusami, K. R., & Chinnaswamy, P. (2005). Effect of chronic alcoholism on male fertility hormones and semen quality. *Fertility and Sterility, 84*(4), 919–924.

Myrup, C., Westergaard, T., Schnack, T., Oudin, A., Ritz, C., Wohlfahrt, J., et al. (2008). Testicular cancer risk in first- and second-generation immigrants to Denmark. *Journal of the National Cancer Institute, 100*(1), 41–47.

Oldereid, N. B., Rui, H., & Purvis, K. (1992). Life styles of men in barren couples and their relationship to sperm quality. *International Journal of Fertility, 37*(6), 343–349.

Paulozzi, L. J. (1999). International trends in rates of hypospadias and cryptorchidism. *Environmental Health Perspectives, 107*(4), 297–302.

Phillips, K. P., & Tanphaichitr, N. (2008). Human exposure to endocrine disrupters and semen quality. *Journal of Toxicology and Environmental Health. Part B, Critical Reviews, 11*(3–4), 188–220.

Prener, A., Engholm, G., & Jensen, O. M. (1996). Genital anomalies and risk for testicular cancer in Danish men. *Epidemiology, 7*(1), 14–19.

Priskorn, L., Holmboe, S. A., Jacobsen, R., Jensen, T. K., Lassen, T. H., & Skakkebæk, N. E. (2012). Increasing trends in childlessness in recent birth cohorts—a registry-based study of the total Danish male population born from 1945 to 1980. *International Journal of Andrology, 35*, 449–455.

Rajpert-De Meyts, E. (2006). Developmental model for the pathogenesis of testicular carcinoma in situ: Genetic and environmental aspects. *Human Reproduction Update, 12*(3), 303–323.

Ramlau-Hansen, C. H., Thulstrup, A. M., Aggerholm, A. S., Jensen, M. S., Toft, G., & Bonde, J. P. (2007a). Is smoking a risk factor for decreased semen quality? A cross-sectional analysis. *Human Reproduction, 22*(1), 188–196.

Ramlau-Hansen, C. H., Thulstrup, A. M., Storgaard, L., Toft, G., Olsen, J., & Bonde, J. P. (2007b). Is prenatal exposure to tobacco smoking a cause of poor semen quality? A follow-up study. *American Journal of Epidemiology, 165*(12), 1372–1379.

Richiardi, L., Bellocco, R., Adami, H. O., Torrang, A., Barlow, L., Hakulinen, T., et al. (2004). Testicular cancer incidence in eight northern European countries: Secular and recent trends. *Cancer Epidemiology, Biomarkers & Prevention, 13*(12), 2157–2166.

Richter, C. A., Birnbaum, L. S., Farabollini, F., Newbold, R. R., Rubin, B. S., Talsness, C. E., et al. (2007). In vivo effects of bisphenol a in laboratory rodent studies. *Reproductive Toxicology, 24*(2), 199–224.

Richthoff, J., Rylander, L., Jonsson, B. A., Akesson, H., Hagmar, L., Nilsson-Ehle, P., et al. (2003). Serum levels of 2,2',4,4',5,5'-hexachlorobiphenyl (CB-153) in relation to markers of reproductive function in young males from the general Swedish population. *Environmental Health Perspectives, 111*(4), 409–413.

Schettler, T. (2006). Human exposure to phthalates via consumer products. *International Journal of Andrology, 29*(1), 134–139.

Schlumpf, M., Schmid, P., Durrer, S., Conscience, M., Maerkel, K., Henseler, M., et al. (2004). Endocrine activity and developmental toxicity of cosmetic UV filters—an update. *Toxicology, 205*(1–2), 113–122.

Schnack, T. H., Zdravkovic, S., Myrup, C., Westergaard, T., Christensen, K., Wohlfahrt, J., et al. (2008a). Familial aggregation of hypospadias: A cohort study. *American Journal of Epidemiology, 167*(3), 251–256.

Schnack, T. H., Zdravkovic, S., Myrup, C., Westergaard, T., Wohlfahrt, J., & Melbye, M. (2008b). Familial aggregation of cryptorchidism—a nationwide cohort study. *American Journal of Epidemiology, 167*(12), 1453–1457.

Shah, M. N., Devesa, S. S., Zhu, K., & McGlynn, K. A. (2007). Trends in testicular germ cell tumours by ethnic group in the United States. *International Journal of Andrology, 30*(4), 206–213.

Shen, H., Main, K. M., Andersson, A. M., Damgaard, I. N., Virtanen, H. E., Skakkebæk, N. E., et al. (2008). Concentrations of persistent organochlorine compounds in human milk and placenta are higher in Denmark than in Finland. *Human Reproduction, 23*(1), 201–210.

Skakkebæk, N. E., Berthelsen, J. G., Giwercman, A., & Müller, J. (1987). Carcinoma-in-situ of the testis: Possible origin from gonocytes and precursor of all types of germ cell tumours except spermatocytoma. *International Journal of Andrology, 10*(1), 19–28.

Skakkebæk, N. E., Rajpert-De Meyts, E., & Main, K. M. (2001). Testicular dysgenesis syndrome: An increasingly common developmental disorder with environmental aspects. *Human Reproduction, 16*(5), 972–978.

Sobreiro, B. P., Lucon, A. M., Pasqualotto, F. F., Hallak, J., Athayde, K. S., & Arap, S. (2005). Semen analysis in fertile patients undergoing vasectomy: Reference values and variations according to age, length of sexual abstinence, seasonality, smoking habits and caffeine intake. *São Paulo Medical Journal, 123*(4), 161–166.

Storgaard, L., Bonde, J. P., Ernst, E., Spano, M., Andersen, C. Y., Frydenberg, M., et al. (2003). Does smoking during pregnancy affect sons' sperm counts? *Epidemiology, 14*(3), 278–286.

Suzuki, T., Kitamura, S., Khota, R., Sugihara, K., Fujimoto, N., & Ohta, S. (2005). Estrogenic and antiandrogenic activities of 17 benzophenone derivatives used as UV stabilizers and sunscreens. *Toxicology and Applied Pharmacology, 203*(1), 9–17.

Swan, S. H., Elkin, E. P., & Fenster, L. (1997). Have sperm densities declined? A reanalysis of global trend data. *Environmental Health Perspectives, 105*(11), 1228–1232.

Swan, S. H., Elkin, E. P., & Fenster, L. (2000). The question of declining sperm density revisited: An analysis of 101 studies published 1934–1996. *Environmental Health Perspectives, 108*(10), 961–966.

Swan, S. H., Brazil, C., Drobnis, E. Z., Liu, F., Kruse, R. L., Hatch, M., et al. (2003). Geographic differences in semen quality of fertile U.S. Males. *Environmental Health Perspectives, 111*(4), 414–420.

Swan, S. H., Main, K. M., Liu, F., Stewart, S. L., Kruse, R. L., Calafat, A. M., et al. (2005). Decrease in anogenital distance among male infants with prenatal phthalate exposure. *Environmental Health Perspectives, 113*(8), 1056–1061.
Toppari, J. (2008). Environmental endocrine disrupters. *Sexual Development, 2*(4–5), 260–267.
Toppari, J., Larsen, J. C., Christiansen, P., Giwercman, A., Grandjean, P., Guillette, L. J., Jr., et al. (1996). Male reproductive health and environmental xenoestrogens. *Environmental Health Perspectives, 104*(Supplement 4), 741–803.
Toppari, J., Kaleva, M., & Virtanen, H. E. (2001). Trends in the incidence of cryptorchidism and hypospadias, and methodological limitations of registry-based data. *Human Reproduction Update, 7*(3), 282–286.
Tuomisto, J., Holl, K., Rantakokko, P., Koskela, P., Hallmans, G., Wadell, G., et al. (2009). Maternal smoking during pregnancy and testicular cancer in the sons: A nested case-control study and a meta-analysis. *European Journal of Cancer, 45*(9), 1640–1648.
United Nations. (2007). *World population prospects: The 2006 revision*. New York: United Nations.
Vine, M. F., Margolin, B. H., Morrison, H. I., & Hulka, B. S. (1994). Cigarette smoking and sperm density: A meta-analysis. *Fertility and Sterility, 61*(1), 35–43.
Vine, M. F., Setzer, R. W., Jr., Everson, R. B., & Wyrobek, A. J. (1997). Human sperm morphometry and smoking, caffeine, and alcohol consumption. *Reproductive Toxicology, 11*(2–3), 179–184.
Vinggaard, A. M., Hass, U., Dalgaard, M., Andersen, H. R., Bonefeld-Jørgensen, E., Christiansen, S., et al. (2006). Prochloraz: An imidazole fungicide with multiple mechanisms of action. *International Journal of Andrology, 29*(1), 186–192.
Weidner, I. S., Møller, H., Jensen, T. K., & Skakkebæk, N. E. (1999). Risk factors for cryptorchidism and hypospadias. *Journal of Urology, 161*(5), 1606–1609.
Welsh, M., Saunders, P. T., Fisken, M., Scott, H. M., Hutchison, G. R., Smith, L. B., et al. (2008). Identification in rats of a programming window for reproductive tract masculinization, disruption of which leads to hypospadias and cryptorchidism. *Journal of Clinical Investigation, 118*(4), 1479–1490.
Welshons, W. V., Nagel, S. C., & vom Saal, F. S. (2006). Large effects from small exposures. III. Endocrine mechanisms mediating effects of bisphenol a at levels of human exposure. *Endocrinology, 147*(Suppl 6), S56–S69.
WHO (World Health Organisation). (2010). *WHO laboratory manual for the examination of human semen and sperm-cervical mucus interaction* (5th ed.). http://whqlibdoc.who.int/publications/2010/9789241547789_eng.pdf

Chapter 8
The Sexual Behavior of Adolescents and Young Adults in Japan

Ryuzaburo Sato and Miho Iwasawa

8.1 The Sexual Revolution in Japan

The sexual revolution, defined as the increased prevalence and social acceptability of premarital sex, started in Western Europe during the latter half of the twentieth century, spread to Southern Europe, and continued on to Eastern Europe and Japan in the course of the 1970s and 1980s (Billari et al. 2007). High economic growth and a rise in higher-education enrollment rates during the postwar period contributed to young Japanese people's increased independence (Raymo 1998; Sato et al. 2010), weakening the constraints of traditional values. The 1970s, however, marked the beginning of a transformation in the social lives of young Japanese, one characterized by increased affluence, a massive extension of tertiary education, and the advent of the "information age" (Yamamoto 2009). The mean age at first marriage started to rise for both men and women, and that led to a longer period between puberty and marriage, and to the increased probability of having premarital sexual relationships (Iwasawa 2004).

The results of surveys on sexual behavior of young Japanese conducted by the Japanese Association for Sex Education (JASE) reveal that the percentage of sexually active university students, most of whom are unmarried, has dramatically increased for both sexes since the 1970s (Fig. 8.1).

Attitudes toward premarital sex have also changed. According to the Japanese National Fertility Surveys conducted by the National Institute of Population and

---

R. Sato (✉)
National Institute of Population and Social Security Research, Tokyo, Japan
e-mail: sato.ryuzaburo@gmail.com

M. Iwasawa
Department of Population Dynamics Research, National Institute of Population and Social Security Research, Tokyo, Japan

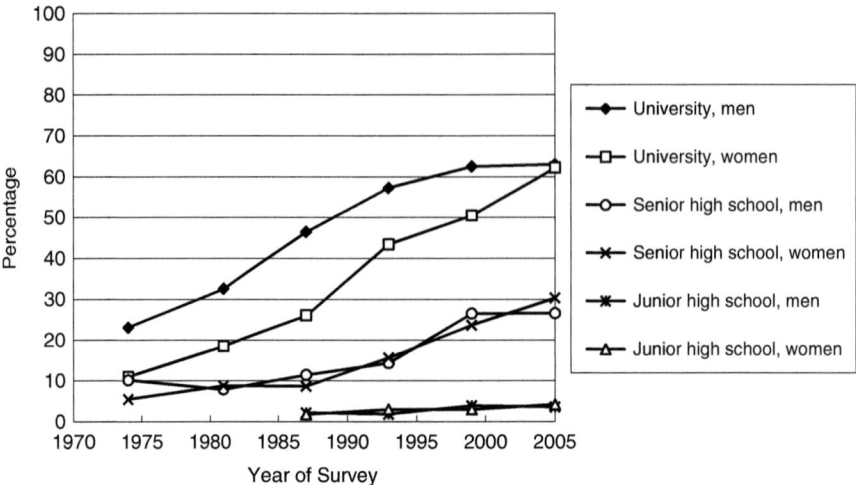

Fig. 8.1 Percentages of students having experienced sexual intercourse, by gender and educational level: Japan, 1974–2005 (Source: Surveys on Sexual Behavior among Youth (JASE 2007))

Social Security Research, tolerance toward premarital sex by never-married people between the ages of 18 and 34 years was already at 78 % for men and 73 % for women in 1992. By 2005 these figures had risen to 84 % and 82 %, respectively for men and women (Kaneko et al. 2008a). Increased social tolerance of premarital sexual relationships can reinforce the trend of delayed marriage. The formation of a youth culture, seen in popular media that portray positive images of premarital sex, have paralleled this normative change.

Although this phenomenon has occurred throughout the developed world, Retherford et al. (2001) point out that, in Japan, sexually explicit material appears in many popular publications and "love hotels" have become common in cities and along highways in the countryside. Although most unmarried Japanese live with their parents, "love hotels," by providing privacy, make it is easy for unmarried couples to have sex. Retherford et al. suggest that the increased prevalence of premarital sex is one of the factors that have led to a rise in the mean age at marriage.

Two characteristics of sexual behavior are unique to Japan. First, the main method of contraception for married couples is condoms (Sato and Iwasawa 2006). A low-dosage oral contraceptive was not approved by the government until 1999. Under the circumstances, condoms were the main method of contraception for unmarried people even before concern arose over HIV/AIDS (JASE 2007). Thus, the context for condom use in Japan is different from that in Europe. The other unique feature concerns partnership formation. In most Western countries, the rise in age at marriage was accompanied by an increased prevalence of premarital cohabitation (Kiernan 2002). In Japan, however, although premarital cohabitation has been increasing, it has done so at a much lower rate than in European countries (Raymo et al. 2009).

In the following sections, we first examine whether a drop in the age at first sexual intercourse and the convergence of sexual behaviors of men and women, both of which are evident in Western societies, are observed in Japan as well. Next, we describe how sexual intercourse has become detached from marriage and reproduction in Japan. Then, to identify people who have a higher risk of unintended pregnancy and sexually transmitted infections, we apply multivariate regression models of premarital sexual experience and the nonuse of contraception for never-married men and women.

8.2 Data

The longitudinal data, following cohorts of young men and women over time, are more suitable for discerning trends in sexual behavior. However, such data are not available for Japan. We use data from the Japanese National Fertility Surveys (JNFS) in 1987, 1992, 1997, 2002, and 2005. The data refer only to the heterosexual behaviors. The JNFS are nationally representative cross-sectional surveys of unmarried men and women between the ages of 18 and 49, and of married women below age 50. The valid response rate for the surveys of unmarried men and women ranged between 70 and 84 %, and that for couples ranged between 86 and 93 %. For this chapter, we limited the sample to men and women below age 35. Accordingly, the sample size is around 10,000–14,000 in each survey. The overview of the results of these surveys is reported in Kaneko et al. (2008a, b).

To investigate the sexual experience of adolescents below age 18, we used individual data from the Surveys on Sexual Behavior among Youth, conducted by the Japanese Association for Sex Education in 1981, 1987, 1993, 1999, and 2005. These are school-based surveys of junior high school students (12–15 years old), senior high school students (15–18 years old), and university students (18–22 years old) living in both large cities and provincial towns. The sample of junior high school students was collected in the third and later survey waves. The sample size of each survey is approximately 5,000. An overview of the results is reported in JASE (2007) and Yamamoto (2009).

8.3 Sexual Intercourse Among Adolescents and Young Adults

8.3.1 Trends in the Age at First Sexual Intercourse

As shown in Table 8.1, the proportion of those who experienced sexual intercourse before age 17.0 has increased sharply regardless of respondents' sex. In the 1970 birth cohort, fewer than 10 % had sexual intercourse before the age of 17.0

Table 8.1 Cumulative percentages of those having sexual intercourse before each specified age, by sex: Japan, various birth cohorts

	Approximate year of birth (birth cohort)								
	1955	1960	1965	1970	1975	1980	1985	1990	
Sex, marital status, and age	(1953–1957)	(1958–1962)	(1963–1967)	(1968–1972)	(1973–1977)	(1978–1982)	(1983–1987)	(1988–1992)	
All women									
13.0 (12–13)						2.1	1.5		
15.0 (14–15)				2.6	1.3	4.0	6.1	6.8	
17.0 (16–17)			10.2	7.7	14.9	22.4	22.4	26.0	
19.0 (18–19)				21.6	23.7	29.6	34.8		
22.5 (20–24)			45.6	52.2	61.5	65.9			
27.5 (25–29)		81.0	80.2	82.0	84.3				
32.5 (30–34)	95.0	93.2	93.4	92.3					
Never-married women									
19.0 (18–19)				19.9	22.6	28.9	33.4		
22.5 (20–24)			34.7	44.7	55.5	60.8			
27.5 (25–29)		44.2	51.8	63.5	70.2				
32.5 (30–34)	48.0	55.9	68.4	69.4					
All men									
13.0 (12–13)					1.6	0.9	1.7		
15.0 (14–15)				4.1	4.1	3.3	6.9	6.2	
17.0 (16–17)			8.3	9.2	13.4	24.4	24.4	22.8	
19.0 (18–19)				28.0	29.5	31.3	33.3		
22.5 (20–24)			57.9	60.1	65.7	67.1			
27.5 (25–29)		81.8	83.4	81.9	81.8				
32.5 (30–34)	91.4	92.1	90.5	88.8					

Never-married men						
19.0	(18–19)			27.2	29.0	30.9	33.1
22.5	(20–24)		54.5	57.5	63.0	64.2	
27.5	(25–29)	70.1	74.7	73.3	73.1		
32.5	(30–34)	71.3	76.0	75.8	73.6		

Sources: For ages 13.0, 15.0, and 17.0, the figures are based on the Surveys on Sexual Behavior among Youth, conducted by the Japanese Association for Sexual Education in 1981, 1987, 1993, 1999, and 2005. For ages 19.0 and older, the figures are based on the Japanese National Fertility Surveys (JNFS), conducted by the National Institute of Population and Social Security Research in 1987, 1992, 1997, 2002, and 2005

Notes: Actual birth cohorts do not necessarily correspond to the midpoint of calendar years that are shown in the column headings. In particular, in the case of age 19.0, the birth cohorts correspond to calendar years of birth that are 1.5 years less than the midpoint of calendar years that are shown in the column headings. Although the JNFS does not ask about the sexual experiences of married people, we assume that all married people have experienced sexual intercourse regardless of sex, whereas this figure was 26 % for females and 23 % for males born in 1990. The percentage of women who had had experienced sexual intercourse by the age of 19.0 was 34.8 % for the 1985 birth cohort, approximately a 13-point increase from 21.6 % for the 1970 birth cohort. The percentage of women who had had sexual intercourse by the age of 22.5 was 65.9 % for the 1980 birth cohort, approximately a 20-point increase from 45.6 % reported by the 1965 birth cohort. The percentage of men who had had sexual intercourse by the age of 19.0 was 33.3 % for the 1985 birth cohort, 5 % greater than that for the 1970 birth cohort (28.0 %).[1]

Compared with that of women, the proportion of men who had had sex before age of 19.0 was already high for the 1970 birth cohort; thus, the rise in the proportion is more modest for them than it is for women. The percentage has even declined slightly for men in their late twenties and above. It is true that the percentages of men who experienced sex have always been higher than those for women, but the difference between men and women has narrowed for younger birth cohorts. In the 1985 birth cohort the proportion of women who had had sexual intercourse before the age of 19.0 was higher than that of their male counterparts. The convergence in the ages at first sexual intercourse among men and women observed in Japan is similar to that witnessed in the US and European countries (Teitler 2002).

The panels of Table 8.1 showing the corresponding percentages for never-married persons indicate that, for women, the percentage of those experiencing sexual intercourse has been rising significantly at all ages. For example, while the percentage of never-married women who had had sexual intercourse before the age of 27.5 was less than 50 % for the 1960 birth cohort, it was over 70 % for the 1975 birth cohort. The percentage for never-married men has increased at ages up to the early twenties and is higher than for never-married women at every age except in the 1985 birth cohort; the percentage levels off in the late twenties and above. In summary, as in Western countries, Japan has experienced the following changes: a drop in the age at which first sexual intercourse is experienced; normative transformation of premarital sex from deviant behavior to acceptable behavior, with more than 60 % of never-married men and women having had sex by the age of 22.5 years; and the convergence in the prevalence of sexual experience between men and women of the same age, approximately 65 % of both men and women in the 1980 birth cohort having had sexual intercourse by the age of 22.5.

---

[1]Kunio Kitamura of the Japan Family Planning Association and his colleagues conducted four rounds of a Survey on Life and Consciousness of Men and Women in 2002, 2004, 2006, and 2008 (Kitamura 2009). These were nationally representative sample surveys on the sexual behavior of Japanese; their sample size was small, however: approximately 1,500 men and women aged 16–49 responded in each round. The proportions of men and women who had experienced sexual intercourse by their teens, twenties, and thirties reported by these surveys approximate our estimation in the current study.

8.3.2 Detachment of Sexual Behavior from Marriage and Childbearing

To understand more comprehensively the changes that have taken place in the sexual experiences of young Japanese adults, in the following sections we focus on changes in two related behaviors: couple relationships (an important precursor to sexual intercourse) and reproductive behaviors (possible consequences of sexual intercourse). We observe the association between the experience of sexual intercourse and couples' relationships at the time of the survey, bearing in mind that not all events of sexual intercourse reported by respondents occurred in their current relationships. Some may have occurred in a previous relationship or other temporary relationships, including ones involving commercial sex.

8.3.2.1 Couple Relationships

To define couple relationships at the time of the survey, we first divided respondents into two groups according to their experience of marriage. Those who had ever been married we further classified as currently married, divorced, or widowed. Never-married people were further classified into the following categories according to the type of relationship they had with a partner: cohabiting, engaged to be married, romantic partner *(koibito)*, just a friend of the opposite sex *(isei no yujin)*, and no relationship. Figure 8.2 shows the distributions of couple relationships among young adults by sex, age group, and birth cohort, and the percentages of those who had experienced sexual intercourse. Although Fig. 8.2 is based on information at the time of each survey and does not allow us to infer a relationship between sexual experiences and current partnership status, the trends suggest several possibilities.

First, most Japanese in their late twenties and early thirties, particularly women, are currently married, and the proportion of those who have had sexual experience levels off at over 80 %. For younger cohorts, however, the proportion of currently married people has decreased over time, suggesting that the linkage between marriage and sexual experience is weakening.

Second, for those between the ages of 18 and 24, the percentages of those who are currently married remains low, but the percentages of those who have had sexual experience have increased steadily, especially among women. This is more evidence of the detachment of sex from marriage.

Third, while the proportion of married people has declined, the proportion of people who have a romantic partner has been increasing. This finding is consistent with the hypothesis that socially condoned premarital sex leads to an increase in unmarried couples because securing a sexual partner is no longer an important incentive to marry. According to the JNFS, the average duration from the first encounter with a potential partner to marriage was 2.5 years for couples married in the mid-1980s; and this was extended to 3.8 years for couples married in the

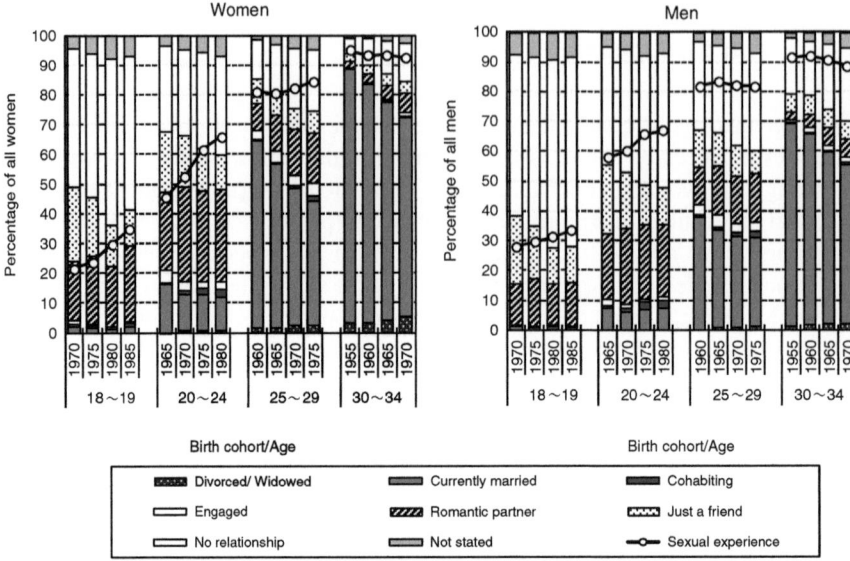

Fig. 8.2 Types of couple relationships and cumulative percentages of sexual experience by gender, age, and approximate year of birth (Sources: The 1987, 1992, 1997, 2002, and 2005 rounds of the Japanese National Fertility Survey. Note: The calendar year of birth of each age group shown in the figure approximately represents the mid-point of that birth cohort. In the case of ages 18 and 19, the cohort corresponds to calendar years of birth that are 1.5 years less than the midpoint of the calendar years shown)

early 2000s (Kaneko et al. 2008b: 25). Interestingly, unlike the situation in Western countries, the proportion of nonmarital cohabiting couples in Japan has not changed and still remains very low.

Fourth, on the other hand, the major change among 18–24-year-olds is a decline in the "just a friend" group and an increase in the proportion of those who reported "no relationship." This trend is noteworthy in two ways. First, the fact that the increased prevalence of sexual experience is not accompanied by an increased prevalence of intimate relationships indicates that sexual relationships have become more casual for the youngest generation than they were for older ones. For young people today, a sexual relationship is not the goal of a romantic relationship, but rather just a gateway to it. Second, the proportion of people who reported "no relationship" is higher than in Western countries. According to a survey conducted by the Japanese government in 2006 (Japan, Cabinet Office 2006: 74), while the proportions of men in their twenties who were then currently not in any romantic relationship were 35% and 30 % in Sweden and the US, respectively, the proportion of those in Japan was over 52 %. This finding is consistent with Atoh's (1998) view that young Japanese today are not actively looking for partners in the free (love and marriage) market. He attributes their behavior to an "undeveloped dating culture" (Atoh 1998).

Accordingly, although sexual relationships are more easily experienced by some young people, for others it may be difficult even to form a friendship with someone of the opposite sex. This bifurcation seems pronounced among women of ages 18–19 and men of ages 20–24.

8.3.2.2 Reproductive Behaviors

Figure 8.3 shows the trends in marriage, induced abortion, and parenthood among all women as well as the trends in sexual experience at given ages.[2] We also look at their status during the experience of childbearing. Using vital statistics data, we classified the transition to parenthood into three patterns: (1) nonmarital birth, (2) marital birth resulting from premarital pregnancy (childbirth within 8 months of marriage), and (3) marital birth resulting from postmarital pregnancy. We calculated the experience of induced abortion from the cohort cumulative rates for age-specific induced abortion rates based on government statistics on induced abortion.[3]

Both the percentage of those who experienced marriage and the percentage of those who experienced parenthood have declined at all ages. The percentages of women who experienced induced abortion by 19 years of age and those who did so by 22.5 years of age are generally higher for the birth cohorts of 1975 and later than they are for older cohorts. The percentages of women who experienced marriage and parenthood in their late twenties and early thirties have dropped sharply. There has been little change, however, with regard to the trend in sexual experience, and the percentage of women who experienced sexual intercourse by their late twenties shows a slight increase.

Our findings suggest that the timing of marriage and parenthood has tended to be delayed for Japanese women of later birth cohorts, whereas the age at which first sexual intercourse is experienced has dropped, resulting in an increase in premarital sexual intercourse. In addition, the rise in the percentages of women who experienced premarital sexual intercourse in their teenage years and those who did so in their early twenties is linked to an increase in the percentage of women who experienced induced abortion. Interestingly, the percentage of women who experienced induced abortion by their late twenties and their early thirties is declining. According to Sato et al. (2008), two critical factors are affecting this trend: the declining percentage of married women, whose frequency of sexual intercourse is assumed to be higher than that of unmarried women, thus leading

---

[2] We calculated the experience rates for first marriage and first childbearing from age-specific first-marriage rates and age-specific first-birth fertility rates using data from Japanese vital statistics. In calculating age-specific first-marriage rates, we made a correction for underestimation because of the registration of first marriage is often delayed.

[3] We treated repeated abortions by the same person as single abortions by other women. Thus, it should be noted that, with regard to older women, the estimated experience rate may be higher than the actual rate.

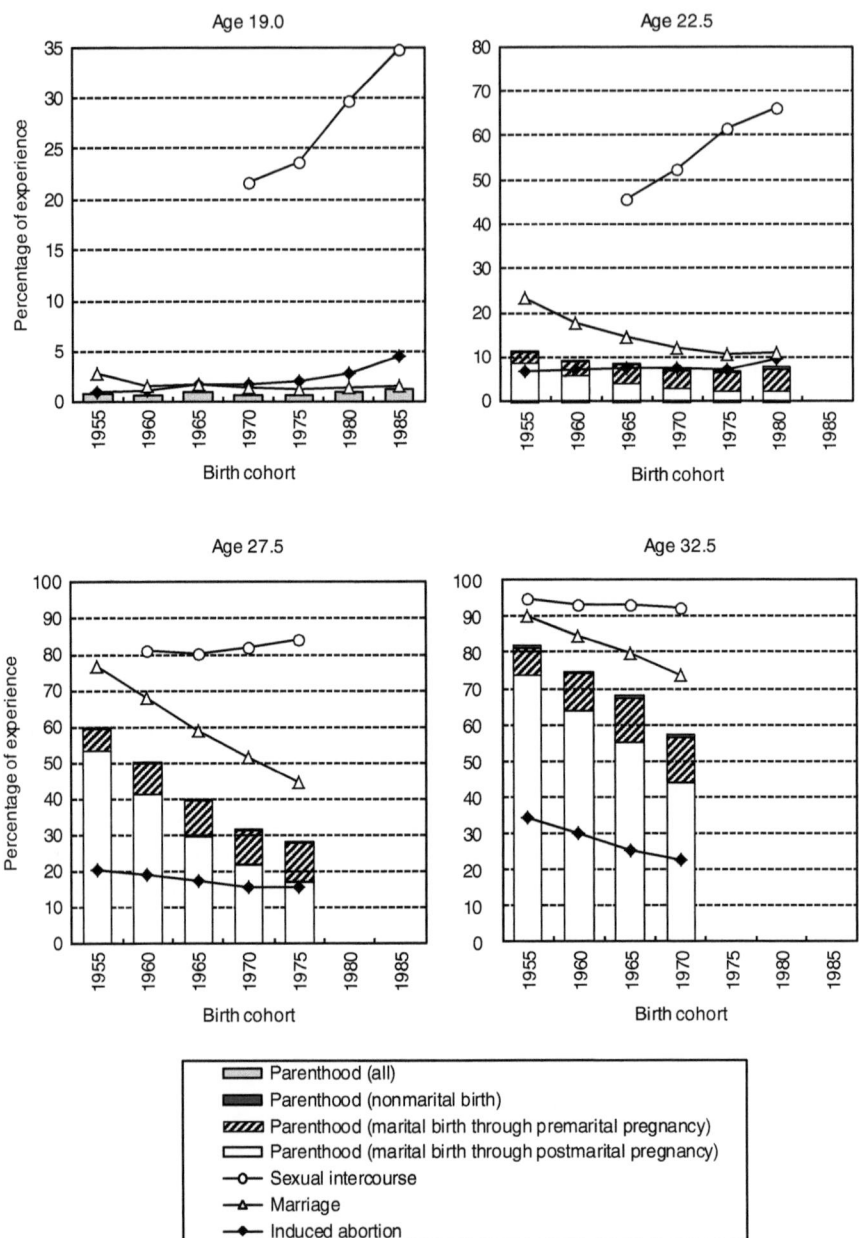

Fig. 8.3 Percentages of women having experienced sexual intercourse, marriage, parenthood, and induced abortion before each specified age: Japan, various birth cohorts (Sources: For experience of sexual intercourse, calculations are based on data from the Japanese National Fertility Survey in 1987, 1992, 1997, 2002, and 2005. For marriage and parenthood, estimates are based on the vital statistics of Japan (Japan, Ministry of Health, Labour and Welfare 2010). For induced abortion, estimates are based on the Maternal Body Protection Statistics/Report on Public Health Administration and Services (Japan, Ministry of Health, Labour and Welfare 2008))

to a decrease in the incidence of pregnancy, and the increasing proportion of women who have not achieved their planned fertility because of delayed childbearing, thus leading to a decrease in the incidence of pregnancy ended by induced abortion.

As Raymo and Iwasawa (2008) have pointed out, the rise in the percentage of women who have experienced childbirth through premarital pregnancy means that the issue of reproductive behavior concerns not only married but also never-married people. This is a recent development in Japan.

Although we do not show the results for men here, the timing of marriage and parenthood is being delayed for men as well as for women. Conversely, the experience of sexual intercourse by those in their early twenties is rising.

8.4 Factors Influencing Sexual Behavior and Risk Behaviors Among Never-Married Men and Women

To deepen our understanding of increased premarital sexual intercourse in Japan and its consequences for reproductive health, we examined several factors related to never-married people's sexual behavior. We also explored risk behaviors that could affect their sexual and reproductive health.

Using multivariate models, we first examined the factors related to the experience of sexual intercourse. Next, we analyzed the factors that relate to the nonuse of any contraception and specifically the nonuse of condoms, as the use of condoms is an effective method for preventing the spread of sexually transmitted infections as well as unwanted pregnancy. We used data from five rounds of the JNFS from 1987 to 2005 that included men and women in the age range of 20–34 years. We limited the survey sample to those of at least 20 years of age because we could not determine the highest education level completed or begun, enrollment being a benchmark of educational attainment, for those still in senior high school or who failed an entrance exam for college and were preparing for the next exam. We also limited the sample to never-married men and women because the JNFS does not have information on the experience of premarital sex for married people. It should be kept in mind that our sample excludes people who had premarital sex and then married.

8.4.1 Determinants of Premarital Sexual Intercourse Among Never-Married Men and Women

Although few studies have been done on the antecedents of young adults' sexual experiences in industrialized countries, several studies have examined the antecedents of adolescents' sexual initiation, and most of these studies are relevant to the sexual experiences of young adults. Studies by Kirby (2002), Buhi and Goodson (2007), and Coppola (2007) have identified important factors related to the sexual initiation of adolescents. Being older, being male, having parents with low education, having less parental control, having older siblings and friends, having a romantic relationship, and having lower school attendance are all considered to have a positive effect on sexual initiation.

Using pooled data from five rounds of the JNFS survey, we first examined the association between sexual behavior and such characteristics of individuals as age, birth cohort, educational attainment, living arrangement with parents (an indirect measure of parental control or interaction), birth order and sex composition of siblings, and attitude toward their own family formation. Retherford et al. (2001) used data from the National Survey on Family Planning conducted by the Mainichi Newspapers to study the factors that could affect unmarried woman's sexual conduct. They found that premarital sexual intercourse was more frequently experienced by women living alone than by those living with their parents, and the proportion of unmarried women who had had sexual experience was higher among younger than among older generations. Following that study, we estimated a binomial logistic model of sexual experience and first reexamined how the experience of sexual intercourse varied by birth cohort after controlling for other factors.

Second, to find out how socioeconomic attributes affect the chance of being sexually experienced, we examined the effect of educational attainment. We expected the influence of educational attainment to work in both directions. That is, we assumed, on the one hand, that being a student at a college or university would increase a person's chances of meeting people of the opposite sex through daily contact and result in more opportunities to have sexual relationships than would having already completed school. On the other hand, we hypothesized that higher education might be associated with normative behaviors that would negatively affect the initiation of premarital sex. If so, the positive influence of education on sexual initiation might be offset. In fact, the research by Retherford et al. (2001) reveals no differences by educational attainment.

Third, we examined the association between sexual behavior and the types of couple relationship that existed among respondents at the time of the survey. Ideally, the range of couple relationships should include relationships prior to sexual initiation, but the JNFS captures only the current relationship; it does not reflect the cumulative experience of all the previous relationships experienced before sexual initiation.

Fourth, we examined the relationship between sexual behavior and living arrangements with parents, assuming that living arrangements would reflect the strength of parents' control and supervision. This assumption was based on previous studies, which have found that parents' increased tolerance toward children's romantic and sexual relationships contributes to the decline in the age of first sexual intercourse (Teitler 2002).

Fifth, we included sibling structure in the model. We examined how young people's sexual experiences vary with the presence of an elder brother or sister or the presence of a sibling of the same or opposite sex.

Finally, we studied the association between sexual experience and never-married people's current marital intentions and their fertility intentions – that is, their desired number of children.

Table 8.2 shows the predicted percentages of respondents who had experienced sexual intercourse, calculated on the basis of the estimated logistic model. It indicates how the predicted probabilities differ by variable category, based on the assumption that all other variables are set at average levels.

Regardless of gender, older respondents and those from later birth cohorts have a greater likelihood than others of having experienced sexual intercourse. In regard to the association with education, for women the probability of having experienced sexual intercourse is significantly higher among junior and senior high school graduates than among college or vocational school graduates, and it is lowest among university graduates. For men, the likelihood is also significantly low among university graduates. Although having access to higher education is considered an advantage in finding sexual partners, the analysis shows that, in Japan, higher education is negatively associated with premarital sexual behavior, especially for women. Given that the JNFS surveys have found little difference in attitudes toward premarital sex among Japanese of lower and higher educational levels, there is no reason to assume that people with higher levels of education tend to underreport their sexual experiences. It is possible that a portion of highly educated women who have had premarital sex were excluded from the sample we analyzed because they had already married, but our result is consistent with Tsuya's (2009) study that included married people, which found that premarital cohabitation is less common among highly educated women than among women with less education.

We found a significant association between the type of current couple relationship and respondents' sexual experience. Cohabiting women have the greatest likelihood (97.6 %) of having experienced sexual intercourse, followed by those who reported having a romantic partner (84.2 %) and those engaged to be married (75.5 %). The probability is lower, but still higher than 50 %, among women who have just a friend of the opposite sex. It is significantly lower among women who reported having no relationship with someone of the opposite sex. Similar patterns are observed among men, although in each category the probability of sexual initiation is slightly higher for men than for women.

As for the association between living arrangement and sexual experience, the probability of having had sexual intercourse is higher among unmarried people living apart from, rather than with, their parents, regardless of gender. This finding suggests that parental intervention limits opportunities for sexual intercourse or that those who are interested in having sexual relationships choose to live apart from their parents. Alternatively, nonregular workers may be more likely than other unmarried people to co-reside with their parents and, as Genda and Kawakami (2006) suggest, for that reason may be excluded from the "romantic relationship market" and have fewer chances to form sexual relationships. In any case, our finding suggests that keeping one's distance from parents provides unmarried people more opportunity to experience sexual intercourse at an earlier age. According to the JNFS, although the percentage of never-married people between ages 18 and 34

Table 8.2 Predicted percentages of those having experienced sexual intercourse, by predictor variable: never-married Japanese men and women of ages 20–34, 1987–2005

	Predicted percentage	
Predictor variable	Female	Male
Age		
21	41.4***	58.3***
24	59.7***	71.4***
27	72.6***	79.2***
30	80.1***	83.1***
33	83.9***	84.4***
Birth cohort		
1960	33.5***	67.8***
1965	44.1***	70.2***
1970	55.2***	72.5***
1975	65.8***	74.7***
1980	75.0***	76.8***
Education		
Junior high school	70.0**	73.0
Senior high school	64.2**	75.7
Junior college/Vocational school[a]	59.7	75.1
University	49.7***	68.8***
Current couple relationship		
Cohabiting	97.6**	98.1**
Engaged	75.5***	88.9*
Romantic partner[a]	84.2	92.3
Friend of opposite sex	54.1***	73.2***
No relationship/not stated	31.8***	53.8***
Living with parent(s)		
Yes[a]	53.4	67.9
No	76.9***	81.5***
Eldest child		
Yes	58.0*	71.0**
No[a]	60.3	74.2
Same-sex sibling(s)		
Yes	60.0	73.1
No[a]	58.3	72.2
Opposite-sex sibling(s)		
Yes	60.2#	73.0
No[a]	57.9	72.4
Marital intention		
Want to marry soon	60.1#	71.7
Yes, if appropriate partner	64.0***	76.6***
Not yet[a]	56.4	71.7
Won't marry/not sure	47.3**	65.1**

(continued)

Table 8.2 (continued)

	Predicted percentage	
Predictor variable	Female	Male
Desired number of children		
0 or 1	59.3	70.6*
2[a]	58.6	73.4
3 or more	60.6	72.7
N	*11,613*	*13,613*
Likelihood-based pseudo R-square measure	0.285	0.193

Notes: We use pooled data from the 1987, 1992, 1997, 2002, and 2005 rounds of the JNFS. A sample of never-married women and men between the ages of 20 and 34 was used for the estimate. Predicted percentages were computed by a logistic regression model based on the assumption that all other variables were set at average levels. In the logistic regression, age is specified by two continuous variables, age and age-squared. The coefficients are both significant at the level of 0.1 %
***$p < 0.001$; **$p < 0.01$; *$p < 0.05$; #$p < 0.1$
[a] Indicates the reference category

who live with their parents has remained at the 70 % level (70.3 % among men and 76.4 % among women in the 2005 survey), it is higher among those who work at jobs offering little security (80 % among men and 87.7 % among women working part time) (Kaneko et al. 2008a: 67). If economic stagnation increases among those who live with their parents, or causes more young adults to live with their parents, the proportion of never-married people who are not sexually active may increase.

As for the influence of sibling structure, we found that regardless of gender, the likelihood of premarital sexual experience is significantly lower among those who do not have any elder siblings than among those who do. In the case of women, the probability of premarital sexual initiation is significantly higher among those having a male sibling, but for both sexes the presence of a sibling of the same sex does not make a difference in the timing of sexual initiation. This may indicate that unmarried people obtain information from an elder sibling or a sibling of the opposite sex that increases their interest in sexual activity, or it could mean that parents are stricter with older siblings than with younger ones. Very low fertility in Japan since the 1990s has resulted in a decrease in the number of young people with siblings and an increase in the number having neither an elder sibling nor a sibling of the opposite sex. It is conceivable that the presence of a sibling of the opposite sex has not only a direct effect on sexual experience but also an indirect effect on it through the parents' attitudes toward their children's gender roles or sexual behavior.

Examining the associations between premarital sexual behavior and marital and fertility intentions, we found that, regardless of gender, the probability of premarital sexual experience is highest among people who wish to marry soon (within 1 year) and those who have a partner considered to be appropriate for marriage. These results suggest that a sexual partner is not always considered to be a marriageable partner. In general, the weaker the marital intention, the lower is the probability of having a premarital sexual experience. As for an association between premarital sexual experience and desired number of children, we found no significant association among women and only a weak one among men. Because childbearing outside marriage is still rare in Japan, the view that childbearing should occur within marriage remains the norm, and our result supports this norm.

8.4.2 Determinants of Contraceptive Use Among Never-Married Men and Women

Our model estimated the nonuse of contraception and specifically of condoms during the sample's last exposure to nonmarital sexual intercourse. According to Kirby's (2002) review of the antecedents of adolescent contraceptive use in the US, factors favoring use include better neighbor quality, having a family with more resources, being older, having a better relationship with one's family such as greater parental monitoring, greater attendance at school including receiving sex education, having a closer and egalitarian relationship with a partner such as a monogamous relationship, and greater female empowerment in the relationship. Being older when having the first sexual experience and greater frequency of intercourse are also positively associated with contraceptive use. Nonuse of contraception is associated with poor health, low self-esteem, and, for females, having an older male partner. Although our study focuses on never-married young adults in Japan and we do not limit our observations to adolescents, these findings seem relevant. We examined whether age, access to education, type of relationship, and relationship with parents is also associated with contraceptive use.

Using only data obtained through the 2005 JNFS for these models, we examined the influence of the above-mentioned predictor variables, excluding birth cohort. The analysis focused on a sample of respondents who had experienced sexual intercourse during the previous year. Before discussing the results, we examine the practice of contraception based on descriptive statistics.

Table 8.3 shows the percentage distribution of currently sexually active, never-married women and men in Japan and selected Western countries in recent years who had had sex during the past year by whether they had used contraception during the most recent sexual intercourse. Of never-married Japanese women aged 18–34, 83.3 % had used some form of contraception. Condoms were the most popular method, used by 73.9 %. Withdrawal and oral contraceptives were used by 9.4 % and 1.6 %, respectively. Of never-married Japanese men, 85.1 % used contraception. For them, condoms were also the most popular method (80.1 %), whereas withdrawal was used by 5.6 %. Only 0.8 % of men replied that their partner had used the pill.

The JNFS asked only about contraceptive use during the last sexual intercourse. According to an international student survey conducted by Billari and his colleagues during 2001–2003, in which Japanese university students were asked about contraceptive use when they *first* and *last* had sexual intercourses, there is little change in contraceptive use between the first and last times (Sato 2007). In light of this finding,

8 The Sexual Behavior of Adolescents and Young Adults in Japan

Table 8.3 Percentage distribution of never-married sexually active women and men by the methods used when last having intercourse: Japan and selected Western countries

Sample	Ages	Women		Method						Men		Method			
		%	(N)	Used contraception	Contraceptive pill	Condom	Withdrawal	Rhythm	Injectable/implant/IUD	%	(N)	Used contraception	Contraceptive pill	Condom	Withdrawal	Rhythm
Japan (2005)																
Never married women	18–34	100.0	(1,293)	83.3	1.6	73.9	9.4	1.5	–	100.0	(1,367)	85.1	0.8	80.1	5.6	0.4
	18–19	100.0	(157)	82.8	0.6	80.3	2.6	0.6	–	100.0	(110)	88.2	0.0	83.6	5.5	0.0
	20–24	100.0	(562)	84.0	2.1	74.7	8.7	1.1	–	100.0	(468)	87.4	1.3	83.8	4.9	0.9
	25–29	100.0	(397)	84.1	1.8	73.6	10.8	2.0	–	100.0	(505)	85.5	1.0	79.2	6.3	0.0
	30–34	100.0	(177)	79.7	0.0	66.1	14.7	2.3	–	100.0	(284)	79.2	0.0	74.3	5.3	0.4
Sweden (1996)	18–19	100.0	–	93.5	49.9	24.1	{17.3}		2.1							
France (1992,1994)	15–19	100.0	–	83.1	59.2	28.4	{0.6}		0.0							
Canada (1995)	15–19	100.0	–	–	63.7	{23.1}										
Great Britain (1990–1991)	16–19	100.0	–	95.9	67.5	23.3	{3.8}		1.3							
US (1995)	15–19	100.0	–	80.0	32.5	33.0	{5.2}		9.3							

Notes: For Japan, based on the 2005 rounds of the JNFS. For never-married persons who had sexual intercourse during the last year. The figures in the method category are the results of multiple answers, showing the percentages of the total. A blank cell indicates that the method was not available to the sample or the number of cases is unknown. The use of low-dose contraceptive pills was approved in Japan in 1999. For other countries, sexually active women may include married or cohabiting women (see Darroch et al. 2001) we presume that contraceptive use during the first sexual encounter is similar to that during the last. More than 80 % of never-married sexually active young adults in Japan and of sexually active teenage women in several Western countries reported using some form of contraception, but only in Japan did a majority of them rely on condoms.

In our multivariate analysis, we identified never-married sexually active young adults who tended not to use contraception. Table 8.4 shows the predicted percentages of nonusers of any contraceptive method for the last sexual intercourse calculated on the basis of the estimated binomial logistic model.

By educational attainment, nonuse of contraception was remarkably high (over 22 %) among women with only a junior or senior high school education. For men, the percentage of nonusers was higher among senior high school graduates than among junior high school and junior college and vocational school graduates.

As for the type of couple relationship, the probability of nonuse of contraception was highest (22.8 %) among women who were engaged to be married, suggesting that some of those women wished to begin family formation early in their marriage. The probability of not using contraception was also significantly higher (18.4 %) among women who did not currently have a romantic partner than among women who did have one. It is possible that some of these women had a romantic partner when having the unprotected sex. Even so, the finding suggests that women in unstable relationships have a higher risk of unintended pregnancy than other women. For men, nonuse of contraception was significantly higher (34.7 %) among those who were cohabiting with a partner than among those defined by other relationships.

Regardless of the respondent's sex, we found no association between the nonuse of contraceptives and the living arrangement with parents. The presence of a sibling of the same sex was associated with a higher percentage of nonuse of contraception for men. For women, the presence of a sibling of the opposite sex was associated with a lower percentage of nonuse.

As for the association between marital intention and contraception, the probability of nonuse of contraception was significantly high (26.1 %) among women who wished to marry within 1 year. This result leads us to assume that many of those women wished to become pregnant. The fact that the proportion of premarital pregnancies to all marital births has been increasing in Japan and one-fourth of marital births fall into this category (Japan, Ministry of Health, Labour and Welfare 2010: 14) would support this hypothesis. Meanwhile, we observed no significant association between male respondents' marital and fertility intentions and the probability of their nonuse of contraception.

Condom use can prevent sexually transmitted infections and unwanted pregnancy, especially when people change sex partners frequently or have multiple sex partners. We were therefore interested in knowing the characteristics of people who did not use condoms as a means of contraception. The results of this analysis are not shown in Table 8.4, but we included the same antecedents as in the model for the nonuse of contraception. The probability of not using condoms was high among women with a senior high school or lower level of education, those who were engaged to be married, and those who intended to marry within 1 year.

Table 8.4 Predicted percentages of the nonusers of contraception during the last time of sexual intercourse, by background characteristic, among never-married women and men of ages 20–34 having sexual intercourse during the previous year: Japan, 2005

Predictor variable	Predicted percentage	
	Female	Male
Ages		
20–22	15.7	14.7#
23–25[a]	15.6	9.7
26–28	12.2	13.4
29–31	15.1	18.5**
32–34	12.6	16.1#
Education		
Junior high school	28.7*	14.2
Senior high school	22.1**	20.9#
Junior college/ Vocational school[a]	12.5	14.2
University	11.4	10.0
Current couple relationship		
Cohabiting	12.1	34.7**
Engaged	22.8*	17.1
Romantic partner[a]	12.4	14.2
Friend of opposite sex	16.9	13.4
No relationship/not stated	18.4#	10.7
Living with parent(s)		
Yes[a]	14.0	12.9
No	16.3	15.3
Eldest child		
Yes	13.9	13.8
No[a]	15.1	13.6
Same-sex sibling(s)		
Yes	14.3	15.6#
No[a]	14.9	11.3
Opposite-sex sibling(s)		
Yes	11.9**	14.6
No[a]	19.3	12.7
Marital intention		
Want to marry soon	26.1***	13.3
Yes, if appropriate partner	15.8*	15.8
Not yet[a]	9.6	12.2
Won't marry/not sure	15.1	15.9
Desired number of children		
0 or 1	20.7#	15.5
2[a]	13.8	13.1

(continued)

Table 8.4 (continued)

	Predicted percentage	
Predictor variable	Female	Male
3 or more	14.1	14.1
N	*1,100*	*1,179*
Likelihood-based pseudo *R*-squared measure	0.071	0.047

Note: We use data from the 2005 round of the JNFS. A sample of never-married women and men between ages 20 and 34 who had sexual intercourse during the previous year were used for the estimate. Predicted percentages were computed by a logistic regression model based on the assumption that all other variables were set at average levels
***p < 0.001; **p < 0.01; *p < 0.05; #p < 0.1
[a]Indicates the reference category

The probability was also low among women who lived apart from their parents. The probability of not using condoms was high among men 26 years old or older, senior high school graduates, and men cohabiting with a partner.

8.5 Summary and Discussion

Our analysis of nationally representative data for Japanese birth cohorts between 1955 and 1990 has documented that the age at which first sexual intercourse is experienced has dropped regardless of sex, and that the gender difference regarding this age has narrowed mainly because of a dramatic rise in women's sexual experience. At the same time, sexual initiation has been increasingly experienced prior to marriage. This statistical evidence supports the idea that the sexual revolution that started in Western industrialized countries has spread to Japan. The decline in the age at which first sexual intercourse is experienced and the increase in premarital sex among young women have provoked interest in risk factors associated with the human papilloma virus (HPV), which causes uterine and cervical cancer. The Japanese government has recently made plans to begin a program to prevent this type of cancer by giving HPV vaccinations to young women who have not experienced sexual intercourse. Demographic studies on sexual behavior, in particular the timing of first sex, number of sexual partners, and use of condoms and other forms of contraception, are expected to contribute greatly to the improvement of the cancer-prevention plan.

The increase in premarital sex among never-married persons is partly explained by the rise in age at marriage, which inevitably leads to more premarital sex among persons who otherwise would have married at a younger age. As we have discussed, however, the causation also goes the other way and involves a positive feedback loop, inasmuch as socially tolerated premarital sex removes a reason for marrying (Bumpass 1990; Retherford et al. 2001). The proportion of never-married persons who are in a romantic relationship without being married has been increasing, regardless of gender. Nonetheless, the opportunity for having a romantic partner is not available for all never-married persons. While the proportion of men and women who are in any kind of romantic relationship is increasing, the proportion of those who do not have even a friend of the opposite sex is also increasing. Traditionally, couple formation in Japan was largely supported by social systems such as the arranged marriage and, in the twentieth century, matchmaking through the workplace (Iwasawa and Mita 2007). The increase in premarital sex has been accompanied by a decline in marriage, but it may also be accompanied by less intimate interpersonal relations between men and women. For some young adults, sex may be increasingly experienced as unplanned, haphazard, spontaneous, and occasional.

Furthermore, the increase in premarital sex has altered traditional patterns of reproduction. Although childbearing is decreasing and nonmarital childbearing is still rare in Japan, both the proportion of childbearing resulting from premarital pregnancy and the proportion of women who have experienced induced abortion have been increasing among Japanese 25 years of age and younger. There has also been an upward trend in induced abortions across cohorts for women between 19 and 22.5 years of age, most of whom have never been married.[4] In this age group, one in seven women who have experienced sexual intercourse has experienced induced abortion. Preventing unintended pregnancy among never-married young adults is thus a critical issue.

In regard to contraceptive behavior, nearly 20 % of never-married young people did not practice contraception at the time they last had sex; and among users, condoms were the most popular means of contraception, followed by withdrawal. Neither of these two methods is highly effective at preventing pregnancy. Furthermore, our multivariate analysis suggests that the probabilities of contraceptive and condom use are lower among sexually active never-married young people with lower levels of education than among the better educated. College and university students can easily access health care services through their institutions, but those who do not enroll in tertiary education tend to be excluded from these types of service. Sexual and reproductive health programs, including sex education, should focus more on young people with lower educational attainment.

Sexual behavior is increasingly common among unmarried persons in various types of couple relationships today. The increase in premarital sex is generally considered to be the result of long-term cultural and material trends such as economic development and increased freedom of personal choice made possible by advanced education, which often tends to encourage couple relationships based on individualism and gender symmetry. Unless young people develop autonomy and self-control, however, their exposure to premarital sex can increase their risk of contracting life-threatening sexually transmitted infections and worsening their general well being. Since individualism and gender symmetry are considered to be

---

[4]The incidence of induced abortion has decreased among teenagers since 2000 and among women in their early twenties since 2006, however. As a result, the incidence of abortion among birth cohorts after 1990 may fall below that of the preceding cohorts and reverse this trend.

rather weak in Japan and perhaps in other Asian countries, the increase in premarital sex in these countries may negatively influence the sexual and reproductive health of young adults.

Whereas the sexual behavior of married persons tends to be stable in the sense that intercourse is experienced with a steady partner and conception is usually planned, for unmarried people intercourse tends to be unstable and conception unplanned, suggesting that unmarried people are more vulnerable to sexually transmitted infections and unmarried women have a higher risk of unintended pregnancy. Nevertheless, most programs that promote sexual and reproductive health have targeted mainly adolescents and mothers.[5] Measures that deal with sexual and reproductive health issues need to be expanded to cover unmarried young adults as well as adolescents and married couples.

Acknowledgments We are grateful to the National Institute of Population and Social Security Research for providing data from the Japanese National Fertility Surveys used in our analysis. Data from the Surveys on Sexual Behavior among Youth, conducted by the Japanese Association for Sex Education, were provided by the Social and Opinion Research Database Project, organized by the Faculty of Social Information, Sapporo Gakuin University. We also thank them for their kind assistance.

References

Atoh, M. (1998). Traditional family values of unmarried women: In relevance to the phenomenal rise in the proportion never married. In Mainichi Shimbun Population Problems Research Council (Ed.), *The future of the family: Beyond gender* (pp. 117–149). Tokyo: Mainichi Shimbun.

Billari, F. C., Caltabiano, M., & Dalla Zuanna, G. (2007). The heirs of the sexual revolution. In F. C. Billari, M. Caltabiano, & G. Dalla Zuanna (Eds.), *Sexual and affective behaviour of students: An international research* (pp. 1–47). Padua: G. CLEUP.

Buhi, E. R., & Goodson, P. (2007). Predictors of adolescent sexual behavior and intention: A theory-guided systematic review. *Journal of Adolescent Health, 40*, 4–21.

Bumpass, L. (1990). What's happening to the family? Interactions between demographic and institutional change. *Demography, 27*, 483–498.

Coppola, L. (2007). Determinants of age at first intercourse: A comparison between nine countries. In F. C. Billari, M. Caltabiano, & G. Dalla Zuanna (Eds.), *Sexual and affective behaviour of students: An international research* (pp. 251–271). Padua: G. CLEUP.

Darroch, J., Singh, S., & Frost, J. J. (2001). Differences in teenage pregnancy rates among five developed countries: The roles of sexual activity and contraceptive use. *Family Planning Perspectives, 33*(6), 244–250. 281.

---

[5] In 2001 the Japanese government started a national health promotion program called "Healthy Parents and Children 21." The program set goals for sexual and reproductive health, such as decreased induced abortion rates among teens, decreased incidence rates of sexually transmitted infections among teens, and decreased incidence rates of postpartum depression. Since these plans target mainly adolescents and mothers in their pregnancy and childcare period, they tend to ignore unmarried young adults.

Genda, Y., & Kawakami, A. (2006). Shugyo nikyokuka to sei kodo (Divided youth employment and sexual behavior). *Nihon Rodo Kenkyu Zasshi, 556*, 92–105.

Iwasawa, M. (2004). Partnership transition in contemporary Japan: Prevalence of childless non-cohabiting couples. *The Japanese Journal of Population, 2*(1), 76–92.

Iwasawa, M., & Mita, F. (2007). Boom and bust in marriage between coworkers and the marriage decline in Japan. *The Japanese Economy, 34*(4), 3–24.

Japan, Cabinet Office. (2006). *Shoshika shakai ni kansuru kokusai ishiki hikaku chosa hokokusho*. Tokyo.

Japan, Ministry of Health, Labour and Welfare. (2008). *Report on public health administration and services*. Tokyo.

Japan, Ministry of Health, Labour and Welfare. (2010). *Heisei 22 nendo shussho ni kansuru Tokei no gaikyo*. Tokyo.

JASE (Japanese Association for Sex Education). (2007). *Wakamono no sei hakusho: Dai 6 kai seishonen no seikodo zenkoku chosa hokoku*. Tokyo: Shogakukan.

Kaneko, R., Sasai, T., Kamano, S., Iwasawa, M., Mita, F., & Moriizumi, R. (2008a). Attitudes towards marriage and the family among Japanese singles: Overview of the Thirteenth Japanese National Fertility Survey: Singles. *The Japanese Journal of Population, 6*(1), 51–75.

Kaneko, R., Sasai, T., Kamano, S., Iwasawa, M., Mita, F., & Moriizumi, R. (2008b). Marriage process and fertility of Japanese married couples: Overview of the Thirteenth Japanese National Fertility Survey: Married couples. *The Japanese Journal of Population, 6*(1), 24–50.

Kiernan, K. E. (2002). Cohabitation in Western Europe: Trends, issues and implications. In A. Booth & A. Crouter (Eds.), *Just living together: Implications of cohabitation on families, children, and social policy* (pp. 3–31). Mahwah: Lawrence Erlbaum Associates.

Kirby, D. (2002). Antecedents of adolescent initiation of sex, contraceptive use, and pregnancy. *American Journal of Health Behavior, 26*(6), 473–485.

Kitamura, K. (2009). *Dai 4 kai danjo no seikatsu to ishiki ni kansuru chosa kekka no gaiyo* (Major findings from the fourth round survey on life and consciousness of men and women) *Kazoku to Kenko*, No. 659. Tokyo: Japan Family Planning Association.

Raymo, J. M. (1998). Later marriages or fewer? Changes in the marriage behavior of Japanese women. *Journal of Marriage and the Family, 60*(4), 1023–1034.

Raymo, J. M., & Iwasawa, M. (2008). Bridal pregnancy and spouse pairing patterns in Japan. *Journal of Marriage and Family, 70*(4), 847–860.

Raymo, J. M., Iwasawa, M., & Bumpass, L. (2009). Cohabitation and family formation in Japan. *Demography, 46*(4), 785–803.

Retherford, R. D., Ogawa, N., & Matsukura, R. (2001). Late marriage and less marriage in Japan. *Population and Development Review, 27*, 65–102.

Sato, R. (2007). Japan. In F. C. Billari, M. Caltabiano, & G. Dalla Zuanna (Eds.), *Sexual and affective behaviour of students: An International Research* (pp. 133–153). Padua: G. CLEUP.

Sato, R., & Iwasawa, M. (2006). Contraceptive use and induced abortion in Japan: How is it so unique among the developed countries? *The Japanese Journal of Population, 4*(1), 33–54.

Sato, R., Shiraishi, N., & Bando, R. (2008). *Induced abortion in Japan: A demographic analysis of its trends and causes* (Working Paper Series E, No. 22). Tokyo: National Institute of Population and Social Security Research.

Sato, R., Shiraishi, N., Beppu, M., & Tanaka, K. (2010). Changing transition to adulthood: Youth and postwar social and demographic transformation in Japan. In R. Sato (Ed.), *The changing transition to adulthood in Japan: Current demographic research and policy implications* (pp. 139–154). Tokyo: National Institute of Population and Social Security Research.

Teitler, J. O. (2002). Trends in youth sexual initiation and fertility in developed countries: 1960–1995. *Annals of the American Academy of Political and Social Science, 580*, 134–152.

Tsuya, N. (2009). Gakureki to koyo anteisei no parutonerushipu keisei heno eikyo (The impact on the formation of partnership between workers' educational background and stable employment). *Jinko Mondai Kenkyu, 65*(2), 45–63.

Yamamoto, B. A. (2009). A window on trends and shifting interpretations of youth sexual behaviour: The Japan Association of Sex Education's '*Wakamono no Sei*' *Hakusho* Reports from 1975 to 2007. *Social Science Japan Journal, 12*(2), 277–284.

Chapter 9
Sexless Marriages in Japan: Prevalence and Reasons

Yoshie Moriki, Kenji Hayashi, and Rikiya Matsukura

9.1 Introduction

We explore the determinants of the frequency of sexual intercourse to reveal the background characteristics of "sexless" marriages. In 1994 the Japan Society of Sexual Science described a couple as being "sexless" "if, despite the absence of unusual circumstances, there has been no consensual intercourse or other sexual contact between them for a month or longer and it is expected that such a state will further persist over a longer period of time" (Abe 2004: 18). Likewise, we define "sexless" couples here as those who are married or cohabitating and have not had any sexual intercourse with the spouse or partner for more than 1 month. Such "sexless" couples have been reported to be more numerous in Japan than one might think, and the reasons for their sexless status have been hypothesized in various magazines and books. However, there have been only a few sociodemographic studies on the topic, partly because of the difficulty of collecting representative data; and as a result little is known about the sexual lives of Japanese couples.

According to studies by biological demographers, the frequency of intercourse and fecundability, which is the monthly probability of conception for a couple who are not trying to avoid pregnancy, are directly and positively related (Bongaarts and Potter 1983; Wood 1994). The probability of conception per menstrual cycle

Y. Moriki (✉)
College of Liberal Arts, International Christian University,
3-10-2 Osawa, Mitakashi, Tokyo 181-8585, Japan
e-mail: moriki@icu.ac.jp

K. Hayashi
National Institute of Public Health, Saitama, Japan

R. Matsukura
Population Research Institute, Nihon University,
Misaki-cho 1-3-2, Chiyoda-ku, 101-8360 Tokyo, Japan

(roughly 1 month) is estimated, for example, to be around 20 % for fertile prime reproductive-age couples who "regularly" engage in unprotected and random intercourse (Bongaarts and Potter 1983: 31–35). Given this probability of conception for sexually active couples, how much the widely discussed prevalence of sexless marriages contributes to Japan's consistently low fertility rates is a natural research question.

The socioeconomic causes of low fertility in Japan, including women's educational levels and their labor force participation rates, have been relatively well studied. Most studies, however, have paid little attention to the linkage between the frequency of marital sexual activity and fertility; the assumption has been that sexual intercourse among married couples of reproductive age occurs with sufficient frequency to result in normal rates of fertility unless the couples use contraception. If sexless marriages in fact prevail among reproductive-age couples, this assumption must be questioned. Current pronatal policies in Japan focus on socioeconomic causes of low fertility; some, for example, aim to create environments in which childrearing and work are more easily combined. These policies may not be very effective if sexual activity is lacking to begin with. In that event, policy attention will have to be shifted, taking into account the nature of and reasons for sexually inactive marriages.

In this chapter we provide an empirical overview of the frequency of sexual intercourse among married Japanese and attempt to determine the actual prevalence of sexless marriages in Japan. We also explore the background of inactive marital sexual life. In doing so, we attempt to shed light on the seemingly "cold" Japanese marital relations and to offer insight into a possibly overlooked cause of Japan's very low fertility. In the following section, we briefly review past studies on the frequency of sexual intercourse within marriages to put the issue into perspective and consider possible reasons for the determinants of this frequency. Next, we explain the data and statistical models that we have used to analyze the background of "sexless" marriages. After discussing the quantitative and qualitative results of the analyses, in the last section we outline a possible link between the low frequency of intercourse and marital fertility rates in Japan.

9.2 Previous Studies

Social scientists have been interested in identifying the factors associated with the frequency of sexual intercourse. Among the factors considered, age has so far received the most attention. Using US data from the 1965 National Fertility Survey (NFS) and controlling for the age of the spouse, parity, and social class, James (1974) reported that the age of males significantly contributed to a commonly observed decline in the frequency of sexual intercourse over time. In contrast, Udry and Morris (1978), comparing the frequency of intercourse reported in the 1965 and 1970 NFS and in the 1974 Family Planning Evaluation Project, suggested that the age of females, rather than that of male partners, was more important, especially in the 1974 survey, when they controlled for the other factors. Udry et al. (1982)

further examined the relative influence of male and female age cross-nationally, using data from Belgium, Japan, Thailand, and the US. The authors confirmed the earlier finding that female age is a significant factor and hypothesized that the aging of women and associated changes in their hormone levels was responsible for the decline in sexual intercourse over time.

Other studies have suggested that age-related decline in sexual intercourse is a function of marital duration. According to Udry (1980), length of marriage was the significant factor explaining the rate of change in intercourse frequency as reported in the US panel data over the period 1974–1978. James (1983) proposed a "honeymoon effect," whereby rates of sexual intercourse decline quickly (by nearly half) during the first year of a marriage, after which the rates halve again over the next 20 years. Greenblat (1983) reported a similar observation from a small-scale survey in the US using open-ended questions: the frequency of intercourse dropped rapidly after the first year of marriage, once the initial "novelty" of sexual activity wore off. Rao and Demaris (1995), using data from the 1988 National Survey of Families and Households (NSFH) in the US and controlling for other sociodemographic variables such as age, parity, education, health status, and religious preference, also found consistently negative effects of the duration of the relationship on the frequency of intercourse.

Which factors—the husband's age, the wife's age, or the duration of marriage—are more important, however, is not yet clear given the interrelations among them. Brewis and Meyer (2005) attempted to untangle the relationship using data from the Demographic and Health Surveys. They confirmed a universal decline in sexual intercourse over the life course in all 19 countries examined in Asia, Africa, and the Americas; but the variable (husband's age, wife's age, or duration of marriage) that best accounted for the decline varied by country. The significant predictor was husband's age in 11 countries, wife's age in 10 countries, and marriage duration in 7 countries. The authors noted that changing reproductive status (e.g., increasing parity) could be confounding the issue, making it more difficult to see the relationship between age-related time variables and patterns of sexual intercourse.

It has been suggested that the current marital context better explains the frequency of sexual intercourse than do typically used "background" variables such as age, education, income, or religious affiliation. According to Edwards and Booth (1976), a perceived decline in spousal affection was one of the most important variables accounting for the reduced frequency of intercourse among married people in Toronto, Canada. Except for age, background characteristics such as husband's occupational status, spouses' education, and wife's employment status did not appear to be significant. Greenblat (1983) further elaborated on this issue, relying on qualitative data. In her study, such indicators as education and religion had little importance in explaining the present rates of sexual intercourse. Interestingly, what explained the current rate of intercourse most was the frequency in the first year of a marriage; couples set a pattern of intercourse during the first year. Even so, the initial rate, whatever it was, usually declined with time as a married couple became involved in daily life filled with work and parenting responsibilities and grew less interested in making time for sexual intercourse.

In a more recent study exploring the notion that couples become "too busy to have sex" with the passage of time and their increasing involvement in married daily life, Genda and Kawakami (2006) investigated the relationship between work patterns and the frequency of sexual intercourse in Japan. Their results suggest that long working hours suppress the frequency of intercourse among married Japanese: the longer the working hours, the lower the frequency. There has also been a suggestion that not only the duration of work, but also the work atmosphere, affects the frequency of sexual intercourse in the work-conscious society of Japan. According to Genda and Saito (2007), the experience of work-related problems such as losing a job decreases the desire to have sex, whereas a positive work environment is associated with a higher frequency of sexual intercourse. These findings indicate that social systems can have significant effects on such a private matters as the frequency of sexual intercourse, and thus call for more attention to the sociocultural context of the issue.

9.3 Data

Our data come from the National Survey of Work and Family, conducted by the Nihon University Population Research Institute in cooperation with the World Health Organization in April 2007. The survey covered a wide range of topics related to the work and the family life of the Japanese, including information about the demographic and socioeconomic characteristics of the respondents and their spouses, marriage decisions, childbearing and rearing, old-age care, birth history, working conditions, contraceptive use, experience of infertility, and sexual activities. This was the first scientific survey in Japan that asked married and cohabiting respondents about the frequency of sexual intercourse with their spouse or the cohabiting partner, making it possible to estimate the frequency of sexual intercourse within marriage.[1]

The target population of the survey was men and women aged 20–59 living in Japan. A total of 9,000 people randomly selected by means of a two-stage cluster sampling method were contacted about completing the survey questionnaire. A copy of the questionnaire was left for each respondent to fill in and was picked up at a later date. After the first round of data collection, people whose responses could not be collected (in most cases because they were away from home when the questionnaires were collected) were contacted through the mail. Respondents from

---

[1] We are aware of only two other scientific and representative datasets that have information on the frequency of sexual intercourse in Japan. One is derived from the Japanese General Social Surveys of 2000 and 2001, which targeted men and women 20–89 years old. It asked about the frequency of sexual intercourse over the preceding year without specifying the sexual partner. The other is from the Survey on Life and Attitudes of Men and Women conducted in 2004, 2006, 2008, and 2010, with a target population of men and women aged 16–49. That survey asked respondents who had ever had sex about the number of sexual encounters they had had within the previous month.

the original round of data collection and those from the follow-up period were not statistically different in their characteristics. The final response rate of the survey was 51.4 % (number of returned questionnaires divided by the number of cases contacted). For the following analysis, we weighted the sample to match the age–sex profile of the Japanese population in 2007.

Adopting the definition of "sexless" used by the Japan Society of Sexual Science mentioned earlier, we define "sexless" married persons as those who are married or cohabiting and have not had any sexual intercourse with the spouse for more than 1 month. Our survey contained one structured question asking about the frequency of sexual intercourse, and it was answered by only one partner. The answer to this question, "How often have you had sexual intercourse *with your spouse* during the past year?" was used to identify the sexless couples. The answer categories were (1) almost every day, (2) two or three times a week, (3) approximately once a week, (4) approximately once in 2 weeks, (5) approximately once a month, (6) approximately once in 2 months, (7) approximately once or twice in 6 months, (8) not at all, and (9) other. The respondents giving answers 6, 7, or 8 were considered to be sexless.

Several points about the data should be noted. First is the low overall response rate (51.4 %). Given the increasing difficulty of obtaining cooperation from survey respondents in Japan, especially in urban areas, we believe that the response rate is acceptable. Second, as one might expect, the question about the respondent's frequency of sexual intercourse had a fairly high nonresponse rate (13 %), causing the overall response rate to be even lower, 44 %.[2] By comparison, in the Japanese General Social Survey, 46.8 % of respondents said they did not want to answer a similar question on the frequency of intercourse (Genda and Kawakami 2006: 85), showing the difficulty of obtaining this sort of information. Nonetheless, we have tested whether the missing cases affected the logistic results and did not find any significant effects.

9.4 Frequency of Sexual Intercourse and the Prevalence of Sexless Marriages

Tables 9.1, 9.2 and 9.3 provide an overview of the frequency of sexual intercourse during the year prior to the survey, as reported by the respondents who were married or cohabitating with the current partner for the first time and who had been in the relationship for longer than 12 months. Surprisingly, the highest percentage of respondents (24 %) indicated they did not have any intercourse over the past year (Table 9.1). Among those who did have sexual intercourse over the past year, 15 % said it was about once or twice in 6 months. If the reported information is accurate—and we find no reason to believe it is not—45 % of respondents (the sum

---

[2] $(1 - 0.13) \times 0.51 = 0.44$.

Table 9.1 Frequency of marital intercourse during the past year (percentage distribution): Japan, 2007

Reported frequency (weighted %)	Men	Women	Both sexes
Every day	0	0	0
2–3 times a week	4	3	3
Once a week	11	11	11
Once in 2 weeks	15	12	13
Once a month	14	13	13
Once in 2 months	6	6	6
Once or twice in 6 months	16	13	15
Not at all	22	26	24
Other	1	1	1
No answer	11	15	13
Total	100	100	100
N	1,095	1,369	2,464

Table 9.2 Frequency of marital intercourse during the past year (percentage distribution), by wife's age: Japan, 2007

	Age group				
Reported frequency (weighted %)	20s	30s	40s	50s	Total
Once a week or more	29	19	12	8	14
Once in 2 weeks	25	14	12	10	13
Once a month	15	17	13	11	13
Once in 2 months	4	6	8	5	6
Once in 6 months	10	16	15	15	15
Not at all	7	15	24	37	24
Other	2	2	1	0	1
No answer	8	11	15	14	13
Total	100	100	100	100	100
N	143	683	756	844	2,464

of those answering "not at all," "once or twice in 6 months," and "once in 2 months") were "sexless" (not having sexual intercourse for more than 1 month) as defined by the Japan Society of Sexual Science. Although this figure seems extremely high and one may suspect the reliability of the data, it should be emphasized that the percentage found to be sexless in our data is similar to the one found in the Fourth Survey on Life and Attitudes of Men and Women conducted in 2008. That survey, targeting Japanese men and women of ages 16–49, found that 37 % of married respondents were sexless, using the same definition of "sexlessness" (Kitamura 2009: 584)—a percentage comparable to the 39 % of our respondents under age 50 who were sexless. The reported response rate for that survey was 54.1 % (Japan Family Planning Association 2008: p. 1 of the preface).

Table 9.3 Frequency of marital intercourse during the past year among male and female respondents wanting a child or another child (percentage distribution), by age group: Japan, 2007

	Age group			
Reported frequency (weighted %)	20s	30s	40s	Total
Once a week or more	36	20	18	23
Once in 2 weeks	24	18	12	18
Once a month	10	20	12	16
Once in 2 months	7	7	6	7
Once in 6 months	9	13	18	13
Not at all	6	11	21	11
Other	4	3	1	3
No answer	5	9	12	8
Total	100	100	100	100
N	97	289	96	482

It is hard to say what the "normal" frequency of sexual intercourse is, but compared with data from other countries, the frequencies observed in our data seem low. For example, the average frequency of intercourse in the previous month reported in the 1988 NSFH was 6.6 times for males and 7.0 times for females (Rao and De Maris 1995: 142); that US sample was limited to respondents who had entered into their relationship within the previous 5 years. The comparable frequencies for our respondents (obtained by adjusting our respondents to match the NSFH sample) are only 3.3 times for males and 3.4 times for females, implying a notably lower level of sexual activity among Japanese couples.[3] The notion that the Japanese tend to have infrequent sexual intercourse seems to accord with a less scientific study conducted in 2005 by the condom company Durex, using an Internet-based survey (for which recruitment was completely voluntary) covering 41 countries. That study concluded that the Japanese were the least sexually active people among those surveyed. Average frequency of sexual intercourse reported by the survey respondents was 103 times a year globally, whereas for Japanese respondents it was only 45 (Durex Global Sex Survey 2005: 20).

Table 9.2 provides further evidence of Japanese couples' low frequency of intercourse by breaking down the frequency according to the wife's age. Not surprisingly, the frequency declines with age; for example, the percentage of women who did not have any intercourse over the past year increases from 7 % among wives 20–29 years old to 15 % (ages 30–39), 24 % (ages 40–49), and 37 % (ages 50–59). The striking finding is that even women in the major reproductive ages of

---

[3] Udry et al. (1982) reported a higher frequency of marital intercourse in Japan in the 1970s than that found here. Besides differences in social conditions between the 1970s and 2007, the data in their study came from patients at obstetrical hospitals and family planning facilities in the Tokyo–Yokohama area; and because of possible biases associated with the data collection sites, it is hard to compare the frequencies. (See Coleman 1981 for details of the data used by Udry et al.)

the twenties and thirties reported low frequencies of sexual intercourse. Only 29 % of women between ages 20 and 29 had sexual intercourse once a week or more, and 25 % and 15 %, respectively, had intercourse only once every 2 weeks and once a month. More than one fifth (21 %) of women in this age group were in sexless marriages; that is, they had sexual intercourse less often than once a month. Moreover, for women of ages 30–39, significantly fewer of them (19 %) had weekly intercourse, whereas 37 % of them were in sexless unions. Given that a woman's average age of first birth in Japan was 29.1 in 2005, and that the percentage of extramarital births was only 2.0 % in 2005 (Japan, Ministry of Health, Labour and Welfare 2007: 118, 127), the high prevalence of reproductive-age women in sexless marriages should be viewed as a matter of concern for Japanese fertility. This finding also provides support for the argument that the frequency of sexual intercourse among Japanese couples must be low because the very low fertility in Japan was achieved despite a low use prevalence of modern contraceptive methods and declining abortion rates (Sato 2008).

Table 9.3 suggests that even respondents who said they wanted to have a child (or another child), did not necessarily have frequent sexual intercourse with their partner. The data show that less than one fourth (23 %) of respondents desiring a child had sexual intercourse once a week or more, 18 % had intercourse once every 2 weeks, and 16 % had intercourse once a month. Curiously, 31 % appeared to be in sexless marriages, including 11 % of them who reported not having intercourse even once over the previous year. An implication of this finding is that even if the respondents wanting to have a child were physically capable (i.e., not infertile), the probabilistic nature of fecundability implies that some would have to wait for a long time to conceive. According to the fecundability and associated conception-wait estimation model proposed by Bongaarts and Potter (1983: 34), the duration of average conception wait for women in their prime reproductive years is about 12 months when a couple has unprotected intercourse randomly four times per menstrual cycle, whereas the average wait can be as long as 43 months when there is intercourse only once per cycle. In our data, the 11 % of respondents who reported not having had intercourse even once over the previous year would not, of course, have a chance of (natural) conception. In addition, the 20 % who had had intercourse less than once a month and the 16 % who had had intercourse once a month might have to wait more than 3 years, on average, or even longer if the wife was older, unless they deliberately adjusted the timing of intercourse to improve their chances of conception.

To address the growing demand for infertility treatment in Japan, the government has started to subsidize some of the costs. For instance, currently 150,000 yen (about USD 1,500) is provided per in vitro fertilization treatment up to twice a year for a total of 5 years (*The Nikkei* 17 March 2010). Policy measures aimed at helping medically infertile couples conceive are needed and should be welcomed. Nonetheless, we have to be careful about using the terms "infertility" and "infecundity." Both refer to an inability to conceive within a certain period of exposure to unprotected intercourse, but various fields define that period of exposure differently. A 2-year period is recommended as the epidemiological definition by the World Health Organization (Rutstein and Shah 2004: 3). The issue here is that, given the infrequency of exposure to unprotected intercourse among the married couples observed in our data, a Japanese couple can enter an "infertile" state for behavioral rather than biological reasons. Interestingly, the Japanese physician who originally coined the term "sexless couples" has reported that a married patient asked him if there was any way the couple could conceive without having sex (Abe 2004: 21). The picture of sexual abstinence among married Japanese presented in this section suggests that that patient was not necessarily an extreme case. For some Japanese, the act of having sexual intercourse with their spouse may not be a simple issue; indeed, marriage and sexual intercourse are not firmly linked. Thus, in Japan, the status of marriage by itself is probably a poor measure of the exposure to the probability of pregnancy. In the following section, we explore the reasons for the infrequency of sexual intercourse among married couples in Japan.

9.5 Determinants of Sexless Marriages

We estimated the determinants of sexless marriages with a logistic regression model in which the dependent variable was being "sexless" as defined by the Japan Society of Sexual Science—that is, married to or cohabiting with the same partner for longer than 12 months and not having had sexual intercourse for more than 1 month. Because some indicators relate to future fertility intentions, the logistic analysis includes female respondents of ages 20–49 and male respondents of ages 20–59. Respondents who did not indicate the frequency of intercourse or who responded "other" to the multiple-choice question about frequency of intercourse are excluded from the analysis. Reasons given for answering "other" included pregnancy, sickness, and temporary absence of the spouse. It should be noted, however, that not everyone who could have been pregnant or whose spouse could have been absent is excluded from the model because the questionnaire did not specifically ask for that information. The final sample size was 1,432 cases after we limited the sample to applicable respondents.

In addition to demographic and socioeconomic characteristics of the respondents, we included other independent variables in the model to assess the effects of the marital relationship, work, and childrearing responsibilities on the couples' frequency of sexual intercourse. The appendix table (Table 9.7) shows the means and standard deviations of the independent variables.

9.5.1 Demographic Factors

Because the reporting of sexual frequency can differ according to the sex of the respondent (Rao and De Maris 1995), males tending to report greater frequency than females (Levinger 1966), we included the sex of the respondent in the model to control for a possible reporting bias. This variable also controls for potential sampling biases if one sex or the other is more likely to have participated in a survey. Moreover, we included this variable out of a concern that the term "sexual intercourse" could be perceived differently by the two sexes, and husbands and wives might have defined "having sexual intercourse" differently.[4] We thought about dividing the sample by sex, but because of the size limitation of the sample decided not to split it for this study.

To estimate the confounding effects of age, we controlled for the ages of both the respondent and the spouse with categorical variables ranging from less than 35 years, 35–39 years, 40–44 years, 45–49 years, 50–54 years, and 55 years or older. For females, however, we included only respondents (or wives of male respondents) less than 50 years old in the analysis because some independent variables were related to future fertility intentions.

We included as an independent variable the self-assessed health status of both the respondent and his or her spouse, using the categories of healthy and not healthy. Each respondent provided a health assessment for himself or herself, choosing from the following structured responses: "very healthy," "not in perfect health but not sick either," "ill and sometimes having to stay in bed," and "ill and having to stay in bed all day." Respondents answering "very healthy" were considered to be healthy for this model. Rao and De Maris (1995) found that good health in US males was positively and significantly related to their rates of sexual intercourse.

9.5.2 Socioeconomic Factors

For the socioeconomic variables, we chose first the employment status of the husband and wife, as reported by respondents. We divided this variable dichotomously for males as working full-time or other, whereas for females we divided it into four categories: working full-time, working part-time, being self-employed or working in a family business, and being a housewife. According to Genda and Saito (2007), Japanese wives who worked part-time were more likely than wives who worked full-time to have sexless marriages if their husbands were full-time employees, a result indicating that the mere fact that a woman works full-time does not lead to a decrease in sexual intercourse.

We also selected husband's working hours during the previous week as an independent variable. Response categories for this variable were less than 50, 50–59, and 60 or more hours. Since the 1980s the Japanese government has introduced various policy measures to encourage shorter working hours, and the efforts have produced some positive outcomes, including a reduction in the annual average number of working hours to around 1,800 (Ogura 2006). This average, however, disguises the fact that workers are becoming polarized into two groups: part-time

---

[4]Because the survey question specifically asked about the frequency of sexual intercourse with the spouse, the level of reporting should not be statistically different between the sexes if these possible sources of biases are controlled.

workers and full-time workers who work long hours (*The Nikkei*, 15 October 2006). To address the problem of long working hours, the government has been promoting a balance between work and personal life. In the government's policy document (Japan, Ministry of Health, Labour and Welfare 2008), working more than 60 h per week is considered working too long, and reducing the percentage of such workers is one of its targets. About 20 % of Japanese males worked more than 60 h per week in 2006 (Japan, Ministry of Internal Affairs and Communications 2007: calculated from Table 26). Men working long hours have little time to spend at home with their families and may not have enough time or energy for sexual relations with their wives. For example, someone who works 60 h a week is assumed to be working, on average, 12 h a day if he works 5 days a week; in this case, he would be leaving his workplace about 9 p.m., commuting to his home for about 1 h (if he is lucky), and arriving home only after 10 p.m. According to Kitamura (2009: 584), results from the Fourth National Survey on Life and Attitude of Men and Women suggest that two main response categories chosen as reasons for not having more positive attitudes toward sex are "being tired from work" (18.8 %) and "after pregnancy and childbirth, no specific reason" (18.1 %).

Our third socioeconomic variable, husband's yearly income, as reported by the respondent, was included as an indicator for social status. Previous studies (e.g., Greenblat 1983) have not found a clear association between social status and rates of sexual intercourse. A recent US study that specifically examined the relationship between income level, the frequency of sexual intercourse, and the number of partners also did not show significant effects of income (Blanchflower and Oswald 2004). Genda and Saito's (2007) study using Japanese data, however, found that people earning less than 3.5 million yen per year (roughly USD 35,000) had a significantly higher probability of being sexless than those earning more. We did not include the educational level of either the husband or the wife in our final model as it was not a significant indicator in our preliminary analysis.

9.5.3 Family Factors

The family factors we chose for our analysis were duration of marriage (in months), the presence of children, and whether a child (or another child) was wanted. Previous studies have found that the frequency of intercourse declines with the duration of marriage (e.g., Greenblat 1983; James 1983; Udry 1980). We therefore included this variable as a squared term, hypothesizing that couples in longer marriages would be more likely than others to be sexless.

We coded responses to the question about the presence of children into three categories: no children, one or more children under age 3, and children over age 3 only. If parents had children both younger and older than age 3, their responses were coded as the second category. Respondents with infants were expected to have a higher probability of being sexless as they would be busy with childcare tasks and might not have time for sexual activities. Greenblat (1983), analyzing qualitative interview data in the US, concluded that fatigue caused by caring for children reduced the frequency of sexual intercourse. Our original intention in including this variable was to capture the shortage of time and energy during the childrearing years, as shown by Greenblat's study. We hypothesized that the presence of infants would not reduce parents' desire for sexual intercourse but would limit the time available for it. Moreover, in Japanese society parents are encouraged to sleep next to their young children (Caudill and Plath 1974; Small 1999). This practice further reduces opportunities for sexual intimacy. Thus, we theorized that the direction of causation was from the lack of time, energy, and opportunity for sexual intercourse associated with parenting to the state of being sexless.

We considered including parity in the model. As Brewis and Meyer (2005) indicate, however, there is an unclear causal relationship between the number of children and the frequency of sexual intercourse. That is, it is difficult to determine whether having more (or fewer) children influences the frequency of sexual activity or whether instead couples with higher (or lower) frequency have more (or fewer) children. Our preliminary analyses did not show a statistically significant effect for parity, and therefore we decided not to include this variable in the final model. Moreover, as the number of children that the respondents have is correlated with the duration of marriage, inclusion of parity as an independent variable would cause the problem of multicollinearity. We think that the regression model eventually should be fitted separately for respondents by each parity, but that level of specification is beyond the scope of the current study and is reserved for future analyses based on a larger sample. Nevertheless, our model captures some effects of parity by including the question on the presence of children and by specifying three choices of answer.

Our third family factor was whether the respondent wanted a child (or another child). It is common sense to expect that couples who want a child would have a higher frequency of sexual intercourse and be less likely to have a sexless union than those who do not want a child (or more children). As we have seen in Table 9.3, however, only 41 % of respondents who wanted a child or another child were having sexual intercourse once a week or more (23 %) or once in 2 weeks (18 %). Therefore, we included the desire or lack of desire for a child (or another child) in the model to clarify the effects of future fertility intentions.

9.5.4 Marital Quality and Couple Factors

Our model included three factors hypothesized to influence the frequency of sexual intercourse: spouse-related stress, risk of divorce, and the type of marriage. To assess the first, our questionnaire contained the following question: "Do you usually feel stressed out?" Respondents who answered "Yes" or "Yes, to a certain extent" were further asked to identify the reasons for the stress. The three answer categories were "My work is not going well," "Housework and/or childrearing is not going well," and "My relationship with my spouse is not good." Responses indicating spouse-related stress were coded yes for this variable, no otherwise. Drawing on previous findings that the state of marital relations influences the frequency of intercourse (Edwards and Booth 1976), we expected that respondents reporting spouse-related stress would have a higher probability of being sexless than other respondents. We did not include the other two stress-related variables in our model because they typically concern only one partner (i.e., work stress for men and childrearing stress for women).

We included the risk of divorce as an indicator of marital quality. Respondents who had thought about getting divorced were coded as being at risk, whereas those who had not considered divorce were coded as not being at risk. Those in a troubled marriage, we hypothesized, would have less interest in engaging in sexual intercourse with the spouse and would be more likely to be sexless. Of course, it is possible for a sexless marriage to cause a divorce, and a reversal of causation should be considered. In most Japanese marriages, however, sustaining family life, especially when there is a child, is more respected than pursuing the satisfaction of sexual interest; and not having (enough) sexual intercourse is not usually considered a sufficient reason for divorce (Genda and Saito 2007). We therefore included the risk of divorce as a predictor of sexless marriage in the model.

Arranged marriages, called *omiai*, are still practiced in Japan. In our survey, about 10 % of respondents reported that their marriages had been arranged. Their responses to the question about the type of marriage were coded yes, while those who married for other reasons, including romantic love, were coded no. The effect of *omiai* on the frequency of sexual intercourse is hard to predict. Those who marry through *omiai* may be more likely to be sexless, when other factors are controlled, than those who marry for love, as they may have a weaker attachment to their spouse. On the other hand, couples who marry through *omiai* may engage in more sexual activity after marrying than other couples because of the novelty of intercourse with each other.

9.5.5 Other Factors

Finally, we included in our model two other factors thought to possibly influence sexual activity: area of current residence and co-residence with parents. A respondent's current residence was coded as urban or rural. Since urban life offers various attractions that compete with time for engaging in sexual activities, we hypothesized that urban respondents might be less inclined to pursue sexual intercourse with their spouse. They may also have long and stressful commutes on trains, which would reduce time for having sexual intercourse and increase fatigue. The co-residence rate in Japan is still fairly high, with about 15 % of married persons living with either their parents or their in-laws (Japan, Ministry of Internal Affairs and Communications 2008: calculated from Table 16). We included this variable to control for possible interventions by parents or parents-in-law. We hypothesized that co-residents might feel uncomfortable having sexual intercourse in the same house as their parents.

9.6 Results

Table 9.4 presents the results of the logistic regression model estimating the effects of the factors considered important in accounting for Japanese sexless marriages. On the relative importance of age-related variables, the issue discussed extensively in previous studies, husband's age appears to be a significant predictor when we control for other factors including wife's age and the duration of marriage. As expected, the probability of being sexless was higher for men older than 35. Wife's age shows significance only for women in their forties, those aged 40–44 and those aged 45–49 being more likely to be sexless than those less than 35 years old.

Among other demographic indicators included in our model, the respondent's sex and the husband's health status were statistically significant. As expected, husband's good health status was negatively related to sexlessness, while that of the wife was not a significant factor. On the other hand, contrary to the expectation that males might exaggerate the frequency of their sexual intercourse, the percentage of husbands reporting their marriages as being sexless was higher (48 %) than that of wives (42 %). A possible explanation for this result is that the age range specified in the model was higher for males (below age 59) than for females (below age 49). Another interpretation is that husbands and wives perceive the same sexual activities in different ways. For example, more wives than husbands may have considered a sexual act not involving penetration as intercourse. If this interpretation is accurate, it implies that marital sex among some Japanese couples may not necessarily entail intercourse.

This hypothesis is speculative at this point, but a vignette from our focus-group discussions suggests that it warrants investigation. One wife in her thirties who had no children asked the interviewer hesitantly whether it was normal for a husband to request his wife several times a week to provide him with oral sex. She also said that she might be able to conceive if her husband were willing to engage in actual intercourse more often with her.

As hypothesized, spouse-related stress and divorce risk were both significantly and positively related to sexlessness. Our results confirm findings reported by Edwards and Booth (1976) that the immediate marital context rather than respondents' social background (occupational status, educational level, and religious identity) explains the frequency of intercourse. Husband's income level proved not to be statistically significant in our analysis either. When we controlled for the current marriage conditions, the general social status of the couple did not directly affect the frequency of intercourse. This finding was not surprising. Given that sexual intercourse within marriage usually involves communication with the partner and the expression of affection, it is no wonder couples in a troubled marriage have a higher likelihood than others of having a sexless marriage.

Couples with children under age 3 were also much more likely than others to be sexless when marriage quality is accounted for, confirming the Greenblat's (1983) findings. The percentage of those who were sexless increases from 45 % for those without a child to 56 % for those with at least one child under age 3. One

Table 9.4 Results of logistic regression analysis predicting sexless marriages

Predictor variable	Percentage and significance	
Observed percentage of sexless respondents	45	
Respondent's sex		
Male	48	**
Female[#]	42	
Age of husband		
< 35[#]	31	
35–39	51	**
40–44	50	**
45–49	52	**
50–54	50	**
55+	64	**
Age of wife		
< 35[#]	38	
35–39	42	
40–44	49	*
45–49	57	**
Health status of husband		
Healthy	43	*
Not healthy[#]	49	
Health status of wife		
Healthy	44	
Not healthy[#]	48	
Employment status of husband		
Full-time	47	*
Other[#]	40	
Employment status of wife		
Full-time	43	
Part-time	42	
Self-employed	49	
Housewife[#]	53	
Weekly working hours of husband		
< 50 h[#]	42	
50–59 h	43	
60+ h	54	**
Yearly income of husband (ten thousands of yen)		
125	44	
250	45	
350	46	
500	47	
750	49	
1,000	51	

(continued)

Table 9.4 (continued)

Predictor variable	Percentage and significance	
Duration of marriage (in years)		
2	43	
4	44	
6	45	
10	46	
16	48	
21	44	
Presence of children		
No child[#]	45	
One or more children under age 3	56	**
Children over age 3 only	42	
Wanting a(nother) child		
Yes	43	
No[#]	46	
Spouse-related stress		
Yes	58	**
No[#]	44	
Divorce risk		
Yes	54	**
No[#]	40	
Type of marriage		
Arranged	47	
Other[#]	45	
Area of current residence		
Urban	46	
Rural[#]	40	
Co-residence with parent(s)		
Yes	46	
No[#]	45	
Log likelihood = −884.441		
$N = 1{,}432$		

Note: # indicates a reference category
*p < 0.10; **p < 0.05

interpretation of this result is that having an infant increases the risk of being sexless because of time-management problems.

In addition to the time- and energy-consuming aspects of having young children, the presence of a child under age 3 means that the couple has recently produced a child. The relationship between having a child and being sexless requires explanation. There is a possibility that some couples purposefully reduce the frequency of sexual intercourse, depending on the number of children they have, particularly if they are conscious about their reproductive goals.

Table 9.5 Percentages of respondents in sexless unions during the previous year, by respondent's age and parity

	Weighted percentage, by age group				
Parity	20s	30s	40s	50s	All age groups
0	14	34	57	74	44
1	26	44	64	83	52
2	29	40	55	70	56
3+	0	36	43	54	46
N	156	575	544	730	2,005

Table 9.6 Percentages of respondents in sexless union during the previous year for those wanting a child or another child, by respondent's age and parity

	Weighted percentage, by age group			
Parity	20s	30s	40s	All age groups
0	14	25	53	44
1	25	39	51	52
2	42	36	56	56
3+	0	20	35	21
N	124	285	76	485

As Table 9.5 indicates, when sexless status is tabulated by parity, higher percentages of respondents with one child (52 %) and of those with two children (56 %) were in sexless unions than were those without a child (44 %). Curiously, the percentages of sexless unions for childless couples (44 %) and those with more than three children (46 %) were similar, suggesting that the latter was a unique group with as yet unidentified characteristics.

Table 9.6 shows that among respondents who indicated a desire for a child, the percentages in sexless unions were higher for those who already had one or two children than for those who did not have any. Among those in their twenties the sexless rate was 14 % for childless respondents and 25 % for those with one child. Similarly, 25 % of childless respondents in their thirties were sexless, but 39 % were so if they already had a child. These results suggest that respondents' seriousness about conceiving a child depended on whether they already had one or not.

After achieving the desired number of children, or even having just one child, Japanese may not give high priority to engaging in sexual intercourse with their spouse as part of their daily married life. The Japanese tendency to prefer family cohesion to conjugal attachment, including sexual bonds, has been reported by Caudill and Plath (1974). The presence of a child under age 3 in this model probably functions as a good indicator of a couple's propensity for family-building.

Finally, the regressions show that the husband's full-time employment status and weekly work hours significantly contributed to sexlessness. Among husbands who worked longer than 60 h per week, the percentage of sexless was 54 %, compared with those who worked less than 50 h (42 %). The sexless percentage for the husbands who worked 50–59 h was not statistically different from those who worked less than 50 h. This finding supports the result of Genda and Kawakami's (2006) study, based on the Japanese General Social Surveys, suggesting that long working hours suppress the frequency of sexual intercourse. In addition, husbands in our survey who worked full-time were significantly more likely to be sexless (47 %) than those working part-time (40 %).

About 22 % of respondents reported that the husband had worked longer than 60 h during the previous week. The actual percentage of men spending such long hours in work-related activities was probably even higher, since hours spent eating out and drinking with colleagues and business partners—practices commonly observed in Japan—were not likely to be reported as working hours. If we also take into account commuting hours, which were not measured in this survey, work-related hours would have been even longer, leaving fewer hours for family activities, including sexual intercourse.

9.7 Insights from Our Qualitative Data

From focus-group discussions we gained further insights into Japanese sexless marriages. The qualitative data help us better understand the meaning of marriage in Japan and the relationships among work, children, and marital sexual frequency. The focus-group discussion sessions took place in Tokyo in March 2009 with 48 married participants (24 men and 24 women) who resided in the Tokyo Metropolitan Area. Eight discussion groups (four male groups and four female groups), each consisting of six people of various ages, were organized. Male participants aged 20–59 who were working full-time and female participants aged 20–49 who may or may not have been working full-time were selected by a survey company to take part in the discussions. Prior to the start of a session, its purpose was fully explained to the participants, who then gave their consent to take part in the discussion. All discussion sessions were tape-recoded and transcribed by the survey company, ensuring the anonymity of the participants' statements. The sessions with male groups were led by the third author of this chapter (a man), and those with female groups were led by the first author (a woman). We quote below some of the observations made by participants.

Substantiating the time and energy demands of childrearing, some participants said that taking care of young children was tiring, and that they could not consider participating in such a troublesome act as having sex.

> These days, my child has started to be more independent, but when he was smaller, much more care, like breastfeeding, was required. As my wife needs to take care of the child from the moment she wakes up and also has to do housework, she is exhausted. I myself need to go to work early each morning, and after I come home, I have to take care of the child, play with him, give him a bath, and feed him. So I am also tired late at night. Since both of us are extremely tired, having sex is far from our thoughts. [46-year-old man with a 3-year-old child]
>
> If I quit my job and am not racing against time every day, maybe my feelings will change. But right now I am really getting by day-to-day with little extra time; it is really hard for me to do that [have sex] too. [36-year-old woman with two children, 5 and 2 years old]

Participants in virtually every group, both men and women, said that they were not bothered by the fact that their marriage did not involve much sex. They understood that having infrequent sexual intercourse was a natural consequence of the marital and family relationship, and they regarded being sexless as "OK" and "not a serious problem." These participants repeatedly used the phrase "we became a family" to describe their feelings, and some women indicated that being a mother was their primary identity.

> Well, I also do not think there is a problem right now as we function well as a family. But it is rather awkward to answer this type of question [about the frequency of sexual intercourse] since we do not have much of it. [35-year-old man with a 1-year-old child]
>
> We really became family centered. In the beginning, we were not sure if we could raise the child. But after the baby was born, we cooperated well; I feel that we became a family, not like the days when we were cohabitating. [This couple lived together for ten years before marrying. They decided to marry when they found out that she was pregnant.] Both of us became family-centered. For example, meals are cooked at home everyday, household accounts are properly kept. We are even thinking about saving up money to buy a home. [29-year-old woman with a 6-month-old child]
>
> Inside my heart, I used to be a woman before the child was born, but since then, being a mother is the most important part of me. It is like "a mother does not do such a thing" (as having intercourse). [36-year-old woman with two children, 5 and 2 years old]

Many participants thought that sleeping in the same room with a young child (of up to about age 6) was part of being a family, even though the practice discourages sexual intimacy. Thus, the focus-group discussions affirmed the cultural preference of the Japanese to pursue a child-centered lifestyle, which often involves sleeping together; and a sexless marriage may be a part of that arrangement.

> We are now sleeping together, all four of us, using a double and single bed next to each other. Thus we hardly ever have sex. [32-year-old woman with two children, 6 and 4 years old]
>
> I have not felt like having sex since I gave birth to my child. In particular, I am not thinking about having sex in the bedroom, as there is a child next to us. I would decline if I could. As for the frequency, it is rare and I cannot even remember well; maybe about once every six months or so. [26-year-old woman with a 1-year-old child]
>
> Basically, [the frequency of sexual intercourse is] not often. I do not feel like taking the trouble of having sex before going to sleep. This is different from before we had a child. [35-year-old man with a 3-year-old child]

For some participants, however, sexless marital relations were a problem if they wanted to have another child. Indeed, several participants in their twenties were wondering how they could conceive a second child without frequently engaging in sexual intercourse. For them, "planning well" (i.e., having unprotected intercourse at the right time of the month) seemed to be the answer, and older participants agreed that it was the way they had obtained their desired number of children.

> While I was pregnant [with the first child], we could not have sex at all as my stomach tended to tighten up easily. After the birth, I was worried about breastfeeding, so we did not have sex even after the delivery. We probably did not have sex for over one year .... Then, after the first child was weaned, we wanted a second one. Since then, we only had sex for the purpose of making the second child. [39-year-old woman, currently pregnant, with a 2-year-old child]

> As for our second child, we conceived the child because we wanted it. We really made an effort to get pregnant. Because we managed to conceive, we thought we no longer needed to have sex. [At that time when we were trying to conceive,] I took my temperature and checked the day of ovulation. It was more difficult to conceive than we thought it would be. But because I conceived, we do not need to have sex anymore; we already have two children. [36-year-old woman with two children, 6 and 4 years old]
>
> As for the frequency of intercourse itself, I prefer not to do it often .... However, I want a second child. I wonder if it is possible to conceive with pinpoint sex. [26-year-old woman with a 1-year-old child]

It is good when family planning eventually works out, but having sexual intercourse on demand sometimes leads to pressure and potentially to marital discord, especially when women are approaching their "biological limit." For the cases described below, securing the availability and willingness of the husband for sex on a particular day was a critical issue, making sexual intercourse even more of a "child-centered" activity, rather than an expression of affection as a couple. The quoted comments also indicate the importance of controlling personal time when a couple is trying to conceive by having sexual intercourse at the right time of the month.

> As I got older, from about age 29, I started to think about giving birth. Then the frequency of intercourse increased a little bit. I was able to conceive naturally once, but the pregnancy failed. Then my feelings changed. Now my aim [in having intercourse with my husband] is to have a child. I now know the right timing of conception. So, our sex has ended up concentrated during the right period. I send emails to my husband saying "Please come home early tonight," but I have realized that he does not like receiving such messages. [34-year-old woman without a child]
>
> My husband's work requires physical strength, and it is hard on him. So when he comes home tired, he says "Sorry" even on the right day [for conception]. I am not pushing him to make love to me all the time; I am just saying "Today is the right time. I only have a chance every 60 days" [as I have an irregular menstrual cycle]. [28-year-old woman with a 1-year-old child]

Although we need to be careful about generalizing from the statements quoted above, the qualitative data from the focus-group discussions have revealed a certain aspect of Japanese marriages and the meaning of marriage in Japan. Having sex with a spouse does not necessarily constitute an essential part of the Japanese marriage; and thus, in the view of the many Japanese, the sexless marriage may be a comfortable state as long as the partners manage to produce their desired number of children and they function well as a family. The participants of the focus groups also confirmed that the sexless state does not usually lead to divorce, because not having sexual intercourse *per se* does not mean spouses do not have feelings for each other. Nonetheless, focusing exclusively on children and family-building without paying sufficient attention to the bond between spouses may lead to serious marital problems. In this respect, the statement by a woman in her forties—"I think that having sex once a month is necessary as a polite gesture from the husband as long as we continue to be a wife and husband"—indicates that infrequent or no sexual intercourse may have negative consequences.

9.8 Conclusion

This chapter has provided empirical evidence supporting the commonly held view that a high proportion of Japanese couples have sexless unions. According to the statistically representative data used in the study, the frequency of sexual intercourse among married Japanese is quite low: nearly one fourth of respondents reported having had no sexual intercourse for more than 1 year. The finding that Japanese couples have little sexual intercourse within marriage suggests that the fecundability of Japanese couples may be decreasing, and that completed family size, which has been fairly stable at around two children, will dip below that figure among recent birth cohorts (Kaneko 2009). Of course, this study presents data on current frequency of sexual intercourse rather than longitudinal data. Even if sexual frequencies of married Japanese have not changed, however, what has definitely changed is the average age at marriage: married Japanese women who intend to conceive are older than ever before. The fecundability of married Japanese may be decreasing because a woman's age and her fecundability have been found to be negatively associated (Wood 1994). Thus, if we are to understand the effects of the frequency of sexual intercourse on marital fertility rates, we must consider whether the current low rate of intercourse is sufficient to produce couples' desired number of children.

Another aspect of Japanese society that has changed over time is social disapproval of premarital sexual relations. According to Atoh (2000), although the social norm of associating marriage, sex, and reproduction was firmly observed until the 1970s, the practice has been relaxed in recent years. Yamada (2007) reports that Japanese have less incentive to marry now because they can enjoy sexual relations without marrying. Having sex is no longer an entitlement for married people only. The rapidly growing number of so-called shotgun marriages is evidence of the prevalence of premarital sex in contemporary Japan. According to pooled data from various rounds of the National Survey on Family Planning and the National Survey on Work and Family, for about one third (30 %) of couples married in 2005, conception preceded marriage. For many couples, therefore, sexual relations begin before legal marriage; and when a couple eventually marries, the honeymoon period (when sex is a novelty) can be long over. For this reason it is not surprising that marital duration is not a significant factor in the logistic analysis discussed in this chapter. Since couples are engaging in sexual relations before marriage, we need information on the actual starting time of sexual relations with the current partner for more accurate estimations.

An unexpected insight provided by the focus-group discussions was that sexual intercourse tends to be perceived as having the purpose of producing a child, and the frequency of intercourse within marriage is often influenced by the number of existing children. The implication of this finding is that in estimating the fecundability of Japanese married couples, an assumption of the randomness of intercourse is more likely to hold during the period of marriage before the birth of the first child, whereas after the birth of the first child, sexual intercourse seems to be planned for reproduction. In this connection, the working hours of the spouses call for attention. If couples plan intercourse for the sake of conception, their work schedules become an important factor for the success of their plan and resulting fertility rates as a whole. Letting couples control their work schedules, especially hours worked overtime, will not only be a good in itself, but could also help them achieve their desired number of children. Thus, a key to maintaining the current marital fertility rates could be enabling couples to have a lifestyle in which they can better manage their personal time according to their private needs, including time for sexual intercourse.

One result of the observed emphasis among Japanese couples on the utilitarian function of sexual intercourse—that is, to produce children—and on of the centrality of childrearing within marriage is that sexual intercourse is often ignored because of couples' busy schedules, especially after they have achieved their desired family size. Kitamura (2009) argues that the attitude of the Japanese medical profession, which tends to discourage sexual intercourse during pregnancy, is partly responsible for the disappearance of sexual intercourse from the married life. It is possible that couples become used to the absence of intercourse through the course of pregnancy, child birth, and childrearing; and an act that has been discontinued is difficult to resume, even when children are older and there is more time for intimacy.

Further research on the frequency of sexual intercourse and its effects on Japanese fertility should attempt to identify the segments of the population that seriously intend to conceive but are having difficulty doing so. Kaneko et al. (2008) reported that although a major reason for the intended number of children not reaching the ideal number of children is economic, many respondents cited "not being able to conceive" as a reason. Some of those couples would certainly have been infertile and in need of medical treatment for infertility. However, there is a good possibility that some of them were fertile, or at least as fertile as others earlier in their reproductive lives, but had not conceived as a result of infrequent sexual intercourse. To clarify which might be the case, further studies should make an effort to identify those couples who want a child but are unable to have one for the lack of sufficient sexual contact.

Finally, we need to examine the issue in a broader framework. In particular, we should take a serious look at the incidence of extramarital affairs, even though it is a difficult topic to investigate. The prevalence of sexless marriages does not necessarily imply that married Japanese are not having sex. On the contrary, it is possible that they are compensating for the lack of intercourse within marriage by having intercourse outside of marriage. The frequency of sexual intercourse among the Japanese, especially Japanese males, may not be low as compared with the global level, when the frequencies both inside and outside marriage are considered. The current survey, although it offers one of the few representative datasets related to sexual intercourse, can be improved to cover extramarital sexual activities, including those with the sex industry. We need to have a holistic understanding of people's daily lives, based on the reality of marriage and family life in Japan.

Acknowledgments This work was supported by a grant to the Nihon University Population Research Institute from the Ministry of Education, Culture, Sports, Science and Technology, 2006–2010, in the form of a matching-fund subsidy from the Academic Frontier Project for Private Universities.

Appendix

Table 9.7 A weighted means and standard deviations of independent variables included in the analysis of the frequency of sexual intercourse

Variables	Mean	SD
Respondent's sex: male	0.545	0.498
Age of husband		
35–39	0.190	0.392
40–44	0.210	0.407
45–49	0.185	0.389
50–54	0.109	0.311
55+	0.019	0.139
Age of wife		
35–39	0.232	0.422
40–44	0.204	0.403
45–49	0.213	0.409
Health status of husband: healthy	0.678	0.467
Health status of wife: healthy	0.684	0.465
Employment status of husband: full-time	0.789	0.408
Employment status of wife		
Full-time	0.262	0.44
Part-time	0.289	0.453
Self-employed	0.044	0.206
Weekly working hours of husband		
50–59 h	0.226	0.418
60+ h	0.23	0.421
Yearly income of husband (ten thousands yen)	301.0	335.7
Duration of marriage (months)	138.1	90.7
Presence of children		
One or more under age 3	0.194	0.396
Over age 3 only	0.628	0.484
Wanting another child or more children: yes	0.350	0.477
Spouse-related stress: yes	0.100	0.300
Divorce risk: yes	0.356	0.479
Type of marriage: arranged	0.108	0.310
Area of current residence: urban	0.855	0.352
Co-residence with parent(s): yes	0.278	0.448
N	1,432	

Note: Respondents married (or cohabiting with the current partner) for the first time and in the relationship longer than 12 months are included in the sample. For women, only those aged 20–49 are included in the analysis.

References

Abe, T. (2004). *Sekkusuresu no seishin igaku* (The psychiatry of sexlessness). Tokyo: Chikuma Shobo.
Atoh, M. (2000). *Gendai jinkogaku* (Modern demography). Tokyo: Nippon-Hyoron-sha.
Blanchflower, D. G., & Oswald, A. J. (2004). Money, sex and happiness: An empirical study. *Scandinavian Journal of Economics, 106*(3), 393–415.
Bongaarts, J., & Potter, R. G. (1983). *Fertility, biology, and behavior: An Analysis of the proximate determinants*. New York: Academic.
Brewis, A., & Meyer, M. (2005). Marital coitus across the life course. *Journal of Biosocial Science, 37*(4), 499–518.
Caudill, W., & Plath, D. W. (1974). Who sleeps by whom? Parent–child involvement in urban Japanese families. In T. S. Lebra & W. P. Lebra (Eds.), *Japanese culture and behavior: Selected readings* (pp. 277–312). Honolulu: University of Hawaii Press.
Coleman, S. (1981). The cultural context of condom use in Japan. *Studies in Family Planning, 12*(1), 28–39.
Durex Global Sex Survey. (2005). *Give and receive: 2005 Global Sex Survey results, frequency of sex*. http://www.durex.com/en-JP/SexualWellbeingSurvey/Documents/gss2005result.pdf. Accessed 10 Mar 2011.
Edwards, J. N., & Booth, A. (1976). Sexual behavior in and out of marriage: An assessment of correlates. *Journal of Marriage and Family, 38*(1), 73–80.
Genda, Y., & Kawakami, A. (2006). Shugyo nikyokuka to sei-kodo (Divided employment and sexual behavior). *Nihon Rodo Kenkyu Zasshi* (The Japanese Journal of Labor Studies), *556*, 80–91.
Genda, Y., & Saito, J. (2007). *Shigoto to sekkusu no aida* (Between work and sex). Tokyo: Asahi Shimbun Publications.
Greenblat, C. S. (1983). The salience of sexuality in the early years of marriage. *Journal of Marriage and Family, 45*(2), 289–299.
James, W. H. (1974). Marital coital rates, spouses' ages, family size and social class. *The Journal of Sex Research, 10*(3), 205–218.
James, W. H. (1983). Decline in coital rates with spouses' ages and duration of marriage. *Journal of Biosocial Science, 15*(1), 83–87.
Japan Family Planning Association (2008). *Danjo no seikatsu to ishiki nikansuru chosa hokokusho* (The 4th survey on life and attitudes of men and women: Report). Tokyo: Japan Family Planning Association.
Japan, Ministry of Health, Labour and Welfare. (2007). *Heisei 17 nen jinko-dotai-tokei* (Vital statistics of Japan 2005) (Vol. 1). Tokyo: Health and Welfare Statistics Association.
Japan, Ministry of Health, Labour and Welfare. (2008). *Rodo jikan tou minaoshi gaidorain* (Guidelines for reviewing labor time). http://www.mhlw.go.jp/general/seido/roudou/jikan/dl/honbun.pdf. Accessed 31 Mar 2011.
Japan, Ministry of Internal Affairs and Communications, Statistics Bureau. (2007). *2006 Rodoryoku chosa nempo* (Annual report on the Labour Force Survey 2006). Tokyo: Japan Statistical Association.
Japan, Ministry of Internal Affairs and Communications, Statistics Bureau. (2008). *Heisei-17-nen kokusei chosa, Jinko gaikan shirizu No.5* (2005 population census of Japan, Population overview series No. 5). Tokyo: Japan Statistical Association.
Kaneko, R. (2009). Shorai jinko suikei ni okeru shussho katei settei no wakugumi ni tsuite (On the methodological framework for making fertility assumptions in the population projections for Japan). *Jinko Mondai Kenkyu* (Journal of Population Problems), *65*(2), 1–27.
Kaneko, R., Sasai, T., Kamano, S., Iwasawa, M., Mita, F., & Moriizumi, R. (2008). Marriage process and fertility of Japanese married couples: Overview of the results of the Thirteenth Japanese National Fertility Survey, married couples. *The Japanese Journal of Population, 6*(1), 24–50.

Kitamura, K. (2009). Yunikuna shoshika taisaku heno teian: Kiwado wa danjo-kan no komyunikeshon-sukiru no kojo (A proposal for a unique method for dealing with low fertility: Improvement of communication skill between the sexes as the key word). *Koshu eisei* (The Journal of Public Health Practice), *73*(8), 581–586.

Levinger, G. (1966). Systematic distortion in spouses' reports of preferred and actual sexual behavior. *Sociometry, 29*(3), 291–299.

Ogura, K. (2006). Contemporary working time in Japan: Legal system and reality. *Japan Labor Review, 3*(3), 5–22.

Rao, K. V., & Demaris, A. (1995). Coital frequency among married and cohabiting couples in the United States. *Journal of Biosocial Science, 27*(2), 135–150.

Rustein, S. O., & Shah, I. (2004). *DHS infecundity, infertility, and childlessness in developing countries* (Comparative Reports, No. 9). Calverton: ORC Macro and the World Health Organization.

Sato, R. (2008). Nihon no "cho-shoshika": Sono genin to seisaku taio wo megutte (Very low fertility in Japan: Its causes and policy responses). *Jinko Mondai Kenkyu* (Journal of Population Problems), *64*(2), 10–24.

Small, M. F. (1999). *Our babies, ourselves: How biology and culture shape the way we parent.* New York: Anchor Books.

The Nikkei. (2006, 15 October). Koyo ruru kaikaku (Revisions of employment rules).

The Nikkei. (2010, 17 March). Funin chiryo kakei ni zushiri (Infertility treatment: A heavy burden for the family budget).

Udry, J. R. (1980). Changes in the frequency of marital intercourse from panel data. *Archives of Sexual Behavior, 9*(4), 319–325.

Udry, J. R., & Morris, N. M. (1978). Relative contribution of male and female age to the frequency of marital intercourse. *Social Biology, 25*(2), 128–134.

Udry, J. R., Deven, F. R., & Coleman, S. J. (1982). A cross-national comparison of the relative influence of male and female age on the frequency of marital intercourse. *Journal of Biosocial Science, 14*(1), 1–6.

Wood, J. W. (1994). *Dynamics of human reproduction.* New York: Aldine de Gruyter.

Yamada, M. (2007). *Shoshi shakai Nihon: Mo hitotsu no kakusa no yukue* (Japan as a low-fertility society: The future outlook of yet another discrepancy). Tokyo: Iwanami Shoten.

Chapter 10
Community-Level Effects on the Use of Reproductive Health Services in Rural China

Zheng Wu, Shuzhuo Li, Christoph M. Schimmele, Yan Wei, Quanbao Jiang, and Zhen Guo

10.1 Introduction

The World Health Organization (2008) observes that reproductive health (RH) problems account for 20 % of the global burden of disease for women. The spectrum of RH includes contraception, maternal health care, reproductive-tract and sexually transmitted infections, cervical cancers, and other gynecological morbidities. In this respect, reproductive rights, family planning services, safe contraceptive methods, and regular RH checkups are important for ensuring women's well-being. However, systemic deficiencies in access to RH services are a challenge in developing countries. In rural China there is a considerable gap between the prevalence of RH problems and the utilization of RH services (Kaufman and Fang 2002). A lack of public health care funding and uneven patterns of socioeconomic development potentially contribute to these disparities.

Z. Wu (✉) • C.M. Schimmele
Department of Sociology, University of Victoria, Victoria, BC, Canada
e-mail: zhengwu@uvic.ca

S. Li
Population Research Institute, Xi'an Jiaotong University, Xi'an, China

Y. Wei
Institute for Population and Development Studies, Xi'an University of Finance and Economics, Xi'an, China

Q. Jiang
Institute for Population and Development Studies, Xi'an Jiaotong University, Xi'an, China

Z. Guo
Department of Sociology, Huazhong University of Science and Technology, Wuhan, China

The most salient paradigm for understanding patterns of RH uses an individual-centered approach (Price and Hawkins 2007). In most cases, RH behaviors, service utilization, and outcomes are modeled and explained at the individual or household level, with limited or no consideration of community-level circumstances (Stephenson and Tsui 2002). This inattention to community-level (contextual) effects circumscribes our knowledge about RH disparities. A strict focus on individual characteristics is a limited approach because it neglects the processes through which local-level mechanisms influence a person's range of RH choices and options. Local institutions, kinship groups, social networks, cultural norms, socioeconomic conditions, and policies are an important dimension of RH behaviors (Price and Hawkins 2007).

Few studies examine the effects of community-level characteristics on the use of RH services (Stephenson and Tsui 2002). This study uses multilevel models to examine the relationship between village-level or county-level characteristics and the likelihood of married women having an RH checkup in rural China. To our knowledge, only two prior studies, Short and Zhang (2004) and Chen et al. (2007), have used multilevel data to examine the use of RH services in China, and both focus on the use of maternal services. Our study contributes to the literature in several respects. First, our analysis uses a more inclusive measure of RH service use, which includes gynecological exams, breast exams, ultrasound exams, and screening for diseases. Second, it assesses village-level characteristics for their direct and indirect effects on RH checkup. Third, it considers county-level demographics, introducing an additional contextual dimension (a three-level model) into our understanding of RH service use.

The local environment can be conceptualized in two ways (Yen and Syme 1999). In the first, the local environment is a fixed geographic location or a physical place, such as a workplace, an urban ghetto, or a rural village. The co-occupants of a physical place share its tangible features, which can affect their health outcomes regardless of differences in individual characteristics (Macintyre et al. 2002). For example, neighborhood air pollution is a pervasive characteristic because its health-threatening effect does not discriminate between individuals from different social or economic backgrounds. In addition, a village's or neighborhood's physical attributes can either discourage or encourage help-seeking behaviors and is also a determinant of access to health care services (Ellen et al. 2001). Hence, physical context, such as local amenities, distance from medical facilities, residential crowding, or pollution, represents a common condition that can generate location-specific advantages or disadvantages for health outcomes.

In the second way of conceptualizing the local environment, the environment has a social structural dimension, such as a spatial concentration of socioeconomic deprivation or developmental disadvantages. Robert (1999) has reported a relationship between local socioeconomic development and health outcomes. Net of personal socioeconomic status, residing in an impoverished or an affluent community affects the social distribution of disease (Do and Finch 2008; Ross and Mirowsky 2008). Although a sizable proportion of between-area differences accrue from compositional differences (e.g., spatial concentrations of individuals with low income), aggregate-level socioeconomic characteristics have independent effects. Accordingly, residing in an impoverished neighborhood can decrease a rich person's health chances, whereas residing in an affluent neighborhood can improve a poor person's health chances. Community-level socioeconomic context corresponds with the prevailing social environment and levels of services (Robert 1999). A lack of social organization is a characteristic of numerous low-income communities; and this restricts cooperation, such as information-sharing or pooling of resources, which is essential for ensuring group welfare.

10.2 Background

In 1978 the Chinese government began implementing a process of economic reform to increase average per capita income (living standards) and finance industrial and agricultural modernization. The economic reforms represented a general retreat from Maoist political and economic principles and, therefore, the elimination of the commune-based economic organization and redistribution of national wealth (White 1992). The transition to a market-based system exacerbated preexisting disparities and also generated new patterns of uneven socioeconomic development across rural China (Sun and Dutta 1997). As a pullback from socialism, the commitment to economic reform involved a tacit recognition that there would be a trade-off between egalitarianism and rapid economic growth (Hsiao 1995). To be sure, the economic reforms fostered spectacular economic gains, but not without some deleterious side effects, including an intensification of income disparities between individuals and a widening of interregional differences in socioeconomic development (Benjamin et al. 2008; Hussain and Lanjouw 1994; Yao 1999).

Under Mao, the Chinese Communist Party developed the Cooperative Medical System (CMS), an almost universal health insurance program that was supported through collective funds and public resources (Kaufman and Fang 2002). The CMS provided the peasant masses with equitable access to public health programs, preventative treatments, primary health care, and in-patient services (Bogg et al. 2002). Before 1978, the CMS insured 90 % of rural Chinese and delivered health care via a three-tier medical system consisting of county, township, and village-level facilities and services. The central government financed and managed the county hospitals and township health centers (Blumenthal and Hsiao 2005). The lower-tier health facilities were financed through mandatory commune-generated contributions (and small point-of-service co-payments in some cases) and staffed with so-called barefoot doctors (Kaufman and Fang 2002). The CMS is credited for the remarkable improvements in rural health care between 1952 and 1982 and commensurate reductions in communicable diseases and rates of premature mortality (Hsiao 1995). This system, which was a model of efficient and equitable health care for low-income countries, did not survive the economic reforms.

In rural areas, the reforms transferred the locus of health care financing from the national government to local administrative divisions (e.g., counties and villages) through decentralization and deregulation, opening individual-level and regional gaps in access to and use of health services (Short and Zhang 2004). Between 1978 and 1999 the central government's annual contribution to health care decreased from 32 to 15 % of public and private health care spending (Blumenthal and Hsiao 2005). The replacement of commune-based agricultural production with semi-private household-level production (the Household Responsibility System) eliminated the basis of CMS funding, causing the system's near collapse (Hsiao 1995). By 1985, only 5 % of rural communities were still maintaining their cooperative health services, with a user-pay system substituting CMS-supplied insurance in most places. The heavy reliance on user fees to recoup costs—out-of-pocket fees now account for 58 % of total health care spending—has priced many rural people out of health care services (Wang et al. 2007; Yip and Mahal 2008). As much as 50 % of the Chinese population does not seek required health care because of the steep out-of-pocket costs (Blumenthal and Hsiao 2005: 1167). Although the Chinese government has experimented with rehabilitating the CMS, the effect of this effort on reducing out-of-pocket costs has been limited (Carrin et al. 1999).

The economic reforms introduced a *laissez-faire* approach to the health care sector, which is the primary reason behind regional disparities (Hsiao 1995). With decentralization, local taxation became a core source of health-sector funding, and this favored the developed areas with strong taxation bases (Blumenthal and Hsiao 2005). Decentralization also prevented the redistribution of income from rich to poor regions, eliminating an important mechanism for smoothing the negative effects of interregional developmental gaps. As a consequence, there are considerable interregional differences in the sources of financing, levels of services, and access to health care. Hsiao (1995) observes that there are 15 types of organization and financing of health care services across rural China. The sources of funding range from user-pay services to full cooperative services. A linkage exists between the level of socioeconomic development and the quality and breadth of health care available. In poor areas, local authorities often struggle to afford the salaries of health care professionals or outfit their health stations with basic equipment (Fang 2004).

There is growing evidence of interregional disparities in RH services. At the broadest level, Gu (2003) reports regional-level deficiencies in the provision of RH services that correspond to developmental differences. The RH service situation is the most adverse for women residing in the underdeveloped Western region, which includes 11 provinces and one fifth of the national population, in comparison with China's developed regions. Just over one third of western Chinese women have ever received a checkup for reproductive tract infections (RTIs), in contrast with one half of eastern Chinese women, according to 2001 National Family Planning data. Western Chinese women also face structural disadvantages in terms of access to maternal health care. Gu observes that there are more maternal deaths in the western provinces, which suggests a corresponding lack of appropriate maternal health care, such as hospitals or postnatal treatment. There are also interprovincial differences in the number of maternal deaths that may correspond to levels of socioeconomic development. In 2000, 9.7 maternal deaths per 100,000 live births were reported in Beijing and 9.6 in Shanghai, two high-income and well-developed areas, in comparison with 108.8 in Gansu, 141.7 in Guizhou, and 466.3 in Tibet, three of China's poorest provinces (Gu 2003: 71).

Underfunding of the health care sector in poor, rural areas is contributing to gaps in RH services (Fang 2004). Although the RH services receive some central funding through the family planning stations, it is insufficient to offset general heath-sector deficiencies, with the result that RH needs are largely unmet. Fang (2004) indicates that several major problems exist in the RH sector. First, in many areas financial limitations have prevented the expansion of RH services beyond the required national family planning initiatives (i.e., contraception) and basic maternal care. Other basic RH services are unavailable in poor areas, such as testing and treatment for common RTIs. Second, a systemic lack of adequate training of local RH service providers affects the quality of care. For example, in Yunnan, another underdeveloped province, 71–91 % of RH service providers in poor villages have insufficient training to diagnose and treat common RTIs. Third, the need for user fees has negatively affected preventative services, as rural health institutions are now oriented toward selling curative medicines to finance themselves.

Most of the literature on post-reform RH focuses on maternal health (MH). The use of MH services has increased since 1975 because of improvements in overall availability and the dissemination of MH information. From 1975–1979 to 1990–95, the use of prenatal and postnatal services improved from 16.7 to over 60 % (Bogg et al. 2002). However, this general pattern obscures important regional-level and contextual influences on RH service use. The use of prenatal checkup services among low-income women is well known to differ from province to province (Fang 2004). A gap also exists between RH needs and help-seeking that is associated with low-income status. Examining two rural counties in Yunnan Province, Kaufman and Fang (2002) observe that pregnancy-related morbidities are common, affecting from 41 to 62 % of women, depending on the township; but few of these women seek medical treatment. At most, about 52 % seek treatment for RH problems during pregnancy, and as few as 16 % get treatment for postpartum problems.

There are good reasons to suspect that local socioeconomic context could be an important determinant of RH checkups. Examining a national sample of rural villages, Short and Zhang (2004) have demonstrated a significant relationship between maternal services (prenatal visits and delivery assistance) and community-level infrastructure, such as distance from amenities and having tap water or electric power. Their findings indicate that village infrastructure, i.e., running water and electric power, are crucial determinants of MH service use. The likelihood of using MH services is 1.5 times higher in villages with tap water than in villages without it and 3.4 times higher in villages with electric power. Bogg et al. (2002) demonstrate that use of prenatal services is positively correlated with proximity to township hospitals, which is important because it suggests that smaller, more isolated villages face disadvantages in access to services. The rate of prenatal service use is about 74 % in villages located less than 1 km from a township hospital, but 49 % when the distance is 3 km or more.

As noted, a limited amount of research examines community-level effects on RH checkups. Our study uses multilevel models to assess village-level and county-level effects on RH checkup in rural China. Our main objective is to determine whether village-level and county-level characteristics have an effect on individual-level use patterns, and whether this effect is mediated by individual-level characteristics. The Chinese village represents a fundamental unit of social and economic organization and is, in essence, a "natural" neighborhood with clear-cut boundaries and members. China has more than 900,000 villages, ranging from small settlements of fewer than 200 persons to dense communities with 1,000 or more persons (Jin and Li 1992). Given communal ownership of agricultural land and other shared enterprises, villages often function as an economic coalition; and thus the welfare of individuals is embedded in local development (Pei 1996). The level of rural development remains uneven because the economic reforms initiated both rapid growth in overall income and an increase in rural socioeconomic inequalities (Benjamin et al. 2008; Yao 1999). Village-level circumstances account for 37 % of overall variance in income per capita and 45 % of the variance in consumption per capita (Benjamin et al. 2005: 793). These income inequalities appear to be contributing to regionalized patterns of access to health care services (Zhao 2006).

10.3 Data and Methods

10.3.1 Data

Our empirical analysis uses National Population and Reproductive Health Survey (NPRHS) data, collected by the State Family Planning Commission between July and September 2001. The target population of the NPRHS included all Chinese women of reproductive age (15–49) residing in all 31 provinces, autonomous regions, and municipalities. The NPRHS used a stratified multistage cluster sampling design and collected data from a nationally representative sample of 39,586 women from 1,041 villages and urban neighborhoods in 337 counties and cities. Local healthcare or family planning workers conducted the interviews in the respondents' homes. The overall response rate was 98.3 %. (See Pan et al. 2003 for details about the survey design and data collection.) In the NPRHS, respondents were asked whether they resided in a rural village or an urban neighborhood. We used this question to identify our study population, people living in rural areas. In China, villages are geographic units with formal administrative boundaries.

The NPRHS collected detailed information on women's childbearing history, contraceptive use, reproductive health, and sociodemographic characteristics. For rural areas, data were also collected on village-level development, such as the presence of a family planning (FP) station, the presence of a regular medical doctor (MD), village enterprises, and other demographic and economic indicators. Village-level information was provided by village heads. Because national population targets and birth control regulations are implemented at the county level (Chen et al. 2007), we incorporated selected county-level sociodemographic variables into the analysis, which we obtained from the 2000 census. Our study sample is restricted to rural areas and includes 24,611 married women of childbearing age from 830 villages and 307 counties. The number of respondents per site ranges from 4 to 112 (the mean is about 30), with only 2 % of villages ($n = 17$) having fewer than ten respondents. The public-use data file from the NPRHS contains no missing values for the variables used in the current study.

10.3.2 Measures

The dependent variable is a dichotomous variable indicating whether the respondent had an RH checkup in the past 18 months. The respondents were asked if they had had an RH checkup for any reason, and those who answered affirmatively were asked several follow-up questions about the particular checkup or tests received. This variable includes vaginal or uterine exams, mammograms, PAP smears, ultrasounds, and other diagnostic tests. Table 10.1 shows that almost half of the married women of childbearing age (49.2 %) had had an RH examination.

Most couples in China are required to have a premarital medical exam in order to obtain a marriage certificate. The exam includes some RH items (Hesketh 2003). Some RH checkups are also attributable to official monitoring of pregnancies and contraception (Chu 2004). We took four steps to reduce the influence of these involuntary components of RH service use. First, we restricted our study sample to married women, thereby decreasing the variation in RH checkup related to marital status. (The study sample may have included respondents who were unmarried at the time of their checkup; the same can be said for other variables measured at the time of the survey, such as pregnancy and contraceptive use.) Second, we entered statistical controls for pregnancy and IUD use in our multivariate analyses, reducing the influence of maternal RHS needs and official IUD checkups. Third, our multilevel statistical model accounts for village-level and county-level variations in RHS use. Research (e.g., White 2006) indicates that there are local differences in the enforcement of and compliance with family planning policies. Finally, we conducted a series of robustness tests, including modeling strategies to minimize the influence of involuntary RH checkups.

To assess the direct effects of the village-level and county-level variables, the multilevel models account for individual-level variables that may confound or mediate the relationship between village or county context and the RH checkup. These include age, ethnic minority, childbearing history, pregnancy, use of contraception, education, spousal age difference, and husband's RH/FP training. Some of these variables (e.g., childbearing history, contraception, and pregnancy) represent RH needs, which obviously influence the demand for RH checkups. In addition, the literature suggests that women's education and ethnic status are also predictors of RH behavior (Short and Zhang 2004). The variables for spousal age difference and husband's RH or FP training are intended to capture potential differences in RH checkups based on women's bargaining power within households. There is a well-established relationship between women's status and reproductive health

Table 10.1 Definitions and descriptive statistics of the variables used in the analysis: married women (ages 14–49) in the NPRHS, 2001

Variables	Definition	M or %	S. D.
Individual-level variables			
Had a RH checkup	Had a reproductive health checkup in the past 18 months (1 = yes, 0 = no)	49.2 %	–
Age	Age in years	34.94	7.57
Ethnic minority	Dummy indicator (1 = yes, 0 = no)	10.1 %	–
Children			
Childless	Dummy indicator (1 = yes, 0 = no)	4.2 %	–
One boy	Dummy indicator (1 = yes, 0 = no)	20.7 %	–
One girl	Dummy indicator (1 = yes, 0 = no)	12.4 %	–
One boy and one girl	Dummy indicator (1 = yes, 0 = no)	25.2 %	–
Two boys	Dummy indicator (1 = yes, 0 = no)	10.4 %	–
Two girls	Dummy indicator (1 = yes, 0 = no)	5.7 %	–
Three or more children	Reference category	21.4 %	–
Children under 18 months	Having a child < 18 months old (1 = yes, 0 = no)	8.7 %	–
Use of contraception			
Surgical sterilization	Dummy indicator (1 = yes, 0 = no)	51.6 %	–
IUD	Dummy indicator (1 = yes, 0 = no)	37.5 %	–
Other methods	Dummy indicator (1 = yes, 0 = no)	4.7 %	–
Nonuser	Reference category	6.1 %	–
Pregnant	Dummy indicator (1 = currently pregnant, 0 = no)	2.9 %	–
Education			
Illiterate or semi-illiterate	Dummy indicator (1 = yes, 0 = no)	24.3 %	–
Primary school	Dummy indicator (1 = yes, 0 = no)	38.2 %	–
Junior high	Dummy indicator (1 = yes, 0 = no)	32.6 %	–
High school	Dummy indicator (1 = yes, 0 = no)	4.7 %	–
Some college or higher	Reference category	0.2 %	–
Spousal age difference (M–F)	Age difference between spouses (range: −10.0–24.7)	2.238	3.075
Husband's RH/FP training	Husband participated in reproductive health or family planning training (1 = regularly/occasionally 0 = never)	19.8 %	–
Village-level variables			
Village population	Village population size (range: 65–14,580)	1,700.1	1,273.6
Village library	Village has a library (1 = yes, 0 = no)	19.4 %	–
Village licensed doctor	Village has a licensed doctor (1 = yes, 0 = no)	87.2 %	–

(continued)

Table 10.1 (continued)

Variables	Definition	M or %	S. D.
Village FP station	Village has a family planning service station (1 = yes, 0 = no)	80.1 %	–
Village enterprise	Village has an enterprise (1 = yes, 0 = no)	30.8 %	–
Village income	Village net income per capita in 2000 (range: 120–15800 yuan)	2,026.5	1,330.9
County-level variables			
County population	County population size in 2000 (range: 44,624–8,913,965)	788,832	882,414
County TFR	County total fertility rate in 2000 (range: 0.55–3.06)	1.32	0.39
County sex ratio at birth (M/F) × 100	County sex ratio at birth in 2000 (range: 93–192)	119.34	15.26
County urbanization	Percentage of urban population in the county (range: 2.2 %–100 %)	29.53 %	22.25
County female education	County average years of female education (range: 2.12–11.37)	6.81	1.10
N (respondents)		24,611	–
N (villages)		830	–
N (counties)		307	–

(Blanc 2001). Large differences in spouses' ages may reflect higher levels of gender inequality within marriages, and this inequality could constrain women's independent RH choices. In contrast, husbands' participation in RH or FP training may encourage their support of women's RH choices.

Table 10.1 presents the definitions and descriptive statistics for the individual-level and contextual variables. It shows that one tenth of the women included in the study belonged to an ethnic minority, or non-Han, population, a ratio that is comparable to the general population. To reflect the number and gender composition of women's fertility history, we created a seven-level categorical variable to measure respondents' number of children: no children (childless), one boy, one girl, one boy and one girl, two boys, two girls, and three or more children. The modal category was "one boy and one girl" (25.2 %), with only 4.2 % of women having no children and 21.4 % of women having three or more children. We created a dummy variable for having a child under the age of 18 months (8.7 %). The use of contraception was common. The data show that over half of the women had had a tubal ligation or their husbands had had a vasectomy. Thirty-eight percent were IUD users, 5 % used other contraceptive methods, and 6 % were nonusers. About 3 % were pregnant at the time of the survey. Finally, we measured women's education using a five-level categorical variable. We observed that 62.5 % of the women had a primary school education or less and just 4.9 % had a high school or college education.

We also considered two spousal characteristics. We measured the age gap between spouses with a continuous variable by subtracting the wife's age from her husband's age. A positive value indicates marriages in which the husband was older than the wife; a negative value, the converse. Table 10.1 shows that the average (positive) age gap between spouses was 2.2 years. In addition, we used a dichotomous variable to indicate whether the husband had RH or FP training.

The contextual variables that we considered included six village-level indicators. Table 10.1 shows that most villages had a licensed doctor (87.2 %) and an FP service station (80.1 %). These two variables represent physical access to RH services. As discussed above, the distance from these services is a predictor of utilization. Nearly one fifth (19.4 %) of the villages had a library. Close to one third of the villages had an enterprise (e.g., factory, cottage industry, textile mill, or brewery). The presence of a village enterprise is a good indicator of local development, and these enterprises can be an important source of stable revenue for local governments (Chen 1997). The average village income per capita in 2000 was 2,026 yuan. We posited that whether a village had an enterprise and that the per capita income of the village would indicate differences between villages in the ability to finance health care services. The average village population was 1,700, with the populations ranging from 65 to 14,580. We included this variable because "critical masses" are needed to maintain numerous local-level institutions and services (e.g., hospitals and doctors) that could influence access to RH services.

Using the geographic identifier available in the NPRHS, we merged five county-level sociodemographic variables (as measured in the 2000 census because the NPRHS does not provide county-level data) with the study sample. Table 10.1 shows that the average county population was 788,832, with a large variance (s.d. = 882,414). The population of rural townships ranged from 2.2 to 100 % (mean = 29.5 %, s.d. = 22.3). Our assumption about the counties was that, as in villages, the availability of health care services would correspond to the size of the population and their level of urbanization. The mean county-level total fertility rate (TFR) was 1.32 births per woman, ranging from 0.55 to 3.06. We found considerable variation in the sex ratio at birth between counties, with a range of 93 males per 100 females to 192 males per 100 females (mean = 119.3, s.d. = 15.3). Finally, the average number of years of formal education for women was 6.81 (s.d. = 1.1), ranging from 2.12 to 11.37 across the counties. These last three variables—total fertility rate, sex ratio at birth, and years of formal schooling—roughly indicate women's status; that is, a high TFR, high sex ratio, and low level of female education tend to reflect gender inequality. Their status, in turn, could influence their choices and decisions regarding RH service use. To facilitate the convergence of the multi-level models estimated in the study, we used the natural logarithm of village population, village income, and county population in the multi-level regression analysis.

Macro level (contextual) variables tend to correlate with one another, leading to multicollinearity in the regression analysis. We estimated zero-order correlations of all village-level and county-level variables to examine the level of associations between the contextual variables used in the analysis; the results are available upon request. The correlation estimates suggest that the level of correlation was generally low, particularly between village-level variables. A few notable exceptions were the correlations between county-level variables and between village-level and county-level variables. For example, at the county level, women's education was found to be positively associated with urbanization ($r = .625$), but negatively related to total fertility ($r = -.583$). Village income was also correlated with county-level urbanization ($r = .412$), women's education ($r = .369$), and total fertility ($r = -.413$). Although none of the correlation coefficients was excessively large, we first considered the contextual variables one-by-one in our multivariate models and then considered them simultaneously. We compared the changes in the regression estimates due to the changes in the model specifications. In short, it appears that the presence of multicollinearity does not significantly compromise the efficiency of the regression estimates.

10.3.3 Statistical Method

We used multilevel modeling techniques for the empirical analysis. As the dependent variable is binary, we used generalized linear mixed models (GLMM) to estimate the fixed effects of contextual variables and individual-level characteristics, while controlling for the variations of villages and counties (random effects). (See McCulloch and Searle 2001; Schall 1991.)

The GLMM model is an extension of generalized linear models (GLMs) for multilevel data (Breslow and Clayton 1993; McCulloch and Searle 2001; Wolfinger and O'Connell 1993). Like the GLM, the GLMM model assumes that the response distribution (conditional on the random effects) belongs to the exponential family of distributions. Analogous to the GLM, the GLMM relates the conditional mean of the observations (given the random effects) to a vector of covariates and a vector of random variables through a link function. Because our response variable is binary, our GLMM model assumes that it follows the binomial distribution with the *logit* link function. This model is equivalent to the multilevel logistic model, hierarchical generalized linear model, or random-intercept model noted in the literature (e.g., Bryk and Raudenbush 1992; Goldstein 2003). We estimated two-level GLMM models when using only two-level data (i.e., individual-level and village-level or individual-level and county-level data) in the modeling, and estimated three-level GLMM models when using all three levels of the data. We computed robust standard errors to account for cluster effects (correlated errors within villages and counties and unequal variances across these geographic areas) arising from multilevel data (Steenbergen and Jones 2002). We estimated the GLMMs using the HLM program (Raudenbush et al. 2004).

10.4 Results

Figure 10.1 presents the component items that comprise our dependent variable (RH checkup). The figure illustrates the item-specific prevalence of RH service utilization. In some cases, RH service users could have had multiple RH examinations, which Fig. 10.1 partially captures but does not present. The most prevalent type of RH checkup was ultrasound for IUD placement and prenatal care. Almost 68 % of respondents who had had an RH checkup had received such an examination, which could reflect the emphasis on family planning and child development in official policies. About 48 % of RH service users had received a diagnostic ultrasound and 40 % a gynecological (vaginal or uterine) exam. Checkups for the other selected RH service items were much less prevalent. Only 10 % of RH service users had received a mammogram and 9 % a PAP smear, and this could indicate a deficit of RH care unrelated to FP policies or maternal needs.

In the multilevel analysis, we considered individual rural women to be "nested" in villages, which were, in turn, nested in counties. Because our analysis focuses on the effects of the contextual variables and because their effects are viewed as being structural, we hypothesized the contextual variables to have both a direct and an indirect effect on the outcome variables.

Table 10.2 examines the effects of each village-level and each county-level variable on the likelihood of an RH checkup. This table includes bivariate logistic models that estimate the total effect for each of the village-level and county-level variables, and also multivariate models that assess the direct effects of each of these contextual variables, net of the effects of individual characteristics. It presents the odds ratios of the estimated regression coefficients.

According to the bivariate results, the size of a village population and the presence of a village library have nonsignificant effects on the likelihood of an RH checkup. In villages with a licensed doctor, the likelihood of having had an RH

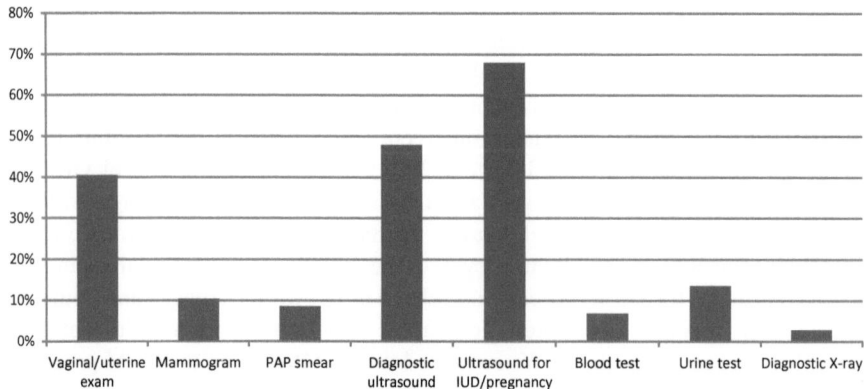

Fig. 10.1 Reproductive health check-up: percentages of married women (ages 14–49) in the NPRHS, 2001 (N = 12,114)

Table 10.2 Multilevel logistic regressions of reproductive health checkup on selected village- and county-level indicators: married women (ages 14–49) in the NPRHS, 2001 ($N = 24,611$)

Contextual variables	Bivariate model OR		Model with individual-level controls[a] OR	
Village-level variables				
Village population (ln)	1.001	–	1.024	–
Village library (1 = yes)	1.132	–	1.083	–
Village licensed doctor (1 = yes)	1.303	*	1.227	
Village FP station (1 = yes)	1.532	***	1.828	***
Village enterprise (1 = yes)	1.291	***	1.171	
Village income (ln)	1.598	***	1.490	***
County-level variables				
County population (ln)	1.328	**	1.442	***
County TFR	0.436	***	0.532	***
County sex ratio at birth (M/F) × 100	0.993	*	1.001	
County urbanization	1.009	**	1.005	
County female education	1.335	***	1.265	***

*p < .05; **p < .01; *** p < .001 (two-tailed test)
[a]Model controls for individual-level variables shown in Table 10.1

checkup is 1.3 times, or 30 %, higher ($[1.303-1] \times 100$) than in villages without a licensed doctor. The likelihood of an RH checkup increases with the presence of both an FP station and a village enterprise. The likelihood of an RH checkup increases as village net income per capita rises. At the county level, the likelihood of an RH checkup is higher in more populous and urbanized counties and also in counties with higher aggregate levels of female education. Both a higher county-level TFR and a higher male/female sex ratio at birth decrease the likelihood of having had a RH checkup.

In assessing the direct effects of the village and county variables, we used the multivariate models to account for individual-level characteristics that could influence the likelihood of having had an RH checkup. In the multivariate analysis the effects of a village licensed doctor and a village enterprise become non-significant. This result suggests that the contextual effects of these variables are indirect, operating wholly through the selected individual-level variables. Although the effect of village income remains significant, its effect on the likelihood of an RH checkup weakens, suggesting that its effect operates partially through individual-level characteristics. The effect of a village FP station becomes stronger in the multivariate model. This suggests that the effect of an FP station is entirely direct and that individual-level characteristics suppress the effect (importance) of an FP station on an RH checkup, although the increase (difference) in the effect of an FP station between the bivariate and multivariate models is not statistically significant ($p > .05$). The effects of a county's sex ratio at birth and its urbanization level become nonsignificant in the multivariate models. Hence, their effects are wholly indirect. The effect of aggregate female education remains significant, but the size of the effect decreases, and thus its effect may operate partially through individual-level characteristics. Some of the effects of a county's population and its TFR are suppressed by individual characteristics.

Table 10.3 presents the logistic regressions (odds ratios) of an RH checkup on village- and county-level indicators. Building on the results of Table 10.2, Model 1 in this table assesses the direct effects of all village-level indicators simultaneously, net of individual characteristics. Model 2 assesses the direct effects of all county-level indicators simultaneously, net of individual characteristics. Model 3 combines Models 1 and 2, simultaneously considering the effects of all village- and county-level variables. For the sake of comparison, we re-estimated Model 3 as a generalized linear model (ordinary logistic regression model). The results are presented in the last column (Model 4) of Table 10.3. A quick comparison of Models 3 and 4 suggests that, without specifying it as a multilevel model, the magnitudes of the regression estimates (in most cases) and the levels of significance (in virtually all cases) are inflated.

Looking first at the intercept and the random components at the bottom of Table 10.3, we see that the estimated intercept in all models is statistically significant, meaning that the average log-odds (across villages or counties) of having an RH checkup (when all predictors are set at 0) is significantly different from zero. The variance components show that there are significant differences in RH checkups between villages and between counties.

Turning to the contextual effects, in Model 1, we find that only the presence of a village FP station and the level of village income have direct (statistically significant) effects. A village FP station and higher village income have strong direct effects and increase the likelihood of an RH checkup. In Model 2, we observe that both a larger county population and a higher level of aggregate female education increase the likelihood of an RH checkup. A high male/female sex ratio at birth decreases the likelihood of an RH checkup. In Model 3, none of the village-level variables has significant (direct) effects on an RH checkup. This indicates that our selected county-level variables account for the direct effects of a village FP station and village income observed in Model 1. Moreover, in this model the effects of country population and female education remain similar to those in Model 2. The effect of county urbanization now becomes significant and contradicts the finding (positive effect) reported in Table 10.2. This suggests that it has a positive indirect effect on an RH checkup.

Across all models, the effects of the individual-level variables have fairly consistent effects. Notably, having one child (either a boy or a girl) increases the likelihood of an RH checkup. In addition, having two girls also increases the likelihood of having an RH checkup. Having a child under the age of 18 months or being pregnant also increases the likelihood of an RH checkup. The use of nonsurgical contraception increases the likelihood of an RH checkup. These are unsurprising results and likely reflect RH needs, family-size preferences, and the

Table 10.3 Logistic regressions of reproductive health checkup on individual-, village-, and county-level Indicators: married women (ages 14–49) in the NPRHS, 2001 ($N = 24{,}611$)

	Multi-level logistic						Ordinary logistic	
	Model 1		Model 2		Model 3		Model 4	
Variables	OR		OR		OR		OR	
Individual-level variables								
Age	1.047		1.036		1.037		1.118	***
Age squared	0.999	***	0.999	**	0.999	**	0.998	***
Ethnic minority (1 = yes)	0.842	*	0.921		0.911		0.661	***
Children								
Childless	1.201		1.161		1.144		1.854	***
One boy	1.664	***	1.605	***	1.617	***	1.991	***
One girl	1.615	***	1.538	***	1.555	***	1.959	***
One boy and one girl	1.066		1.060		1.065		1.022	
Two boys	0.982		0.986		0.983		0.940	
Two girls	1.194	**	1.212	**	1.196	*	1.201	**
Three or more children[a]								
Children under 18 months	1.592	***	1.612	***	1.590	***	1.941	***
Use of contraception								
Surgical sterilization	1.006		0.994		0.980		1.503	***
IUD	2.913	***	2.940	***	2.916	***	3.750	***
Other methods	2.397	***	2.350	***	2.376	***	3.031	***
Nonuser[a]								
Pregnant (1 = yes)	1.727	***	1.722	***	1.736	***	2.018	***
Education								
Illiterate or semi-illiterate	0.498		0.461		0.486		0.687	
Primary school	0.600		0.558		0.588		0.716	
Junior high	0.665		0.605		0.643		0.799	
High school	0.751		0.681		0.726		0.892	
Some college or higher[a]								
Spousal age difference (M − F)	0.983	***	0.985	**	0.984	***	0.969	***
Husband's RH/FP training	1.598	***	1.620	***	1.600	***	2.216	***
Village-level variables								
Village population (ln)	0.929		–		0.953		0.926	***
Village library (1 = yes)	0.943		–		1.156		1.010	
Village licensed doctor (1 = yes)	1.074		–		1.018		1.052	
Village FP station (1 = yes)	1.695	***	–		1.176		1.494	***
Village enterprise (1 = yes)	1.029		–		1.026		0.967	
Village income (ln)	1.423	***	–		1.090		1.214	***

(continued)

Table 10.3 (continued)

Variables	Multi-level logistic			Ordinary logistic
	Model 1	Model 2	Model 3	Model 4
	OR	OR	OR	OR
County-level variables				
County population (ln)	–	1.332 **	1.307 *	1.255 ***
County TFR	–	0.667 *	0.705	0.757 ***
County sex ratio at birth (M/F) × 100	–	1.000	0.999	0.998
County urbanization	–	0.993	0.992 *	0.993 ***
County female education	–	1.262 **	1.248 **	1.195 ***
Intercept	−2.586 ***	−3.846 **	−4.065 **	−5.200 ***
Random effects (variance component)				
Village	2.104 ***	–	0.430 ***	–
County	–	1.873 ***	1.699 ***	–

$*p < .05; **p < .01; *** p < .001$ (two-tailed test)
[a]Reference category

preference for at least one male child. As expected, a spousal age gap decreases the likelihood of an RH checkup, whereas a husband's RH or FP training increases the likelihood.

10.5 Robustness Analysis

To examine the sensitivity of our findings under different scenarios and assumptions, we conducted several analyses of robustness. For example, we considered the possibility that some or many of the ultrasound tests were done for the purpose of sex-selective abortion. Table 10.4 reruns the models presented in Table 10.3, excluding ultrasound checkups for IUD placement and prenatal care. In general, the results from this reanalysis suggest that the findings in Table 10.3 are indeed robust. The effect of an FP station, however, is notably stronger in all the models in Table 10.4.

To account for, or at least reduce, the probability that some RH checkups could have been involuntary, we estimated three supplementary GLMM models, redefining the study population by excluding women whose RH checkup was free of charge (Model 1), women whose checkup was organized through their employer (Model 2), and women whose checkup was both free of charge and organized through their employer (Model 3). These models should sort out a large proportion of involuntary RH checkups and focus mainly on user-financed and discretionary checkups. In general, with respect to the contextual effects, the results, presented in Table 10.5, do not seriously undermine the findings presented in Table 10.3.

Table 10.4 Logistic regressions of reproductive health checkup on individual-, village-, and county-level indicators, excluding ultrasound checkups for IUD placement and prenatal care ($N = 21{,}201$)

	Multilevel logistic						Ordinary logistic	
	Model 1		Model 2		Model 3		Model 4	
Variables	OR		OR		OR		OR	
Individual-level variables								
Age	1.036		1.026		1.028		1.099	***
Age squared	0.999	**	0.999	*	0.999	**	0.998	***
Ethnic minority (1 = yes)	0.768	***	0.844	*	0.835	*	0.633	***
Children								
Childless	1.174		1.126		1.122		1.771	***
One boy	1.562	***	1.518	***	1.511	***	1.787	***
One girl	1.540	***	1.477	***	1.474	***	1.770	***
One boy and one girl	1.077		1.066		1.066		1.019	
Two boys	0.984		0.997		0.982		0.924	
Two girls	1.173	*	1.174	*	1.155	*	1.194	*
Three or more children[a]								
Children under 18 months	1.452	***	1.483	***	1.453	***	1.783	***
Use of contraception								
Surgical sterilization	1.094	***	1.089	***	1.076	***	1.556	***
IUD	2.503	***	2.508	***	2.502	***	3.300	***
Other methods	2.387		2.328		2.374		3.213	***
Nonuser[a]								
Pregnant (1 = yes)	1.357	*	1.318	*	1.339	*	1.661	***
Education								
Illiterate or semi-illiterate	0.368	*	0.350	*	0.603	**	0.493	
Primary school	0.461		0.444		0.752		0.585	
Junior high	0.532		0.499		0.848		0.691	
High school	0.607		0.571		0.967		0.765	
Some college or higher[a]								
Spousal age difference (M − F)	0.982	***	0.984	**	0.983	***	0.970	***
Husband's RH/FP training	1.635	***	1.641	***	1.631	***	2.429	***
Village-level variables								
Village population (ln)	0.888		–		0.939		0.932	**
Village library (1 = yes)	0.982		–		1.146		1.056	
Village licensed doctor (1 = yes)	1.029		–		1.015		1.001	
Village FP station (1 = yes)	1.909	***	–		1.239	*	1.726	***
Village enterprise (1 = yes)	1.077		–		1.010		1.010	
Village income (ln)	1.482	***	–		1.095		1.238	***

(continued)

Table 10.4 (continued)

Variables	Multi-level logistic						Ordinary logistic	
	Model 1		Model 2		Model 3		Model 4	
	OR		OR		OR		OR	
County-level variables								
County population (ln)	–		1.276	*	1.256	*	1.230	***
County TFR	–		0.561	**	0.606	**	0.642	***
County sex ratio at birth (M/F) × 100	–		0.999		0.999		0.997	**
County urbanization	–		0.996		0.995		0.995	***
County female education	–		1.217	*	1.168	*	1.134	***
Intercept	−3.058	***	−3.695	**	−3.851	**	−5.260	***
Random effects (variance component)								
Village	1.985	***	–		0.454	***	–	
County	–		1.795	***	1.564	***	–	

*p < .05; **p < .01; ***p < .001 (two-tailed test)
[a]Reference category

Table 10.5 Multi-level logistic models of reproductive health checkup on individual, village, and county-level indicators: a robustness analysis of involuntary checkups

Variables	Model 1		Model 2		Model 3	
	OR		OR		OR	
Individual-level variables						
Age	1.000		1.044		1.043	
Age squared	0.999		0.999	**	0.999	**
Ethnic minority (1 = yes)	0.844	*	0.846		0.811	*
Children						
Childless	1.254		1.676	**	1.625	**
One boy	1.127		1.356	**	1.079	
One girl	1.182		1.481	***	1.325	**
One boy and one girl	1.023		1.045		0.962	
Two boys	0.947		0.912		0.885	
Two girls	1.023		1.090		1.029	
Three or more children[a]						
Children under 18 months	1.806	***	2.410	***	2.382	***
Use of contraception						
Surgical sterilization	0.790	*	0.816		0.754	*
IUD	1.726	***	1.931	***	1.628	***
Other methods	1.864	***	2.143	***	2.037	***
Nonuser[a]						
Pregnant (1 = yes)	1.764	***	2.155	***	2.154	***

(continued)

Table 10.5 (continued)

Variables	Model 1 OR		Model 2 OR		Model 3 OR	
Education						
Illiterate or semi-illiterate	0.323	*	0.246	**	0.192	***
Primary school	0.374	*	0.320	*	0.252	**
Junior high	0.430		0.373	*	0.302	**
High school	0.533		0.459		0.397	*
Some college or higher[a]						
Spousal age difference (M - F)	0.984	**	0.990		0.989	
Husband's RH/FP training	1.499	***	1.754	***	1.809	***
Village-level variables						
Village population (ln)	1.001		0.974		0.995	
Village library (1 = yes)	1.191		1.034		1.032	
Village licensed doctor (1 = yes)	0.906		0.923		0.926	
Village FP station (1 = yes)	1.039		1.134		1.005	
Village enterprise (1 = yes)	0.968		1.035		1.017	
Village income (ln)	1.082		1.018		1.085	
County-level variables						
County population (ln)	1.238		1.149		1.094	
County TFR	0.702		0.875		0.838	
County sex ratio at birth (M/F) × 100	0.994		1.006	*	1.003	
County urbanization	0.990	*	0.989	**	0.990	**
County female education	1.161		1.296	**	1.237	*
Intercept	−4.517	**	−3.319	**	−3.543	**
Random effects (variance component)						
Village	0.412	***	0.178	***	0.108	***
County	1.778	***	0.757	***	0.781	***
N	17,548		15,967		15,062	

Note: Model 1 removes women whose RH checkup was free of charge; model 2 removes women whose checkup was organized through their employer; model 3 removes women whose checkup was free and organized by their employer
*p < .05; **p < .01; ***p < .001 (two-tailed test)
[a]Reference category

10.6 Conclusion

Illnesses related to women's reproductive systems are a major health problem in China, and RH checkups are important for diagnosing such disorders. The transfer of funding responsibilities for the provision of health care from the central government to local authorities has created serious deficiencies in China's health services. In particular, disparities in access to reproductive health care related to the collapse of the Cooperative Medical System have produced disparities in met

RH needs. Among rural Chinese women, access to RH checkups varies widely (Kaufman and Fang 2002). Personal income inequalities often translate into unequal health care access because of the privatization of services.

Considering that individual welfare could be a function of local development, we examined whether village development influenced women's use of RH checkups. We also considered the effects of county-level sociodemographic context on their use of checkups.

Low use of RH checkups could be associated with shortcomings in available services. Our study found that only 49 % of rural married women of reproductive age had had an RH checkup. What is also troubling is the low overall use of services unrelated to maternal care. For instance, just 4 % of the women in our study had received a PAP smear and 5 % a mammogram, both of which are basic medical screens for cervical and breast cancers. These diseases are among the leading causes of premature mortality among women in developing countries, and early detection through regular screening is essential for their prevention and treatment. Yet, as Fang (2004) observes, there is a glaring absence of services for the diagnosis and treatment of such disorders in China. The main focus of Chinese RH services is family planning and maternal care, and prevention of reproductive diseases is given much lower priority.

Our results demonstrate that the measures we selected of village-level development did have effects on the likelihood of RH checkup use, although the effects were indirect. The observed (total) effects of the selected village-level variables were explained away by either individual-level or county-level variables. This finding suggests that the influence of village context depends on who you are and in what county the village is located. At the county level we found both direct and indirect effects. All selected county-level variables had an effect, although the effects of the county-level total fertility rate and the sex ratio at birth were primarily indirect. In addition, our ancillary (robust) analysis indicates that our findings are generally robust and consistent.

Between-county differences appear to be more relevant than between-village differences for predicting RHS utilization. We found that a regional effect accounted for (or mediated) village-level differences in the use of RH checkups. After selected county-level variables were introduced into the regression models, the effects of having a village FP station and the level of village income (the only two direct village-level effects observed) attenuated to nonsignificant levels. This could be considered a surprising finding, given that one would expect RH checkups to increase with the presence of a village FP station and higher village income, as these variables represent access to services and the ability to pay for them. However, the county-level context could have an overriding influence for two reasons. First, in numerous cases, the responsibility for health care was decentralized to the country level after the 1979 economic reforms (Hsiao 1995; Liu et al. 1995; Zheng and Hillier 1995). Hence, the scope and quality of services and the level of user fees are linked to county-level funding and policies. Second, women's status is another predictor of RH checkups, and it is more likely to differ at the regional than the subregional level.

Our results also suggest that women's status is a crucial dimension of RH checkup use. We estimated women's status through examining both individual-level variables, such as women's education and husband's involvement with FP or RH training, and contextual variables, such as county-level TFR and women's aggregate level of education. Of course, these are somewhat imperfect measures of women's status, and further research is needed to confirm our tentative findings; but they present some interesting insights nonetheless. The total fertility rate is an indicator of women's social position in developing countries (Oppenheim-Mason 1987). In addition, it is plausible to infer that a husband's involvement in FP or RH training is conducive to his wife having an RH checkup. Our findings indicate that a low TFR, husband's involvement in FP or RH training, and higher aggregate education all increase the likelihood of an RH checkup. In a surprise result, we found that a woman's educational level was not a significant factor. This finding is at odds with results from previous studies (e.g., Short and Zhang 2004) and could be a result of the way we measured individual-level education. In particular, the high prevalence (95 %) of respondents with less than a high school education in our study sample could mask a potential positive effect of higher education on RH checkups.

Our findings have several limitations. The first concerns our dependent variable, which is a global measure of RH checkups. Although this measure captures a range of services, it was impractical to separate them from one another in our multilevel models. This implies that an overall RH checkup could be loaded on one or two specific items that comprise our global measure, meaning that there could be greater disparities than our analysis observes. For example, certain types of RH services are common (e.g., ultrasound for IUD placement and maternal care), whereas other services (e.g., PAP smears) are uncommon (see Fig. 10.1). In this respect, our dependent variable is somewhat imprecise because it cannot capture such nuanced between-village differences. Moreover, the dependent variable does not capture RH-related curative services, a subject for future research. Our analysis is further limited because we could not measure individual-level income, and the village-level income effects should therefore be interpreted with caution.

Acknowledgments An early version of this chapter was presented at the International Conference on Low Fertility and Reproductive Health in East and Southeast Asia Tokyo, Japan, November 12–14, 2008. We thank Robert Retherford and the conference participants for their helpful comments and suggestions, and also thank Feng Hou for research assistance.

References

Benjamin, D., Brandt, L., & Giles, J. (2005). The evolution of income equality in rural China. *Economic Development and Cultural Change, 53*(4), 769–824.

Benjamin, D., Brandt, L., Giles, J., & Wang, S. (2008). Income inequality during China's economic transition. In L. Brandt & R. G. Rawski (Eds.), *China's great economic transformation* (pp. 729–775). Cambridge: Cambridge University Press.

Blanc, A. K. (2001). The effect of power in sexual relationships on sexual and reproductive health: An examination of the evidence. *Studies in Family Planning, 32*(3), 189–213.

Blumenthal, D., & Hsiao, W. (2005). Privatization and its discontents—The evolving Chinese health care system. *New England Journal of Medicine, 353*(11), 1165–1170.

Bogg, L., Wang, K., & Diwan, V. (2002). Chinese maternal health in adjustment: Claim for life. *Reproductive Health Matters, 10*(20), 95–107.

Breslow, N. E., & Clayton, D. G. (1993). Approximate inference in generalized linear mixed models. *Journal of the American Statistical Association, 88*(421), 9–25.

Bryk, A. S., & Raudenbush, S. W. (1992). *Hierarchical linear models.* Newbury Park: Sage.

Carrin, G., Ron, A., Yang, H., Wong, H., Zhang, T., Zhang, S., et al. (1999). The reform of the rural cooperative medical system in the People's Republic of China: Interim experience in 14 pilot counties. *Social Science and Medicine, 48*(7), 961–972.

Chen, H. (1997). The transition in TVEs' ownership structure: A valuable reference for the reform of SOEs. In G. J. Wen & D. Xu (Eds.), *The reformability of China's state sector* (pp. 131–155). Singapore: World Scientific Publishing.

Chen, J., Xie, Z., & Liu, H. (2007). Son preference, use of maternal care, and infant mortality in rural China, 1989–2000. *Population Studies, 61*(2), 161–183.

Chu, J. (2004). Prenatal sex determination and sex-selective abortion in rural Central China. *Population and Development Review, 27*(2), 259–281.

Do, D. P., & Finch, B. K. (2008). The link between neighborhood poverty and health: Context or composition? *American Journal of Epidemiology, 168*(6), 611–619.

Ellen, I. G., Mijanovich, T., & Dillman, K. (2001). Neighborhood effects on health: Exploring the links and assessing the evidence. *Journal of Urban Affairs, 23*(3–4), 391–408.

Fang, J. (2004). Health sector reform and reproductive health in poor rural China. *Health Policy and Planning, 19*(S1), i40–i49.

Goldstein, H. (2003). *Multilevel statistical models* (3rd ed.). London: Edward Arnold.

Gu, B. (2003). Population, reproductive health, and poverty in China. In *Population and poverty: Achieving equity, equality, and sustainability* (pp. 63–77). New York: United Nations Population Fund.

Hesketh, T. (2003). Getting married in China: Pass the medical first. *British Medical Journal, 326*, 277–279.

Hsiao, W. C. L. (1995). The Chinese health care system: Lessons for other nations. *Social Science and Medicine, 41*(8), 1047–1055.

Hussain, A., & Lanjouw, P. (1994). Income inequalities in China: Evidence from household survey data. *World Development, 22*(12), 1947–1958.

Jin, Q., & Li, W. (1992). China's rural settlement patterns. In R. G. Knapp (Ed.), *Chinese landscapes: The village as place* (pp. 13–34). Honolulu: University of Hawaii Press.

Kaufman, J., & Fang, J. (2002). Privatisation of health services and the reproductive health of rural Chinese women. *Reproductive Health Matters, 10*(20), 108–116.

Liu, Y., Hsiao, W. C. L., Li, Q., Liu, X., & Ren, M. (1995). Transformation of China's rural health care financing. *Social Science and Medicine, 41*(8), 1085–1093.

Macintyre, S., Ellaway, A., & Cummins, S. (2002). Place effects on health: How can we conceptualise, operationalise, and measure them? *Social Science and Medicine, 55*(1), 125–139.

McCulloch, C. E., & Searle, S. R. (2001). *Generalized, linear, and mixed models.* New York: Wiley.

Oppenheim-Mason, K. (1987). The impact of women's social position on fertility in developing countries. *Sociological Forum, 2*(4), 718–745.

Pan, G., Zhang, H., & Wang, G. (2003). *Theses collection of 2001 National Family and Reproductive Health Survey.* Beijing: China Population Publishing House.

Pei, X. (1996). Township-village enterprises, local governments, and rural communities: The Chinese village as a firm during economic transition. *Economics of Transition, 4*(1), 43–66.

Price, N. L., & Hawkins, K. (2007). A conceptual framework for the social analysis of reproductive health. *Journal of Health, Population and Nutrition, 25*(1), 24–36.

Raudenbush, S. W., Bryk, A. S., Cheong, Y. F., & Congdon, R. (2004). *HLM 6: Hierarchical linear and nonlinear modeling.* Lincolnwood: Scientific Software International.

Robert, S. A. (1999). Socioeconomic position and health: The independent contribution of community socioeconomic context. *Annual Review of Sociology, 25*, 489–516.

Ross, C. E., & Mirowsky, J. (2008). Neighborhood socioeconomic status and health: Context or composition? *City & Community, 7*(2), 163–179.

Schall, R. (1991). Estimation in generalized linear models with random effects. *Biometrika, 78*(4), 719–727.

Short, S. E., & Zhang, F. (2004). Use of maternal services in rural China. *Population Studies, 58*(1), 3–19.

Steenbergen, M., & Jones, B. (2002). Modeling multilevel data structure. *American Journal of Political Science, 46*(1), 218–237.

Stephenson, R., & Tsui, A. O. (2002). Contextual influences on reproductive health service use in Uttar Pradesh, India. *Studies in Family Planning, 33*(4), 309–320.

Sun, H., & Dutta, D. (1997). China's economic growth during 1984–93: A case of regional dualism. *Third World Quarterly, 18*(5), 843–864.

Wang, H., Xu, T., & Xu, J. (2007). Factors contributing to high costs and inequality in China's health care system. *Journal of the American Medical Association, 298*(16), 1928–1930.

White, G. (1992). *Riding the tiger: The politics of economic reform in post-Mao China*. Palo Alto: Stanford University Press.

White, T. (2006). *China's longest campaign: Birth planning in the People's Republic, 1949–2005*. New York: Cornell University Press.

Wolfinger, R., & O'Connell, M. (1993). Generalized linear mixed models: A pseudo-likelihood approach. *Journal of Statistical Computation and Simulation, 48*(3–4), 233–243.

World Health Organization. (2008). *Sexual and reproductive health*. www.who.int/reproductive-health/index.htm. Accessed 31 May 2010.

Yao, S. (1999). Economic growth, income inequality and poverty in China under economic reforms. *Journal of Development Studies, 35*(6), 104–130.

Yen, I. H., & Syme, S. L. (1999). The social environment and health: A discussion of the epidemiological literature. *Annual Review of Public Health, 20*, 287–308.

Yip, W., & Mahal, A. (2008). The health care systems of China and India: Performance and future challenges. *Health Affairs, 27*(4), 921–932.

Zhao, Z. (2006). Income inequality, unequal health care access, and mortality in China. *Population and Development Review, 32*(3), 461–483.

Zheng, X., & Hillier, S. (1995). The reforms of the Chinese health care system: County level changes: The Jiangxi study. *Social Science & Medicine, 41*(8), 1057–1064.

Index

A
Abortion
  induced, 5, 8, 103, 105, 123, 124, 145–147, 157, 158
  rates, 2, 8, 123, 145, 158, 168
Africa, 54, 101, 102, 104, 105, 109, 129, 163. *See also* African continent
African American, 129
African continent, 101
Age
  compositional transformations, 32
  gap between spouses, 196
  profiles, 42
  retirement, 42, 113
  structural shifts, 42
  structure, 33, 42, 77, 111–113
Aged, the, 32–34, 42, 47, 52, 63–66, 80–84, 86, 87, 108, 111–113, 142, 152, 164, 174, 178, 183. *See also* Elderly, the
Americas, the, 163
Analysis
  trend, 76
Androgen, 125, 126
Angel Plan, the
  new, 36, 60
Anogenital distance (AGD), 127
Antiandrogen, 125–127
Antinatal, 25
Areas
  rural, 4, 94, 105–107, 173, 176, 189, 191–193
  urban, 4, 60, 62, 64, 92, 94, 107, 165, 173, 176, 183

ART. *See* Assisted reproductive technologies (ART)
Asia, 1–5, 8–9, 11–14, 16–18, 22, 25, 27, 31–55, 75, 87, 93, 103, 104, 112, 117, 120, 121, 158, 163
Assisted reproductive technologies (ART), 6, 24, 103, 109–112, 117, 123, 124, 129
Attitude
  toward having children, 69, 148, 151
  toward marriage, 85
  toward premarital sex, 85, 137, 149
Australia, 16, 21, 27
Austria, 21, 23, 27, 51, 91, 94, 110

B
Baby boomers
  generation, 32, 86
Beijing, 190
Belgium, 21, 27, 110, 163
Bequests, 44, 46. *See also* Inheritance
Biomarkers, 127
Biomedicine, 3
Births
  extramarital, 85, 168
  live, 108, 123, 124, 190
  marital, 145, 146, 154
  nonmarital, 145, 146
  number of, 12, 27, 76, 77, 110, 123, 124
Bubble
  economy, 40

C

Canada, 21, 27, 101, 112, 153, 163
Cancer
　breast, 206
　cervical, 156, 187
　testicular (TC), 6, 117, 120–122, 125–129
Capital markets, 35
Care giving, 3, 5, 16, 19, 25, 39, 42, 60, 61, 80, 108, 157, 164, 178, 187, 188, 190, 192, 196, 198, 202, 203
Care of elderly, 3, 5, 23, 25, 39, 42, 61
Cash transfer, 13–15
Celibacy, 92, 95
Census, 7, 192, 196
Central Europe, 27
Childbearing
　delayed, 82, 147
　history, 7, 192, 193
　ideals, 81, 95, 96
　trends, 82
Childbirth, 16, 18, 61, 66, 69, 117, 145, 147, 171. *See also* Births
Child Care Leave Act (Japan), 36, 60
Child/children
　care, 3, 25, 36, 178
　desire for having, 61, 62, 64, 66, 70, 172, 177
　ideal number of, 37, 80, 82, 83, 87, 97, 104, 182
　intended number of, 37, 80, 182
Childless, 2, 3, 14, 24, 25, 81, 123, 177, 194, 195, 201, 203, 204
Childrearing
　costs, 48, 49, 54
China, People's Republic of, 105, 108
Chinese
　Communist Party, the, 189
　government, 36, 106, 189, 190
　population, 190
Cholesterol levels, 114
CMS. *See* Cooperative Medical System (CMS)
Cohabitation, 2, 8, 23, 82–84, 88, 89, 95, 96, 138, 149
Columbia, 119
Community
　level, 187–207
Conception, 7, 8, 119, 123, 124, 158, 161–162, 168, 180, 181. *See also* Model, conception-wait estimation
Condom, 138, 147, 152–154, 156, 157, 167
Congenital, 6, 109, 117, 120–122, 124
Consumerism, 3, 22, 25

Consumption
　education, 39, 40
　health, 114, 192
　per capita, 38–44, 192
　private, 38–43
　public, 38–43
Contraception, 2, 5, 6, 8, 61, 80, 103–105, 114, 117, 119, 123, 138, 139, 147, 152–157, 162, 164, 168, 187, 191–195, 200, 201, 203, 204
Contraceptives
　method, 6, 8, 154, 168, 187, 195
　use, 61, 80, 103, 104, 152–156, 164, 192, 193
Cooperative Medical System (CMS), 189, 190, 205
Copenhagen, 119, 120
Co-residence, 63, 149, 173, 176, 183
Correlation, 15, 19, 21, 53, 66, 70, 72, 77, 87, 172, 191, 196, 197
Cost
　of children, 3, 4, 13, 15, 16, 18, 22, 23, 25, 26, 31, 32, 37, 38, 47–49, 51–55, 60, 87, 95
　of the elderly, 32, 38, 46, 47, 52, 53
Costa Rica, 42, 50, 51
County, 7, 8, 105, 188, 189, 191–193, 195–207
Couples. *See also* Sexless, couples
　married, 2, 5, 20, 80, 138, 158, 162, 163, 169, 181
Croatia, 21, 27, 110
"Crowding out" effect, 4, 32, 38, 52, 53, 55
Cryptorchidism, 117, 121, 122, 125, 127, 129
Cultural
　norms, 19, 188
　revolution, 106

D

Daycare center
　availability of, 62, 70
　provision of, 61, 65, 68–70, 72
　use, 4, 59–72
Decentralization, 7, 189, 190
Demographic
　dividend (first and second), 36, 42, 43, 51–52, 55
　factors, 7, 77, 169–170
　and Health Surveys (DHS), 104, 108, 114, 115
　outlook, 1
　transformations, 1
　transition, 42, 75, 113
　transition multiplier (DTM), 75

Index

Demography, 1, 6, 7, 25–27, 32, 34–36, 42, 43, 51–52, 55, 61, 62, 75–77, 79, 80, 93, 94, 103, 107, 108, 112, 113, 115, 130, 156, 161, 163, 164, 169–170, 174, 188, 192, 196, 206
Denmark, 21, 27, 94, 110–112, 120–122, 124
Deregulation, 189
Determinants of low fertility, 2, 11
Developing countries/nations, 12, 54, 96, 103, 104, 108, 109, 112–114, 187, 206, 207
Dichotomous, 170, 193, 196
Dioxin, 126, 127
Disability, 106, 114
Disaggregation, 35
Disease
  chronic, 6, 103, 105, 113
  communicable, 103, 114, 189
  infectious, 109, 114
  noncommunicable, 6, 103, 113, 114
Disparity/ies. *See also* Income, disparity
  interregional, 65, 190
Divorce, 85, 95, 96, 143, 144, 172–174, 176, 180, 183
Drug exposure, 109

E
Earnings
  female, 13, 55
  male, 86
East Asia, 2–5, 9, 11, 12, 31–55, 87, 103, 112
East Asian economies
  societies, 3, 9, 50
Easterlin hypothesis, 85, 89, 90
Eastern Europe, 12, 13, 16, 18, 19, 137
Economics, 47, 55
  aspirations, 77, 88–89
  growth, 1, 40, 42, 50, 77, 137, 189
  indicators, 192
  mechanism of low fertility trap, 4, 5, 77, 94, 95
  model of fertility, 13, 22
  outlook, 77
  reform, 189–192
  support ratio (ESR), 42, 51, 52, 54
  theory, 38
Edinburgh, 119, 120
Education
  college, 91, 147–149, 154, 157, 194, 195, 201, 203, 205

  higher, 137, 148, 149, 207
  high school (lower), 63, 91, 147, 149, 150, 154, 155, 194, 195, 201, 203, 205, 207
  levels, 82, 86, 91, 93, 95, 96, 147
  median, 92, 93
  primary school, 107, 194, 195, 201, 203, 205
  private cost, 4, 31, 36–47, 54
  public cost, 4, 31, 36–46
  tertiary, 6, 15, 91, 96, 137, 157
Educational attainment, 147, 148, 154, 157
Elderly, the, 2–5, 23, 25, 31–55, 61
Employees
  full-time, 4, 36, 66, 67, 170
  part-time, 4, 36, 66, 67, 170
Employers, 19, 87, 202, 205
Employment
  stability, 87
  status, 4, 5, 61, 66, 67, 163, 170, 175, 177, 183
Endocrine-disrupting chemicals/endocrine disrupters, 2, 6, 117–130
Endogeneity, 72
England, 75
English-speaking
  countries, 12, 16, 24, 27
  region, 15
Enterprise, 90, 192, 195, 196, 199, 201, 203, 205
Environment, 2, 36, 77, 85, 87, 94, 96, 125–127, 129, 162, 164, 188, 189
  contaminant, 126
  hazard, 6, 109
Estimation
  results, 4, 65, 69–71
Estrogen, 126, 127
Eurobarometer survey, 24
Europe, 4, 12, 13, 15, 16, 18–20, 23, 24, 27, 50, 75, 76, 79, 80, 82, 88–90, 118, 137, 138
European countries, 4, 15, 16, 20, 24, 34, 54, 62, 75, 82, 86, 101, 105, 110, 112, 113, 117, 122, 138, 142
Exam, 3–5, 7, 8, 11, 12, 31, 48, 50, 51, 54, 55, 60, 119, 123, 127, 139, 147, 148, 151, 152, 163, 171, 182, 188, 191, 193, 197, 198, 202, 206, 207. *See also* Medical, exam
  breast, 7, 188, 206
  gynecological (vaginal, uterine), 7, 188, 193, 198
  ultrasound, 7, 107, 188, 193, 198, 202, 203, 207

Expected family size, 79
Expenditure
   on education, 5, 15, 39
   on health, 39
   private, 15
   public, 40

F
Factor
   anatomical, 109
   demographic, 7, 77, 169–170
   endocrinological, 109
   genetic, 6, 109, 121, 125, 129
   iatrogenic, 109
   lifestyle, 6, 93, 114, 125, 128, 129
   socioeconomic, 3, 170–171
Family
   "incomplete family", 82
   patterns, 76
   planning, 7, 8, 11, 84, 85, 105–107, 148, 162, 167, 180, 181, 187, 190–195, 198, 206
   planning station, 191
   size, 6, 11, 23, 24, 76, 77, 79–82, 94–96, 105, 107, 111, 115, 181, 182, 200
Family Planning Evaluation Program (US), 162
Faroe Islands, 127
Fecundity, 122–124
Fertility. *See also* Total fertility rate (TFR)
   below-replacement, 1, 2, 5, 22, 32, 79, 93, 95, 117
   control, 5, 54, 66, 93, 103, 119, 162, 182
   decline, 1–9, 13, 32–34, 36, 51, 76–79, 85–87, 93, 95, 101, 103, 104, 106, 112, 117, 162
   depressed, 5, 93, 95, 96
   ideals, 23, 76, 79–82, 90, 95, 96
   levels, 5, 6, 12, 13, 15, 22, 54, 76, 79, 81, 85, 93–96, 101, 102
   low, 2–9, 11–27, 31–55, 75–97, 101–115, 130, 151, 162, 168
   lowest-low, 2, 23
   marital, 2, 4, 36, 59–72, 162, 181, 182
   model, 7, 8, 13, 22, 38, 47
   obstacles to, 3, 11–19, 22–26
   overall, 5, 8, 85, 90, 105, 106, 108, 165, 191, 192, 206, 207
   preferences, 13, 16, 22, 26, 79–82, 94, 106, 107, 163, 177, 179, 180, 200, 202
   realized, 2, 81, 82, 96, 180
   reduction of, 2, 32, 68, 69, 71, 76, 78, 103, 104, 118, 171, 189
   total, 1, 12, 15, 16, 26, 27, 34–35, 40, 44, 48, 49, 51, 54, 63–66, 80, 101, 102, 108, 110, 112, 118, 123, 128, 153, 164, 166–168, 190, 198, 206
   trends, 4, 6, 13, 46, 66, 75, 76, 81, 82, 86, 87, 90–96, 101, 103, 106, 117–130, 138–145, 157
Fetus, 107, 125, 127
Financial
   constraints, 13
   crisis, 13, 25
   support, 3, 13–15, 25, 26
Finland, 21, 94, 120–121
Focus group discussion, 7, 174, 178–181
Forecasting, 79
France, 21, 50, 75, 94, 112, 120
Freeters, 87
Frequency of intercourse, 7, 145, 152, 161–173, 177–182. *See also* Intercourse
Fukushima Nuclear Power Plant, 97

G
Gansu, 190
Gender
   differences, 6, 19–20, 26, 35, 151, 156, 195
   inequality, 3, 11, 19–21, 25, 195, 196
   norm, 3, 5, 14, 19, 21, 24–26
   roles, 19, 24, 26, 151
Gene, 6, 109, 121, 125, 129
Generational
   equity, 38, 55, 189
German Population Acceptance Survey, 24
Germany
   under Nazi regime, 105
Globalization, 76
Greece, 21, 27
Guizhou, 190

H
Health. *See also* Reproductive health
   care, 5–7, 35, 38–40, 109, 110, 112–114, 157, 187–192, 196, 205, 206
   care professional, 190
   care spending, 35, 190
   center, 109, 189

of elderly, 4, 5, 35, 38
expenditure, 5, 39, 40
insurance, 24, 189, 190
public, 4, 5, 24, 35, 104, 109, 146, 187, 189–190
station, 7, 190–192, 195, 196, 199–203, 205, 206
Help-seeking
behavior, 188, 191
"Honeymoon effect", 163
Hong Kong, 1, 2, 9, 11, 12, 21, 93, 108
Hormone, 125, 126
Hospital, 117, 167, 189–191, 196
Household
finances, 35, 77–78
Responsibility System, 190
Housewife, 64, 66–67, 170, 175
Housing, 23, 38, 93–94, 173
HPV. *See* Human papilloma virus (HPV)
Human capital
components, 4, 49, 50, 52, 54, 87
per capita child, 49, 50, 52, 54
Human immunodeficiency virus/acquired immunodeficiency syndrome (HIV/AIDS), 9, 138
Human papilloma virus (HPV), 156
Hungary, 21, 27, 50, 51
Hypospadias, 117, 121, 122, 126, 127, 129

I
ICMART. *See* International Committee Monitoring Assisted Reproductive Technologies (ICMART)
Ideal family size, 22, 23, 76, 77, 79–82, 94, 95
Income
absolute, 88
disparity, 7, 189, 190, 207
expected, 77, 85–89, 206
labor, 38–41, 43, 47, 48, 52, 53, 86, 89
per capita, 7, 39–41, 47, 48, 52, 53, 189, 192, 195, 196, 199
redistribution of, 189, 190
relative, 4, 40, 42, 85–87, 89, 90, 95
India, 2, 105
Individual-centered approach, 188
Individualism, 3, 25, 93, 157
Industrialized country/nations, 16, 32, 34, 118, 120, 122, 147, 156
Infant, 2, 5, 64, 127, 171, 172, 176
Infectious disease, 109
Infertility
causes of subfertility and, 109, 121

Information
sharing, 189
Inheritance, 85
Intercourse
consensual, 161
frequency of, 7, 145, 152, 161–174, 177–184
sexual, 6, 7, 108, 138–157, 161–174, 177–184
unprotected, 108, 154, 162, 168, 179
Intergenerational transfers
changing patterns of, 32
International Committee Monitoring Assisted Reproductive Technologies (ICMART), 110
International Conference on Low Fertility and Reproductive Health in East and Southeast Asia, 3
Intracytoplasmatic sperm injection (ICSI), 124
Intrauterine device (IUD), 153, 193–195, 198, 201–204, 207
Intrauterine insemination, 124
Investment, 77
In vitro fertilization, 109, 124, 168
Israel, 110
Italy, 21, 27, 75, 86
IUD. *See* Intrauterine device (IUD)

J
Japan
Family Planning Association, 84, 85, 142, 166
Statistics Bureau of, 20, 34, 39, 78, 87
Japanese
Association for Sex Education (JASE), 137–139, 158
General Social Survey, 164, 165, 178
government, 2, 11, 18, 24–26, 32, 36–38, 59, 60, 64, 76, 94–96, 138, 144, 156, 158, 168, 170, 171
Ministry of Education, Culture, Sports, Science and Technology, 72, 91
National Fertility Survey (JNFS), 37, 80, 137, 139, 141, 143, 144, 146–153, 156, 158
Job
career, 66
discrimination, 16
family conflict, 96
history, 71
security, 16, 25
status, 61, 62, 64, 66–67, 69, 70, 72

K
Kawasaki, 119, 120
Kinship, 188
Korea, North, 1, 12
Korea, South, 1, 2, 4, 9, 11, 12, 15, 16, 18, 21, 23, 24, 26, 31–34, 43, 46–55, 76, 93, 108–110

L
Labor
  force, 4, 117
  force participation, 55, 90, 162
  market, 3, 16, 18, 24–26, 60, 69, 71, 86, 87, 89, 90, 93, 96
  supply, 60, 90
Latin America, 50, 54, 110
Latin American Caribbean Region, 104
Life cycle
  deficit (LCD), 40, 41, 43–54
  surplus, 40
Life expectancy
  at birth, 33, 103
Lifestyle, 6, 93, 105, 114, 117, 125, 128, 129, 179, 182
Life table, 47, 68
Lifetime earnings, 16
Living arrangements, 42, 148, 149, 154
Longevity, 55, 103
Los Angeles, 119
"Love hotels", 138
Lowest-low fertility, 2, 23. *See also* Fertility
Low fertility. *See* Fertility
Low fertility trap (LFT)
  trap hypothesis (LFTH), 4, 75–79, 85, 94, 95
  trap mechanisms, 4, 5, 76, 77, 94, 95

M
Macao, 1, 2
Macedonia (MK), 21, 27, 110
Mainichi Newspaper, 3, 148
Mammogram, 8, 193, 198, 206
Mandatory retirement, 42
Marital
  fertility, 2, 4, 36, 59–72, 151, 154, 162, 181, 182
  status, 140, 193
Market
  based system, 189
Marriage. *See also* Sexless, marriage
  arranged, 63, 66, 82, 83, 157, 173, 176, 183
  decisions, 61, 80, 164
  delayed, 2, 5, 6, 8, 82, 95, 138, 145, 147
  late, 109
  length of, 163
  love, 82, 144
  mean age at (first) marriage, 91, 137, 138
  non-traditional, 82
  postponed, 42, 88, 91, 95
  traditional, 23, 82, 85, 157
Masculinization, 125
Maternal
  care, 191, 206, 207
  death, 105, 190
  health (MH), 187, 190, 191
  smoking during pregnancy, 128
Maternity leave, 16, 17, 25
Medical
  care, 60, 108
  doctor, 192
  exam, 193
  facilities, 188
  system, 189
Medicine
  curative, 191
Method
  contraceptive, 6, 138, 152, 154
  probit, 68, 71
  statistical, 197
Ministry of Health, Labour and Welfare (Japan), 33, 59, 62, 65, 93, 146, 154, 168, 171
Minneapolis, 119
Model
  conception-wait estimation, 168
  Engel, 40
  generalized linear (GLM), 197, 200
  generalized linear mixed (GLMM), 197, 202
  logistic regression, 151, 156, 169, 174, 200
  multilevel, 8, 188, 191, 193, 197, 200, 207
  multilevel logistic, 197, 203
  multivariate, 139, 147, 197–199
  Prais–Houthakker, 40
  random-intercept, 197
  regression, 119, 139, 151, 156, 172, 174, 200, 206
  Rothbarth equivalence scale, 40
  statistical, 7, 162, 193
Mongolia, 2, 9, 12, 109
Morbidity, 2, 5, 105, 187, 191
Mortality
  premature, 189, 206
  transition, 33
Multicollinearity, 66, 172, 196, 197
Myanmar, 1, 12, 75

Index 217

N

National Fertility Survey (NFS) [the US], 162
National Income and Product Accounts (NIPA), 35
National Institute of Population and Social Security Research (NIPSSR) [Japan], 34, 37, 137–138, 141
National Population and Family Planning Commission [China], 105
National Population and Reproductive Health Survey (NPRHS) [China], 7, 192–194, 196, 198, 199, 201
National Survey of Families and Households (NSFH) [the US], 163, 167
National Survey of Family Income and Expenditure (NSFIE) [Japan], 39
National Survey of Population, Families and Generations [Japan], 78
National Survey on Family Planning [Japan], 148, 181
National Survey on Work and Family [Japan], 4, 7, 61, 80–84, 88, 89, 95
National Transfer Accounts (NTA), 4, 5, 32, 34–46, 50, 54, 87. *See also* Japanese, National Fertility Survey (JNFS)
Netherlands, the, 21, 27, 75, 90
New York, 119
Niger, 102
Nihon University Population Research Institute (NUPRI), 3, 61, 164
NIPA. *See* National Income and Product Accounts (NIPA)
Nonparticipant in the labor force, 4
Nordic countries, 12, 13, 16, 18, 19, 27, 94
North-west Europe, 23
Norway (NO), 21, 27, 34, 75, 94
Those Not in Employment, Education, or Training (NEET), 87
NUPRI. *See* Nihon University Population Research Institute (NUPRI)

O

Occupational status, 163, 174
OECD. *See* Organisation for Economic Co-operation and Development (OECD)
Omiai, 173. *See also* Marriage, arranged
Opportunity cost, 3, 16, 18, 25, 60, 76
Organisation for Economic Co-operation and Development (OECD), 13–15, 17, 18, 20, 33, 86, 90

P

PAP smear, 7, 193, 198, 206, 207
"Parasite singles", 77
Parenthood, 23, 145–147
Parenting, 22, 163, 172
Paris, 119, 120
Parity progression
  from the first to a second birth, 69, 70
  ratio (PPR), 62, 68, 88
PCB. *See* Polychlorinated biphenyls (PCB)
Pension
  program, 35, 38
  system, 112, 113
Pensioner, 113
Peru, 105
Pesticide, 126–128
Philippines, the, 12, 50, 51, 75, 76
Physical
  attributes, 188
  context, 188
Policy
  effectiveness, 2, 22, 61, 70
  one-child, 105, 106, 109
Pollution
  air, 188
Polychlorinated biphenyls (PCB), 126, 128
Population
  aging, 32–34, 38, 43, 55, 77, 78, 90, 112–114
  density, 82, 94, 96
  forecaster, 79
  growth, 1, 76, 105, 106
  growth rate, 1
  projections, 42, 76
  pyramid, 111, 112
  rural, 7, 8, 105, 107, 173, 176, 188, 198, 206
  urban, 64, 92, 93, 106, 107, 173, 176, 183, 192, 195
Postnatal, 190, 191
Pregnancy
  premarital, 2, 8, 145–147, 157
  unintended, 139, 154, 157, 158
Prenatal
  check up, 202, 203
  visit, 191
Productivity, 42, 55
Projections, 2, 42, 76, 103, 112–114, 123
Pronatal/pronatalist policies, 11, 25, 26, 32, 36, 54, 111, 162
Purchasing power, 13, 86, 88

R
Rate of natural conceptions (RNC), 123
Reallocation
  asset, 44–46
  resource, 35
Regression
  analysis, 49, 52, 175–176, 196
  estimates, 51, 197, 200
  first and second stage, 69
  multinomial logit, 67
  probit, 68
Religious identity, 174
Reproduction
  reproduction rate, net, 75
Reproductive. *See also* Reproductive health
  age, 4, 5, 7, 37, 76, 78, 79, 81, 95, 108, 162, 167, 192, 206
  choice, 101–115
  development, 126
  disease, 206
  opportunity, 78
  organs, 6, 125
  rights, 112, 187
  technology, 103, 109, 110
  tract, 6, 120–122, 124, 187, 190
  tract infection (RTI), 190, 191
Reproductive health
  behavior, 188, 193
  checkup, 7, 8, 191, 193, 194, 198–207
  choice, 188, 195
  disparities, 7, 188, 190, 205, 207
  examination, 193, 198
  male, 6, 117–130
  problems, 2, 5, 7, 125, 128, 129
  services, 6–8, 187–207
Residential crowding, 188
Retirement. *See also* Age, retirement
  age, 42, 113
  mandatory, 42
Risk behavior, 147–156
RNC. *See* Rate of natural conceptions (RNC)
Russia, 19, 21, 27, 91

S
Sampling
  method, 80, 164
  selection, 69
  size, 62, 69, 139, 142, 169
  stratified multistage cluster, 192
Savings, 23, 43, 179
Second shift, 19
Sector
  private, 60
  public, 40

Self-employed, 66, 67, 170, 175, 183
Semen
  quality, 6, 117–122, 124, 125, 127–129
Sex
  education, 141, 152, 157, 158
  industry, 182
  premarital, 2, 8
  ratio, 7, 106, 107, 195, 196, 199, 200, 204–206
  unsafe, 2, 6, 8, 114
Sexless
  couples, 161, 165, 169
  marriage, 7, 8, 161–183
Sexuality
  activity, 2, 5–8, 61, 151, 162, 163, 167, 171–174, 180
  attitude, 85
  behavior, 7, 137–158
  experience, 85, 139, 141–145, 147–149, 151, 152, 156
  intercourse (*see* Intercourse)
  relations, 84, 95, 137, 138, 144, 145, 148, 149, 171, 181
  relationship, 137, 138, 144, 145, 148, 149
  revolution, 6, 137–139, 156
Sexually transmitted infections (STIs), 2
Shanghai, 190
Sierra Leone, 103
Singapore, 2, 11, 12, 21, 24, 26, 76, 92, 93, 108, 109
Slovenia, 21, 27, 50, 51
Social
  duties and obligations, 82
  economic background, 188
  network, 188
  policies, 6, 113
  security, 37, 77, 78, 113, 137, 138, 141
Socialization, 79, 86
Society, 23, 35, 36, 82, 85, 87, 94, 103, 110, 112, 113, 124, 161, 164–166, 169, 172, 181
Sociodemographics, 161, 163, 192, 196, 206
Socioeconomic
  causes of low fertility, 162
  characteristics, 61, 80, 93, 94, 164, 169, 189
  conditions, 188
  deprivation, 188
  development, 187–190
  factors, 3, 170–171
Southeast Asia, 2, 3, 5, 8, 9, 11, 12, 22, 25, 117
Southern Europe, 12, 14–18, 137
Spain, 21, 27, 87, 110

Sperm
   counts, 2, 9, 118, 128
   density, 118, 119, 128
   motility, 128
   quality, 118, 128
State Family Planning Commission (China), 192
Statistics
   descriptive, 152, 194, 195
   vital, 145–146
Sterilization, 105, 106, 194, 201, 203, 204
Steroidgenesis, 126
STIs. *See* Sexually transmitted infections (STIs)
Sub-Saharan Africa, 101, 102, 104, 105
Substitution of quality for quantity of children, 38. *See also* Trade-off, quantity-quality
Survey on Life and Attitudes of Men and Women (Japan), 164, 166
Survey on Sexual Behavior among Youths (Japan), 137–139, 141
Sweden, 19, 21, 27, 34, 42, 51, 75, 86, 89–91, 94, 129, 144, 153

T
Taiwan, 2, 4, 11, 12, 21, 31–34, 43, 46–55, 108, 109
Tax
   relief, 13–15, 18
TDS. *See* Testicular dysgenesis syndrome (TDS)
Testicular dysgenesis syndrome (TDS), 6, 124–127, 129. *See also* Cancer, testicular (TC)
Thailand, 1, 8, 9, 21, 75, 76, 108, 109, 163
Tibet, 190
Time-use
   survey, 19
Tokyo, 3, 7, 8, 59, 64, 75, 91–93, 137, 167, 178
Toronto, 163
Total fertility rate (TFR), 1, 2, 32, 36, 48–50, 52, 54, 76, 93, 101–103, 111, 112, 195, 196, 199, 200, 202, 204, 207. *See also* Fertility
Township, 189, 191, 196
Trade-off
   between the number and quality of children, 4, 38, 50, 54, 55
   quantity-quality, 4, 48, 50
Transfers
   familial, 32, 35, 44
   intergenerational, 32, 35
   inter vivo, 44
   intrahousehold, 35
   private, 35, 43–46
   public, 43, 45, 46
Transition. *See also* Demographic, transition
   from one to two, from two to three children, 61
Treatment
   and diagnosis, 121, 127, 206
   and prevention, 206

U
Unemployment, 13, 87, 90
United Kingdom (UK), 21, 27, 86, 110–112
United Nations (UN), 76, 101–106, 112, 113, 117
United Nations Population Fund (UNFPA), 3
United States (US), 15, 19, 21, 24, 27, 42, 50, 51, 85, 89–92, 101, 105, 110, 112, 119, 129, 142, 144, 152, 153, 162, 163, 167, 170–172
Urbanization, 76, 82, 90, 93–96, 195–197, 199, 200, 202, 204, 205
Uruguay, 50, 51
US State Supreme Court, 105
Utilization
   daycare center, 71
   healthcare, 192
   RH services, 187, 196

V
Variable
   contextual, 8, 195–199, 207
   dependent, 51, 52, 62, 64, 67, 68, 71, 169, 193, 197, 198, 207
   dichotomous, 193, 196
   dummy, 39, 63, 64, 68, 195
   independent, 169, 170, 172, 183
   instrument, 65, 69, 70
   predictor, 62, 66–68, 150–152, 155, 156, 175–176
   response, 197
Vietnam, 1, 9, 12, 19, 21
Village development, 7, 206

W
Wages
   penalty, 16
Waiting lists for daycare centers, 71
Wales, 75, 91
Water sanitation and hygiene, 114
Wealth, 77, 88, 96, 189

Welfare
 of children, 38, 55, 62, 65
 of elderly, 38
 group, 189
Western countries
 Europe, 12, 14, 15, 17, 18, 80, 90, 101, 137
Woman/women's
 age, 64, 80, 81, 83, 92, 108, 142, 152, 164
 education, 7, 8, 62, 207
 labor participation, 55, 90, 162
 status, 8, 193, 196, 206, 207
Work
 full-time, 67, 170–171, 178
 paid, 3, 11, 16, 17, 19–21, 25, 96
 part-time, 24, 36, 170–171
 unpaid, 3, 11, 19, 25

Worker, 9, 13, 36, 54, 64, 85, 86, 88, 95, 113, 149, 170, 171, 192
World Bank, 103
World Economic Forum, 21
World Fertility Surveys (WFS), 114
World Health Organization (WHO), 3, 105, 114, 118
World Value Survey, 80
World War II, 32, 85

Y
Young, the
 adults, 2, 4–6, 13, 85, 87, 89, 95, 137–158
Youths, 51, 138, 139, 141
Yunnan, 191

MIX
Papier aus verantwortungsvollen Quellen
Paper from responsible sources
FSC® C105338

If you have any concerns about our products,
you can contact us on
ProductSafety@springernature.com

In case Publisher is established outside the EU,
the EU authorized representative is:
**Springer Nature Customer Service Center GmbH
Europaplatz 3, 69115 Heidelberg, Germany**

Printed by Libri Plureos GmbH
in Hamburg, Germany